TO THE ROOF OF THE WORLD

For Susy my adventure that keep going on

To the Roof of the World

Memoir of a Hashish Hippie

Brigitte Axel

Brigitte Axel Publishing

Copyright © 2021 by Brigitte Axel

All rights reserved. No part of this book may be reproduced in any manner whatsoever without written permission except in the case of brief quotations embodied in critical articles and reviews.

First Printing, 2021

CONTENTS

Prolouge ix

1 - THE BEGINNING - ON THE HIPPIE TRAIL . . 1
2 - I'VE BEEN TOLD THEIR STORY SO MANY TIMES 4
3 - A NEW YEAR AND A NIGHT OF PRINCE . . 14
4 - IT IS MY TURN TO BE 20
5 - THE FINE ARTS, AND THE ESTRO HARMONICO 27
6 - MOROCCO-PARIS: HITTING THE ROAD FROM NEW YORK TO MEXICO 39
7 - PARIS ISLE SAINT LOUIS ON MY BOAT . . . 61
8 - ITALY ON A BUDGET 74
9 - PARIS LEFT BANK 79
10 - NEW YORK AND MY FIRST JOINT 85
11 - TRAVELLING MEXICO OVERLAND 93
12 - LE MUTIN SANK AND I AM LETTING GO OF A PREDICTABLE FUTURE 116
13 - STEPPING INTO THE REAL THING 119
14 - MATALA, HIPPIE COVE 125

v

15 - RETURN TO MATALA	148
16 - OLD GULHANI AND THE TURKS	175
17 - TEHERAN AND THE SHAMSHUN HOTEL	204
18 - KABOUL	220
19 - LAHORE, NEW DELHI	237
20 - JAIPUR	263
21 - RETURN TO NEW DELHI	275
22 - AGRA & BENARES	308
23 - YASSARENA	323
24 - KATHMANDU	331
25 - A HIPPIE WEDDING	357
26 - FULL MOON AGAIN AND MORE FOOLS	387
27 - S.T.P. THREE WEEKS AWAKENING AND HOW TO NEVER SLEEP	393
28 - WATCHING PEOPLE IN MIRROR FRAGMENTS	410
EPILOGUE - ALL MY DREAMS CAME TRUE	441

This book is dedicated to all the people in it and the ones who may care about them; and to the lands I traveled in the time of revolution for peace and love. The tide of many memorable seasons swept over this history, transforming and eroding that world. Many of those people are gone and many of the once peaceful lands have been ravaged by war and development. A wonderful world, even today. How once upon a time, I had to find my way.

Listen, to the north – The land of ancestors
Respond to the South – The land of innocence.
Seek to the East – The land of illumination.
Resolve to the West – The land of introspection.

From chaos infinite, I hear the horses roaming across the galaxies. The goddess always comes in time – whether you are ready or not. With the sight of lightning and emptiness, on a road, unless it is a hidden way. Where we march a blind prince is waiting.

I did this translation myself, with a little bit of help from my international friends, Thomas Thirkell, Claudia Wolfers, Christine Hardy. Emily Mac Ivor, Nicky Crooks, Shiv Mirabito, Saba Sams, Vinaya Chaitanya David Timothy and Shweeta Bajaj.

Thank you to Claude Latour for his work designing my cover.

Thank you to Ralph Griffiths and Aslan Mackay for their work editing, compiling, and proofing.

Thank you to Luannah Victoria Arana for her help with the self-publishing process.

PROLOUGE

THE FIFTH DAY OF MARCH 2016

I have just completed my second draft, handwritten in English. It is my translation augmented of the previous relevant history of my continuing hippie experience.

Originally, I wrote this book in French in my early twenties. Over the years I learned and adopted English and 50 years later, I still migrate seasonally, following the sun, in English speaking lands, to my preferred residences.

My first seasonal home has been the same for the last 4 decades – the tropical west coast of Goa in India.

My second home is the hippie palace that we built it in the shape of a pagoda for accommodating paying guests and our family.

It's a retreat nested in a forest hill it overlooks the best protected harbour of the pacific north in supernatural British Columbia the beautiful west coast of Canada.

LAST DAY OF NOVEMBER 2017

Now my draft is all keyed into the computer and I continue to polish my words. I keep telling my hippie saga and continue explaining all there was, which still inspires what still happening in my exceptional hippie generation on that ever-evolving trippy trail.

H - Hashish, hippie, the first hippie trail.

H is my second book published with Flammarion - my French publisher.

I was deported from Kathmandu in November 1969.

I will forever be thankful for the help of Pierre-Paul – A Mauritian student of medicine who got in touch with the Swiss Embassy on my behalf. While I was locked up in the Nepalese feudal prison.

The responsibility for my temporary lost self was to be handed over to my parents in Brussels. With my parents' patient love and protecting concern, still shaken by my near escape, I was able to reintegrate my former (indomitable conquering) self.

My mother's advice to me was to write.

Soon I started writing about the epic adventure that I survived. That proved to be a successful therapy and my ticket to get back on the road again.

This was my second chance at emancipation.

Promising Glory, Contract proposal, negotiations with Flammarion publishing house. Etienne Lalou is my charismatic Literary Director, and misses Claude Dalla Torre my dynamic press agent.

I meet Mr. Ernest Flammarion; all are in a hurry to launch my story. Everyone hopes for a best seller with my second book, ready on the bookstore shelves. In the spring of 1970. Promoting me, a promising young hippie author (now hot, and literate).

My book, it is published at the height of the hippie revolution. In March of 1970 I suddenly represent the psychedelic experience.

I endorse the mission to resurrect the enthralling fame of the Silk Road. I do not display false humility, or abject flattering for the press... after writing my exciting tale, I attend interviews, live on Benelux, Swiss and French television. I am quoted with my picture in the newspapers and weekly magazines. Everyone in the media listens to me and looks at me.

Many daring youth get their back packs on and follow my tracks on the hippie road. With "HASH" my second book at 21, I am expecting that fame and fortune will help my way. I am in a hurry to go back on the road for my real life. I am stunned by the establishment changed views towards us real hippies, now the beautiful people opening all doors.

The professional people milk their share of our penniless globe trotter experiences. Everyone is ready to take acid and smoke dope; one more distraction to add to the consumer list of cool colourful trends.

My hippie peers and I, no longer estranged and different, everyone fashionably endorses the new trend and experience all that alternative reality, we are now leading and included in the mainstream.

I do not stay in Paris long enough to reap real success or fortune. Money still means nothing to me.

At the corner of Saint Germain church, I fall nose to nose, on a young woman with a little kid.

I can't believe it!

She is wearing my Afghan puchinka coat taken from me when I was freaking out. I tell her. You are wearing my coat!

She tells me she bought it from a hippie on Durba square in Kathmandu.

It's on her back, keeping her cozy and warm. That lady is not about to give it back to me. Okay it is my magic coat but the fact that I have seen it walking towards me reinforces my faith in divine synchronicity with personal guidance.

And I must accept to let it go...Then the nameless lady with my coat and her kid, trot quickly away...

I run away from Paris, fearless again, trusting towards my destiny, cutting again a hole in the trapping net.

Press reviews, interviews and television appearances put me in the star light, passersby ask for my autograph in the street, even on the train all the way to the Spanish border.

Even though I am the first one to speak with firsthand experience about the hippy trail and so young I still have quite a lot to say and learn about peace and love. But I am not interested, patient or tolerant of the politics of my time. I ignore the necessary courting of the press and my fleeting fame is short-lived and my gain unsubstantial.

I am in a rush to leave with my advance in royalties and will never secure any more money from my reputable publisher, Flammarion, still owes me for 8000 of the 20000 copies sold

I am surviving by other means, still waiting for the forgotten royalties, due to me. I could still reap those fruits of my labour. Even if it's only a little money.

Life goes on, my chosen way, more in Canadian English.

Here is my story, now, one ancient combat, still going on as I am.

1

THE BEGINNING – ON THE HIPPIE TRAIL

This is the story of my experience.

I want to respect the names of people who took part, and where it took place. We can simply call them hippies. Love and the need for love, there is nothing more we need to justify ourselves.

We gather like shivering famished rats. We try not to tear each other apart too much. We wander from feeling to feeling but we avoid thinking about these feelings. We want to construct something together. We prefer to disintegrate into nothingness than sink in organised shit. I am not concerned about my lasting power.

I wish to transform myself while maintaining my personal rhythm. The air is purer in poor countries; there are fewer cars and no factories. With no land of my own, I come from utopia; I part from it again and again. I want to be in sync alert with the constantly changing world

Previous to my hippie journey, I spent 4 years traveling and experiencing my adventure with the eyes of a dreamer. To solve the riddle of my shared destiny, I must reveal a little of my parents' history who are still a big influence in my life.

All these people who lit my way to the present. Their spark is unforgotten in the narrowing circles of my maturing. Everyone mentioned here, briefly shared my continuing destiny.

This is how I took part in the crusade of my generation with other intrepid full-grown champions. I inherited concern for peace in the world from my grandparents surviving the war; of which I got tired of hearing about as I grew up as a baby boomer.

Now, I am older and still on that same quest. I still try to find my peace, taking my time, passing through the constantly changing world, without any preconceptions.

We had been sent!

We ditched our worn-out shoes and we loved to be welcomed as bare-foot hippies. I thought I cut all ties from a society; I keep coming back to. Very soon, hippies were followed. We set a fire that spread fast, and it engulfed us. We wanted one world with no caste, no religion, and no boundaries for spreading irresistibly the loving peace.

And then came the Himalaya trekkers, the tourists, the businessmen, the drug dealers and we – the hippies, watched the big traffic exchange of a developing world.

Years later, the things that were exclusive to our lives are still the fashion.

2

I'VE BEEN TOLD THEIR STORY SO MANY TIMES

A necklace patiently rethread from several precious scattered pearls kept waiting. Many lost in the dust. You traveled the world. You thought you found nothing. And suddenly a valley where hope and love are born.

To my paternal grandparents who took me for summer holiday in their country refuge since I was four, I owe my centering sense of belonging in nature.

In the spring of 1912, 24-year-old Russian count Illoucha Axel, the youngest of twelve siblings, and his new bride Lili were just about to embark on their honeymoon. His adventurous wife, 20 years old with beautiful squirrel-like eyes and corkscrew curls, was a nursing student of the avant-garde Edith Cavell method.

Upon graduation, earning her diploma with distinction, she celebrated with Illoucha. She celebrated with Il-

Ioucha in his room, smelled the voluptuous perfume of the red roses, ate the great chocolates, drank the Champagne and accepted the diamond ring Illoucha bought for her. She decided to offer her precious virginity that night, therefore she was already pregnant.

Illoucha in Odesa

Lili was the daughter of a Belgian Notary and the youngest of seven siblings. The new couple was booked in first class for their honeymoon – on the maiden voyage of the Titanic. They had the honeymoon suite reserved at the New York Ritz Carlton, but Illoucha's travel papers were a day late and they missed that boat.

Illoucha and Lili embarked instead on the R.M.S Olympic – an ocean liner owned by the same White Star line that owned the Titanic.

At the port of entrance, Illoucha's program was ruined by the USA immigration officers. He could not speak their language. He was an impatient suspect, yelling in French with a heavy Russian accent.

He was arrested and put into quarantine for screening on Ellis Island.

Lili was pregnant and nauseous; she had to wait for him on board with the crew. Illoucha stayed several days in frustrating limbo before returning to his bride. They never set a foot on the land of the free.

When baby Richard, born in Liege, was six months old, Countess Lili and Count Illoucha traveled with him on the Trans-Siberian railroad.

They settled in the Russian port of Odessa. Illoucha was posted there as an aeronautic engineer for the new air fleet of Tsar Nicholas II.

Lili in Odesa

They enjoyed the cosmopolitan black sea town. Mingling with the elite in a modern apartment cocoon where they felt part of the Russian Revolution, with the officers and families of the newly constituted air fleet of Imperial Russia.

Until Tsar Nicholas II's forced abdication soon followed by his assassination made it very clear that they were now in mortal danger.

9 years after Illoucha and Lili made their home in Russia they had to escape it or get killed like their obsolete leaders.

It's Lili who woke up in panic, did not lose hope and took measures to save her family. She begged for her life on her knees to the gallant French submarine captain who used to court her. He accepted to take them on board. They escaped with their nine-year-old son, running through the massacre, lucky to escape the murderous Bolshevik pursuit.

In extremis, Illoucha, Lili and their 9-year-old son embarked on the Pelikan, the last submarine from Odesa to Nizhny Novgorod.

Illoucha only managed to grab his iron safe with his stack of shares of Odesa Tramway and Trans-Siberian Railways and Lili's precious jewels, his Russian dagger with the stamp of his family – a brass hand with the county crest of three swimming horses. Lili seized Michu, Little Richard's teddy bear, and the melancholic Icon of Our Lady of the Immigrant holding Saint Boris and Saint Gleb in their caravel gone to seek fortune and orthodox converts. The saints were sacrificed later by their mad brother - Ivan the Terrible.

My father Richard on a bear skin in Odesa

***

On my other side, my maternal grandparents, elegant with their hats and gloves, only took an interest in me when I was nine, when my grandfather suspected he was dying. To my grandfather Roberto and especially to my grandmother Genia, who we call Mamouche; I owe my initiation to refined European city life and culture.

An Icon of Our Lady of the Immigrant

In the spring of the year 1914, Mamouche met Roberto at the monthly ball in her chic Brussel boarding house. She sat beautifully waiting beside her mother Luna and her brother Sacha.

27 years old and twice divorced, Genia had an eventful life already. She first got married at the age of 20 to Maxim – a first violin student. She met him at La Coupole in Paris in 1909; they were speaking mixed Russian with French, about revolution, with the older visionary exiled from Russia, Vladimir Ilyich Ulyanov, who was also known as Lenin.

But young Genia was still holding in her little heart her first crush for Serguei - a Russian cadet her parents did not approve of. They sent her to study in Paris, where she almost forgot about him, but she never made love with her patient husband Maxim.

Destiny sends Serguei to her again at La Coupole, in Paris. By now, he is a dashing captain who can support her. Genia divorced Maxim to marry Serguei. But Serguei felt unworthy of Genia's virginity and initiated her to a furtive sex life with no frills or satisfaction.

Genia Winspeare - My Maternal Grandmother

He got her pregnant, but their baby is stillborn.

Two years later she is fed up with the hopeless patient boredom of an army wife. She divorced Serguei and returned to her parents' home in Russia.

The Russian Revolution has started. Genia's protective father anticipates turmoil that will destroy their opulent home in Ekaterina Darskaia. He is a famous doctor and ensured the safety of his family.

He sent them off to Brussels and placed all available wealth at their disposal for the years to come.

His wife Luna, daughter Genia, and son Sacha move to French speaking Brussels where Genia completed her education, which was interrupted by 5 years of marriage trials.

Genia was once again ready to find love and independence.

Genia is dreamily sitting waiting for her first dance at The Spring ball in the chic boarding house. Beside her Kalmyk mother and her younger brother Sacha, beautiful Genia is gazing at what's to come next in her world.

27-year-old Genia is writing in French her past romantic story – "The Awakening". Genia is fluent in seven languages. While her brother Sacha just qualified to teach Physics and Math.

27-year-old Roberto looks older than his age with his beard. The Stylish Anglo Jacobin Italian bachelor set his eyes on Genia. At the beginning of the year 1914, Roberto is fluent and can write in nine languages.

Roberto Winspeare - My Maternal Grandfather

His mother, Maria Antonia - a Caraccioli princess, presents him to Luna ex-beauty queen of Ekaterina Dar. Beside her, Genia gets up to curtsy and speak in French with a Russian accent, with a clear high pitch voice.

Maria Antonia, a widow for ten years, still ignores the complex challenges of life. Her late spouse gambled all his wealth away and died a loser. While her ambitious son – Roberto squanders the rest of their fortune. He sold the last of the dowry of his mother – the orange groves of Sicily, ten years ago, when he assumed responsibility for the family at seventeen.

Though Maria Antonia follows Roberto blindly, his business ways are ludicrous. The young baron keeps speculating and branching out in risky ventures.

The princess was easily subjugated. While relieved of responsibility when Roberto told her, "You are a hen chick who hatched an eagle."

Roberto has a majestic and assertive presence. He obliged his two younger brothers to succeed and encouraged them to marry the affluent girls they met.

Francesco, an international lawyer moved to the new world in New York with Florence Caseneuve - his billionaire wife.

While Jacomo, the youngest of the three brothers, became a diplomat who specialized in genealogy. Jacomo commuted between Rome and Berlin with his wife – Erika. Erika was the only daughter of Eric von Danuken - the famous magician who is coaching mass mesmerization to Italy's budding dictator Benito Mussolini and Germany's future Furher - Adolf Hitler.

Roberto bows deeply to ask Luna's permission to invite her daughter Genia for the first dance. Roberto's search for a bride ends here.

Genia - aloof and poised, is a vivacious exotic creature. She sparkles at the spring ball with her classic beauty in the charcoal chiffon dress she designed. She takes Roberto's hand, looking into his blue eyes with childlike grace.

Will he impress her?

Roberto right away knows she will be his wife. He pursues and wins her and soon, they marry in Brussels. They have twin girls, one of which is my mother Sia.

**

I am born on New Years' eve.

Mama delivers me at the same Malibran maternity in Brussels where she was born along with her twin sister – Tata, 28 years before me.

My father, Richard, is pacing up and down the hall. Mama Sia's screams making him concerned enough to disregard all rules and he barges into the delivery room and sees me emerging from her womb.

I am their love baby - a girl, just born out of her great pale pink elastic body and I fiercely start to suckle my mother's tits. Sia never yielded any milk for me and gave up on trying when I managed to draw and suckle one drop of her blood.

"My mother Sia and her twin sister Tata"

The end of the Second World War after the American Allies debarked and liberated Europe, they become idolised saviours for the starved Europeans. It became a fashion to follow the American ways, and everyone believes that is the shortest way to prosperity.

Sia learnt to work and survive at the age of sixteen. She sells her art and assumes the principal responsibility for her family. Sia aspires to find an honest and comfortable life in the rising middle class.

I am the first born of Sia and Richard, but before me Sia had two sons from her first enterprising and disloyal husband.

Me as a baby

She left that first husband for my father knowing she was already pregnant with my half-brother Serge.

Her first baby did not survive. Her children were all unpreventable accidents, none of her eight born children got her milk.

I am nursed with a bottle and baby formula, a new fashionable substitute. Despite this, I grow to be a fat rosy baby with fine strawberry hair and delicate skin.

I grow up unsure to ever gain enough charm to appease all the anxious, mad adults from my good family who are my teachers.

It is a time of struggle in Europe the war ravaged most ancient fortunes, my dysfunctional family, once affluent still dreams of power.

3

A NEW YEAR AND A NIGHT OF PRINCE

All gypsies come from India, so who am I?

For my sixteenth birthday, I design my first womanly dress - a finely woven *pied de poule* in black, grey and white with a revealing cleavage. Black grosgrain piping and black buttons all the way flaring down in pleated fold to mid knee.

Madame Tassel, my mother's seamstress, tailors it perfectly. I had not yet reached puberty, but no one could tell that by looking at me. Under my new dress I slip on black lacy lingerie and black silk stockings with a backseam arrow in the middle. I walk, propped up eight centimeters, on pointy black heels with ankle straps.

I blow at once my sixteen candles on the mocha cake Mama Sia made for the occasion.

Mama, my three younger sisters, and my younger brother have already started to yawn. After the festive dinner they all go to bed.

But not me, I am not tired and so excited to follow Papa and continue the night of the 31st of December. Papa Richard is in the driver's seat of the black Studebaker, me beside him, my big brother Serge with his fiancée Micheline in the back seat.

My mother Sia's portrait by Robert Delbecq

Papa drive to the town center and we descend into his favourite cave; *Les Mille et un nuit*, in English "a thousand and one nights".

Papa is the best looking smouldering dark eyes and dark hair romantic dandy I know. He's dressed up in his black long coat lined with astrakhan over his tuxedo with a white silk scarf and astrakhan top hat just like Omar Sharif, but Papa looks better.

We follow him to the underground cave.

Papa speaks Russian to the door keeper with a warm friendly voice. We step into the dim lit room filled with smoke.

Papa, in Russian, greets with hugs and kisses on the lips, the four musicians, the barman and the patron.

Papa introduces us, me first, it's my birthday.

We reached the oasis for White Russians, Hungarians Romanian Polish, Tzigane's and immigrant bohemians looking for something familiar beyond necessity. Here everyone can quench a thirst inextinguishable with pure vodka and swill down fiery little water to fuel the nostalgia for a past with no more future.

My father Richard's portrait painted by my mother Sia"

Papa is a pal of the musicians and joins in singing out of key, with the lyrics he remembers.

Valia, and Aliocha Dimitrieovitch and their daughter, Natacha. Natacha sings with a deep clear voice and plucks a balalaika, and her handsome mate young Yuri plays the violin.

They greet us with a song, responding to Aliocha calling guitar. Each of them sings a solo first, and then together plays their part. I know some words of all the songs.

The two guitars, tzvef guitarra.
O tchitchornio dark eyes
Gare,gare burn, burn
Raspachol.
Balalaika
Coachman bring your horses, Yamshi niegali, lashaldi.
The lily time...

The chrysanthemum time...
It takes the whole night to play everything.

First toast, Aliocha slowly starts a song, sober, with his deep crackling smoker voice.

Then Valia, the well-worn siren tears at hearts, howls and strikes with her fire branding voice.

Natacha takes part, swelling each song like a strong tide. Injecting confident passion with her drilling echoing voice, she is hopeful; to dominate her unbridled leading parents. She concludes triumphant in solo.

Cigarettes, vodka, champagne, paprika chips and salted nuts.

Papa is offering rounds and rounds. All of us are downing crystals tumblers full of vodka and tossing them over the left shoulder smashing them on the ground.

The empty crystal shatters on the wood floor, the nonchalant sweeper with his broom, keeps the floor free of shards.

I dance between Serge and Micheline, Papa and Valia, Aliocha, Natacha, and Yuri. The four musicians gather melodic speed sing at a gallop and scream hop! Hop!

Each glass crashes with a laughing sound.

We drink, we sing, we talk and dance, Valia sings her stories about the never-ending road, surviving through the good old days and all what happen next still going on.

They're all fuelled with vodka and the flowing champagne, frenetic and delirious, like the guitar, the violin, the balalaika, and the calling voices.

I listen, I speak, we laugh, and I play my part of that passion. I dance on the table; jump on the swept dance floor with cat jumps and pirouettes. Cossack dance and the cancan split.

I smoke cigarettes; I drink thirstily the champagne, down the vodka shots and smash my crystal tumbler.

I add volutes to the smoky dim light. This is my first prince night, with Papa. I am feeling great, underground, unrestricted displaying myself, part of this temporal private court of kings and queens of the night.

Their raspy wailing voices pluck my feelings.

I empathize with the broken promises of love, heartbreak mending and bitter enthusiastic orgasmic regrets, all that encourages me to fly exuberant above it all.

I am drunk but don't realize it until we resurface, with dawn in the morning and I pass out because of the fresh air. Papa disposes of Serge and Micheline at her flat, then carry me safely home.

Maman when she sees me passed out limp in papas arms get furious and she slaps me; but I feel nothing, and I don't even puke. When I wake up around twelve in my bed, I feel fine.

From now on I am not getting taller, except from the eight centimeter high heels I can dance all night in. I am smaller than my mother and my two twin sisters but bigger than Papoum. My eyes are similar to the eyes of my father, but not smouldering dark.

Me and Mamouche at our family's Christmas party

I don't have intense amazing green eyes like my mother, neither her mane of beautiful thick hairs. But I am content to be like I am in the beauty category, sort of classic with golden copper colours. I prefer the company of men and would rather avoid my competitive and pestering sisters.

To build my maturing personality I need some privacy...

In the spring equinox, three months after my sixteenth birthday, like Maman, I bleed for the first time, I am now an officially grown-up woman.

I can start to experiment.

4

IT IS MY TURN TO BE

Papa looks at me and announces I am too old to wear ponytails on top of each ear. At seventeen, I still want to please him, prove myself worthy of life and cease to act like one innocent child.

The night of Fat Tuesday, on the road to Le Zoute, a popular seaside resort on the Belgian Coast, Serge and his fiancée Micheline are drunk with his friend Henry after many Rodenbach with grenadine. It is Serge's favourite beer, although he will never beat his previous record of downing 52. Henry the driver falls asleep and the *deux chevaux*, Citroën's famous economy car, ends up in the muddy ditch.

Serge is not the driver; he is fiddling with the radio trying to keep awake seated at the dead man's place.

My brother Serge, my closest friend and confident, has fallen with his face in the ditch beside the sleeping driver, he is swallowing mud.

His fiancée Micheline in the back seat and the driver suffer from shock. But Serge swallows the mud of the ditch and nobody in the ambulance realize he is drowning.

When they do at the hospital, it's too late and he dies, asking just before to Maman if his face is okay. Maman and Papa were called immediately; they rushed driving to the hospital and arrive just in time to see him before he dies.

Serge is only 22 years old and now gone for life.

Serge and Micheline

I do not realize how important death is. At seventeen I am rebelling and experiencing. Now suddenly I understand there is no time to waste. I want to be immortal now, an artist leading my generation, on my own after Maman.

I drift from school to school. I abandon ancient Greek and Latin for cooking school. After paring and baking a pale calf tongue, I drop out. Then I go to a private cramming school and pass *les jury central*, the essential academic curriculum. There I begin to hang out with rebellious spoiled brats who borrow their father's fast cars.

I sit tensely in the racing cars, around the public park *Bois de la Cambre*, and down to Le Zoute. I hear the roar and feel the speed in controlled sliding on the screeching wheels.

With the Aston Martin of Charlie's father, the Firebird of Bertrand's father, the Porsche of Dany's father, the boys are racing the sports cars, emulating James Dean, risking that life we don't own, and we don't know the value of.

I hang out and experiment with the good-looking boys. But I am not ready, and I find them frustrating. There is nothing to be fascinated about beside fast cars, motorcycles, hockey fields, ski slopes and all what money can buy, they don't give a shit for what I like to do.

I am interested in philosophy, in existentialism, in spiritual anthroposophy. In finding my special way I read voraciously, French, Russian, English and American authors and poets and Eastern masters. I debate ideas and I listen to catch the beat, of gypsy, classical music and jazz beside the mysterious English and American rock and roll, and the Ray Charles and the twist we all dance to.

I parrot the mysterious lyrics of English rock and roll and the American folk music, the Blues, and the Spanish salsa.

I take a typing course.

Maman and Papa built and complete the family home in Uccle where we move. Maman works at home to create wallpaper and textile design in her studio beside the living room in our new house.

She works at painting minute samples from nine in the morning with a break for lunch. She continues from two to five every day, but not on the weekend.

After dinner, Maman sit in front of a brand-new colour T.V. We never had T.V. before.

Maman is happily distracted and relieved to watch the novel little screen intruding in our house. Maman entirely absorbed, forget all about her four daughters and young son.

We monster children are needy, ingrate, lazy, unsatisfied teenagers. We are rebellious, growing apart, showing no solidarity, difficult, unmanageable, unstable.

I don't like the television, it's unable to answer my questions. It interferes and distracts Maman while silencing me.

***

It's a slippery winter day. I am erring by our previous rented town house avenue Albert; I am insulated in the white and rust lynx coat my elegant Russian grandmother Mamouche gave me.

I've got boots and tights on and a fine woolly navy dress, I don't have a penny, just my hands warming in my pockets. I walk following the tram rails; I stand under the roof at the tram stop avenue Albert.

A small unnoticeable man appears to address me, we engage in conversation, he is a hat maker, and he has a shop on the street with a display window he points to.

I confide my auntie, the twin of my mother, now dead, was a hat maker in Rome.

Quiet and ceremonious, the man invites me to warm up at his shop with a drink of port. I am cold and there is slippery ice and grey snowbanks on the sidewalk. I don't have a program, the man is discreetly obsequious, and I don't have to walk further. I may warm up, just here. I follow him careful not to slide.

From the sidewalk I can see his window display with two beautiful feather hats.

A chair, a sofa, a table covered with hats in progress, and a single gas burner and kitchen pot.

Mamouche in her new Lynx coat at the end of the war in Paris

All is looking lonely and wanting, like the fellow, except for the two rounds and perfect swan down feather fluffy hats, one is white, and the other is black, like shadow and light.

The shop is a cold refuge, my nose, my feet, my hands are still cold. The furtive man keeps my cup filled to the brim with sweet port until I fade warming up in a sort of torpor on the uncomfortable chair.

I hear myself slurring, fabulating to this grotesque strange guy creeping closer.

He perceives I am losing control; he dares to touch my legs while he fills up my glass with port. I sink heavily glued to my seat. I swat him away like a pestering fly until I manage, with a great effort, to stand up. I tighten my fur coat, push the creep away, seize firmly the two nice hats from the window display, open the door, and walk away.

I am unsteady and drunk, but I still know my way home, zigzagging all the slippery way, holding to houses and the hats, not to fall. I finally slide on my bottom, on the icy slope beside our garden.

With one hand, I cling firmly onto my hats. I enter the unlocked back door and feel my way across the living room and reach the obscure spiral staircase groping for the walls.

I don't push the timer light on, in the dark I climb feeling each stair on my hands and knees up to my room. I make too much noise and wake up Papa and Maman, who ask where I come from.

I say I come from a costume party, and I won the hats with my number!

***

I hang out with Micheline, Serge's fiancée, although we never speak about Serge, he is gone. Micheline and I are planning our great summer together and teasing our hairs.

The rainy summer is warming up. Every sunny day we spend at the outdoor pool. We swim and lay in our bikinis in the afternoon speaking animatedly. We roll our R's, pretending to be Russian girls.

Once a month I go dazzling my be-speckled generous god-father Pierre, he likes to listen to my arty elucubrations. I distract him from the stock market and insurance policy, and every time he gives me money for my wardrobe.

Papa and Maman escape for three weeks holiday to Saint Tropez; they leave us under their friend Nina's supervision.

Nina is gone all day and reappear inebriated late at night. She enters the house fiddling noisily with her key, chasing our teenaged friends away, screaming at us, interrupting our party, and calls us "purulent shits."

Upon Papa and Maman's return she complains, especially about insolent me leading my younger siblings towards perdition. After her description of everyday surprise party during adult absence Papa furious seizes me by the hair and drags me in the bathroom. He grabs the scissors and chops my ponytail as a punishment in front of Maman, a silent witness.

Papa deaf to my plea, deaf to my outraged opinion, trusts the vile rantings of Nina, his long-time boozer friend.

To teach me discipline and obedience Papa and Mama send me to boarding school in Tournai. My patient and docile learning childhood is over, my depending irresponsible teenager life experiment has become a heavily restricted burden.

I rebel and sabotage all peace in Tournai girl's dormitory. I scream, rant, and rave consistently through the nights. The boarding school is not keeping me. My parents must take me back at home.

I am on strike; I refuse to be forced to trust obediently and blindly follow rules.

5

THE FINE ARTS, AND THE ESTRO HARMONICO

I consent to engage in learning sculpture at the Academy of Beaux Arts in Brussels. I enrol for clay modeling in the morning and stone carving in the afternoon.

My first assignment is to replicate the plaster head of a good-looking roman centurion with his helmet on. I enjoy rotating each angle on my turning round tray, working the humid flexible earth with wooden tools.

Once this centurion replica is done. I tackle original compositions.

I work the clay on my spinning support. The naked model poses just for me, ten minutes each hour the flexible lady assume my suggested contortion.

We are only six in the class in a big airy room with a glass roof flooded with light.

All we need to work with at our disposal. A trough full of clay, two kinds, the yellow smooth potter clay, and the gritty, purplish blue one called chamot.

We are given special casting class with two seasoned masters.

One of my plaster sculptures

I discover the beauty of pure copper thin sheets used to prepare the molds for plaster cast. The master sculptor shows me how to shape stone in the afternoon. I love to push and build my female strength.

I carve, hammer and chip and polish using the special iron tools. I produce two pieces, a bas-relief of a winged male feline bi-ped with a fish, in French cream coloured limestone. And one big ronde-bosse contemplative immature female feline in little granite.

I sculpt; it is a slow, patient and force demanding work.

I take a course in jewelry. And produce non-ferrous metal lacy necklace and bracelets I weld on my copper sheet laces.

I paint oil on canvas.

I tackle my first long book. I am, of course, also dancing and flirting.

When I turned sixteen my brother Serge helped

My plaster and copper leaf sculpture

forge my Identity card to show legal age for dancing in nightclubs.

Now, I follow Serge's prancing dancer circuit where the doormen already know me.

I dance with dancers. And I talk with talkers and drink with drinkers, and I smoke with smokers.

The old baron, Jean de Terlinden, one of my observing mentors who never married; at eighty-two still dashing and looking for perfection in female company. He was admiring my grandmother Mamouche during the war, he was admiring Maman when he met her, two decades later, and it is my turn to be admired now.

Maman, Mamouche, and I, have fun together about this elusive old persistence.

He pays the tab for me and his entourage.

We meet in one Italian restaurant on Waterloo Street to hang out and dine with a group of smart hopeful young beautiful people; it feels civilized with him and all his crew.

I've got nothing to offer beside my inspired originality. When I wear the white and rust lynx coat Mamouche gave me I feel disguised, far away from myself in a masquerade of success.

I am the one who look like Mamouche, corpulence and classic look with one differing aquiline nose. I carefully hide my freckles under a golden peach tinted foundation, my eyes extended with blue kohl and eyeliner. I present a mask imperturbable.

I smoke cigarettes in my long cigarette holder, lucky strike or Craven-A cork tipped. I play poker and if I lose, I never honour the bet. I laugh it off!

I drink, taking my time, sipping my alcohol with self-control. I engage in passionate conversation with knowledgeable professional men, and sometimes women.

I am an optimist projecting success. I feel positive observing and sampling what choices I've got.

Because I produce art, I obtain Papa's permission to change rooms from upstairs, with everybody on the same floor, to downstairs by myself into the vacant art studio.

Now I have my private room with separate entrance on the back garden. I insulate the wall with nine square panels of gyprock covered with pure copper sheets, hemmed in cement painted cobalt blue.

Jean Marie helps me do everything.

He works from 9 to 12 and from 2 to 5, beside me in the class at the academy. He helps carry my heavy sack of plaster, he gives me cigarettes, and from six to nine I share his studio space on Sparrow Street, near our school.

I weld silver and pewter and paint with oil, at lunch time and after five we do art projects in his large, cavernous atelier with good light at the bottom of the courtyard in an ancient abbey.

The walls are made of tightly imbricated stones without mortar, the floor uneven with loose pavement. The skylight in the vaulted ceiling is supported by round columns.

We make a life-size mold plaster cast of my nude statue. I melt pewter on my sculptures. I weld copper leaves and sticks of silver on my barbarian jewelry.

Another sculpture, made of granite

Jean-Marie helps me.

I cook gourmet meal in his second-floor bachelor studio with a kitchenette. He takes sculptural nude pictures of me, and he made a black chamber to develop the films. Jean-Marie monitors my welding, installs my copper walls, paint my floor blue, rent a truck and transport all my statues to my parent's garden and my room.

Jean-Marie makes my oil portrait, nails and screws the frame and stretches the canvas for his and my oil paintings.

Jean-Marie is totally devoted to my whims.

He's got one married mistress from his time in Africa, his age, gone for summer holiday with her husband. She left with him the key for her house and her wine cellar. So, he must feed her cat.

I am feeling free to shine and turn him around my finger. And ignore his feelings for me. With a toast to her health, we drink the best burgundy I ever drank. Three dusty bottles of Venerable Millesime, older than both of us. I dance to the music of the Calchakis improvising a sensational salsa solo.

Jean-Marie helps me plant my new décor, he places my life-size nude statue and my portrait beside me, along with Jean Fouquet's early renaissance master pièce, La Dame de Beaute.

Agnes Sorel's daring virgin show off her nude breast to her nursing child, I put that museum poster in a simple frame of pure copper.

The headboard of my empire bed is carved with a basket of flowers, fruits, and doves tinted in verdigris. The bed covers are flowered cretonne, a heavy cotton fabric, which match the drapes I can draw shut.

My room is lit by wrought iron lamps, perfumed by a swinging church incense burner. One ornate Easter beeswax candle, two meters long, fat, and never lit stands like a guard in a wooden candle holder.

I have appropriated one of two gaily painted metal lanterns on spikes, they were purchased from a Venetian gondolier by my great auntie Florence and great uncle Francesco while they finished gliding on their tour of the great canal of Venice on their honeymoon, long before I was born.

Eve crying

From the Academy I can walk to the Unicorn, a restaurant bar in a perpendicular discreet alley, near avenue Louise. I am welcomed in my spectacular outfits. I meet all kinds of alternative interesting guys to talk to, and a couple of young glamorous dangerous women.

I make cocktail sauce with cream, chive, ketchup, pillipilli and cognac. I am hanging out playing all kind of fun games, with a bunch of five young dandies. Each owns one of five Mercedes with a retractable waterproof canopy.

A burgundy one for unicorn patron Greek Michel, a bottle green one for Pacha dandy Dominique, a charcoal one for Jean-Marie his gentle brother, a midnight blue one for decadent baron Florimont and a black one for fun crazy Andre.

One sunny summer late afternoon I sit in the cushy leather seat beside any one of the elegant drivers. We parade around town in a tranquil convoy showing off with an open hood, like Gatsby the magnificent.

The gallant Andre shows me around town in his glossy polished coupe. I get suitably impressed when Andre enters with his own key at the Estro Harmonico private club. With a bar, restaurant, and art gallery, it is the trendy hang out frequented by Uccle intelligentia.

Andre is the son of an Italian Russian marques and a Chinese mother. He teaches me how to use chopsticks at his mother's Chinese restaurant.

Andre is witty, eccentric and amuses me. He limps with a cane since he jumped from the mezzanine into the fireplace room at the Estro Harmonico.

He says I am his little cane.

I am introduced properly to these social elite. This happening night refuge is a great discovery, near my house at a walking distance.

The jovial patron, Robert captures my complete attention with a thunderous

Flying in the city's grey walls

voice. Robert loves exploding about the promises of life with individual freedom away from duality.

Estro Harmonico is his retirement venture after prospecting in the Belgian Congo now called Zaire.

Robert is newly installed in Brussels with his wife Clairette, a modern, dark short hair blue eyed lady. He calls her proudly a real woman, and they have two young kids together.

Clairette plays piano and sing Boris Vian and Barbara songs after midnight. The couple makes waves with searching unsatisfied people disponible for revolution.

The log fire is always lit with red ambers, ready to grill substantial juicy meat, jacket potatoes, and flambé love apples for a rustic supper after midnight.

...

I am experiencing the situationist individuals taken back as a prospective shopping client.

I distract the staff with Robert and Raoul at my side.

I try on a pile of luxurious garments, while Robert and Raoul fuss loudly about the way I look, while the brunt of the browsing gang nick all they can grab and stuff into ample raincoats.

We all have read Rudolf Steiner, before that.

I go with them three times, my heart beating stronger each time. I was game until I had to run very fast to escape two vendors sprinting at our pursuit.

We share the loot with the gang from Berlin in Brussels.

I join the chorus with Lotte Lenya and sing Kurt Weil three penny opera, Mahogany, Offenbach lyrics of La

Belle Helene, and Karl Orf Carmina Burana. I listen and dance to the Beatles, and Bach cantatas.

We discuss Che Guevara, Mao Dse Tung, Emiliano Zapata and Martin Luther King Jr.

We play chess and poker games. Smoke cigarettes and drink copious amount of alcohol.

I slowly sip a lot of Mandarine Napoleon, Green Chartreuse, or Grand Marnier.

I am lighting one cigarette after the other, between phrases, sucking on my glamourous cigarette holder.

I listen and speak a lot too. I consume steak barely cooked on the wood fire with jacket potatoes, and love apples in foil, flambé with calvados, followed by flambé Irish coffee.

I am dancing steady on my high heels up on the wooden stage landing. Everyone can admire our stamina with our two-hour non-stop gig.

I meet Peter Shtang, a 21-year-old escapee from behind Berlin's wall, who arrived with the gang, and prefers to stay here. I bump into him, while he read Karl Marx walking in my street.

I am reading Montaigne, Rousseau, Jean Paul Sartre, Simone de Beauvoir, and the Marquis de Sade, beside Rudolph Steiner, Musil, Goethe, and Soren Kierkegaart.

My grandfather's eastern master is Bo Hin Ra and I read, Aurobindo, Vivekananda, Yogananda, and Krishnamurti.

I am taken to openings; theater plays and the opera. I am invited to elegant restaurants or bohemian flamenco and Tzigane bistros and dancing. I am exploring city life after working hours.

In the day I have no say in the running of life. I sleepwalk daily to my art class, often very late in the morning. The kind doorman always lets me in.

I believe I own my sleepless night; it helps me invent my maturing self. I put on the parachute dress and open my black lace rounded tapering parasol under the moon, not quite like Mary Poppins.

I practice my art at the academy, and in Jean-Marie's atelier.

I will offer a Moroccan style feast to welcome buyers to my first show. With Robert from the Estro, I enter the slaughterhouse, pinch my nose and brace myself at the smell of fear and carnage. We come to choose and buy a kosher lamb to roast on the pit on the massive open fire at the Club. It is for my Mechoui vernissage.

I showcase necklaces of melted silver on copper. My athletic female form stretching in clay with feline heads baked naked in the kiln of the academy, I dress them later in Jean Marie atelier with welded scales of copper leaf.

Seven oil painting on canvas, feline headed angels with wings in seven elements. One is time, one is

An invitation to my first show

fire, one is earth, one is water, one is air, one is stone, one is ether.

A single painting and a sculpture sold at the opening, by two of my devoted mentors, not the success I hoped for.

This is the proof that I need to build resistant strength somewhere else.

My first epic book all about my everyday life of great expectations catch the interest of Jean Blanzat, first lecture at Gallimard publishing house, prix femina for *"Le faussaire"*, a hero of the resistance.

He believes I am a young visionary, he will recommend my "Voyage Ambigu" to be published, after I correct and clarify my text according to Jean Blanzat's precise minuscule notes.

I am activated like one exploding seed. But I won't root in this city life, and I bounce out of it.

With the boost from platonic admirers buying a token of my art, and footing my extravagant opening bill, I've still got enough cash to purchase my passage from Marseille to Casablanca, a three-day voyage on the mixed cargo ship Azrou of the Paquet Company.

I am invited by my friend Wanda.

I am tired of stagnating in Brussels city distracted by settled professional older men. Securing bourgeois comfort is not my dream.

My heroic attempt at independence through my art production and sale is a failure. Nobody here is free for me. I can't fit in. I want reality.

At the Estro Harmonico all my friends are just riding away for their night escape, it's never for real.

My gliding spirit must land like a seed on fertile earth. To do so, to be it, to play with, to dance, eventually to choose and be chosen,

Night after night, I eat delicatessen and drink sweet liquors with one of my favourite regulars chatting me up.

I pass time listening to experienced voices telling exciting tales. I conclude by my two clever words, even a passionately intelligent tirade: "how cute!"

They are all married, or not married but settled in their way and just seeking a distraction. I honestly like to show what I could do. I won't wait anymore for someone here to go with me. I am wasting my time.

I am nineteen years old now. My hair is long again, and Papa will never lift a punishing hand on me or cut my hair again.

My conduct is on my own shoulders.

Papa asks me with nonchalant inquisition: "what is it, Brigitte?"

"Is that laziness, boredom, obstipation, stupidity, arrogance or neglect?"

My emphatic answer, tit for tat:

"It's heredity!"

6

MOROCCO-PARIS: HITTING THE ROAD FROM NEW YORK TO MEXICO

And here I am, waiting for my love miracle to happen. I feel it is not here.

I am just one escape away from this rainy city where all the important fancy people work behind grey walls, their window opening to grey clouds.

For them I represent the elusive sunshine. I so much want to get away from this malaise. Away from Brussels' perpetual rain, from my parents' drama, from accidental inclusion in a security net. From what is proper, expected from me.

I dive for the unknown invited by my trusted friend Wanda. I will visit her in Morocco.

In his flashy, second-hand, silvery grey Studebaker, Papa drives me to my train ride from Paris to Marseille.

I am wearing low-waisted jeans over my ballet dancer body and demi pointe black slippers.

Twelve hours later I walk in the port of Marseille, all alone, under a sunny blue sky.

The sun shines on me at the Azrou dock.

A rough looking porter put my bag of dresses on his head. He brings me to my cabin on the mix cargo, plonks my bag down on the chair and immediately proceeds to fondle me.

I scream a piercing call and get immediately rescued by several colourful members of the crew.

The black cook gives me red palm oil for tanning my white body on the sun deck where I consciously offer a glimpse of my skimpy bikini as this voyages' mascot to the fascinated and respectful crew.

I get to eat fried garlic with potatoes cooked in red wine and reap many delicate perks from each sailor to me.

I wake up at the crack of dawn with the crew, ignoring my fellow cargo mix passengers. I choose to be a joyful working part of the boat. I get to clean the deck and sing in the intoxicating briny air at sunrise.

After the three days cruise I walk away from the Azrou. With the captain by my side, the first mate carries my bag. Behind us the rest of the crew escorts me to the quay, cheering bye-bye.

Amal sees me coming.

Dhar al Beida, the progressing city of the medieval kingdom of Morocco.

I am welcomed.

I open my eyes to this ocher earth under cloudless blue sky. I perceive better with the sun, the warm and sunny glow steers my desire to merge, waking me up further.

I correct the proofs of my first book: "Le Voyage Ambigu" in Wanda's adopted hamlet I thrive on Moroccan hospitality.

We are in the Ben Slimane army base with French cooperation, between Casablanca and Rabat.

Palm grove in the rift mountains

Here begins my unbounding voyage.

Wanda is called Madame Amal here. She left rainy Brussels, pregnant, for sunny Morocco two years ago.

She married her boyfriend Amal, the best student graduate in gynecology at the Université Libre de Bruxelles where she got her teaching degree. She teaches French at the village school.

Wanda is the daughter of Nina, to whom I owe my unforgotten last forced haircut by Papa when I was seventeen.

By now, wisely maturing, I don't hold any grudge for Wanda's mother.

The great Nina, a tough survivor sarcastic and cruel, a big jolly drinker and jovial talker is still struggling since the Second World War.

Wanda and her whole family are part of my parents' bohemian circle.

Dimitri, Wanda's noble exiled Russian father, artist illustrator draws and paints commercial decors. Wanda's noble exiled Polish mother Nina peddles his work and negotiates commands, surviving with more beer each day.

They can be found a fixture propping the bar in the *Petit Ixelle*, the bistro they live behind, drinking beer and holding court, joking about real struggle with other regular clients.

Nina and Dimitri successfully raised two children: Wanda my friend, now a teacher, the doctor's wife and the mother of little Natacha and Wanda's brother Ivan, now a staff sergeant stationed on the border of Belgium and Germany.

Wanda is a ravishing blond woman, slim and willowy, with a lot of spirit, sparkling mischievous eyes and a feisty sharp tongue.

We have fun and develop a liking for each other since the last costume ball we attended at the Academy, she was a Sabine, and I was a mysterious black cat.

I am glad to see Amal, at the Azrou dock. He is the doctor directing Benslimane hospital. He came to fetch me in his deux chevaux.

On the road in the Deux Cheveux

We drive for one hour to the villa, welcomed by Wanda with the adorable toddler Natacha trotting up by her side.

Nobody forgot that previously Amal tried to kiss me in front of his pregnant fiancée, two years ago, I already bit him.

Amal still finds me exciting like a forbidden fruit, but I do not expect him to kiss me in the mouth again, when I am sunning myself in the courtyard; and I bite his tongue, again.

Still, Wanda, laugh at him with me.

We understand each other. She is glad to see me, we must forgive Amal, but he still must discover respect with clad sophisticated young European women, and he should not forget women are not amusable commodities.

Wanda and I improvise operatic arias mocking Amal's sacrilegious wicked ways.

Every day is full of sun under the blue sky. We sing and laugh and eat good tagin: lamb, potatoes, onions, and tomato stew. And a bottle or two of good cabernet sauvignon, or Gris de Boulaoune, the most popular Moroccan wine for export.

In Ben Slimane Wanda tells me, the young men are calling me a precious marvel. I believe they mean it, when my guide throws his jacket over a muddy puddle for me to walk on.

I am the latest curiosity distracting notables from the entourage of Doctor Amal, we are invited in the countryside on the pretext of presenting me, the young available sister of Madame Amal.

In the souk market before Essaouira

Upon entering the feast in a striped green and red tent we leave our shoes in front of the canvas door.

Wanda and I sit in the middle of the circle, surrounded by a dozen male guests. Everyone sits cross legged at ease on the polychrome thick carpet around a round brass tray heaped with food.

The servant passes a brass basin and pore water to wash our hands, one must use only the right hand for eating. Our host, plucks and tears the finest first bites and hands them to me. I savour the choice morsels of tender lamb from the round tray everyone digs in.

This is the first tray.

Then a plate of tagine for us to eat, soaking the juice with fresh kesra bread.

Next comes a dish of sweet couscous with cinnamon.

Watermelon and delicate sweet *Pastilla*, a pigeon pie with almond and cinnamon.

The modern notables drink a lot of alcohol; they don't follow the religious sobriety which rules bigoted Muslims. The wives who send the feast are waiting for the scraps to eat what is left. They wait hidden in the kitchen.

Wanda and I meet and thank them before we go.

The wine is good with many vineyards around, filled with French grapes planted by French protectorate to blend export wine with.

In Casablanca at the café terrace a gathering of older men sip sweet mint tea and nibbles on *Alami*, snacks of hot roasted almonds in cumin, some cubes of chicken liver, some olives and pickled capsicum, snails in spicy sauce.

Well-nourished while hanging out with friends, they fill their Sebsi pipe, take the toke and pass it on.

They drink the entire metal pot of fragrant syrupy fresh mint tea that the waiter lifts high. The spout forms an arc of warm perfumed sweet tea in gilded glass.

The men pull and puff on the ornate skinny long pipe with minuscule clay bowl they fill up and light every time.

I am interested, I ask Amal about the effects of Kif.

Amal says. "Oh! They smoke, and they smoke more, then they get dry, dry, dry, like this" and he shows me his dry and narrow pinky, "and then they croak...It may take hundred years..."

I must try this!

When I taste that old man's Sebsi full of Kif, a mild pleasant feeling I'd like to repeat, not a dulling, but a subtle change in perception. I become a notch more grounded to earth.

He is funny Amal.

No one drinks alcohol in public.

I repeat many Arabic words, I enjoy repeating the guttural sound, I use the formulas to bargain at the market, count, greet, say thanks.

Wanda presents me to the teachers at the end of the school year party.

I meet Majowsky, her youngest colleague, who is just ending his two years mandatory military service for the French.

Majowsky wants to explore the south of Morocco before he goes back to France and marry his polish Fiancée. He owns a deux chevaux car, he invites me to join him to explore the south.

Majowsky looks like James Joyce, a lightweight ash blond man with round glasses.

He wishes to become a vegetarian, which makes me laugh. In Morocco the blood of lambs is more abundant than water in this slice of parched earth.

Majowsky will have to try later. I am right about that.

Between us we have not quite enough money for the long journey south. But we count on good luck and Moroccan hospitality all the way.

Our first stop the port of Safi with one Old Portuguese fortress, the pottery souk. I don't like to feel like a tourist. I am happy to use my Moroccan Arabic to bargain hard and purchase 12 colourful hand painted ceramic soft boiled egg holders, a perfect gift for my mother.

We explore the green Atlas Rif, then reach Chefchchouane and climb the blue staircase of the blue-sky sanctuary, to the octagonal minaret in the mullah city with blue indigo walls.

Further south, through the ocher road, we pass many abandoned ocher magic castles sculpted of earth and straw. The deserted medinas, partially crumbled, are invaded by termites growing spikey towers. We finally stop to enter one of the ornate walls.

No more water, two curious kids rest in the wall shade, they watch their goats and sheep grazing North Africa's sparse savannah, with a goat mother and kid content to wallow in a puddle of liquid mud still in the bottom of a shallow well.

We can't afford a hotel room or restaurant.

We buy local kesra bread from the splendid ladies, enthroned in front of their big basket full of fresh bread for sale. Dressed like queens in gilded brocade green, red or blue with buttoned kaftans.

In the Medina, we find a table with a bench. We sit beside other hungry people and buy a bowl of thick harira soup to dip our grey fresh bread for one dirham. There is no shade and there are many flies.

We drink sweet mint green tea and big glasses of fresh water poured from the shiny brass pot in brass cups by water vendors dressed in red with red caps, brass bells, and red pompoms.

That's our road rest when we refuel the deux chevaux and our dusty self. We are entirely ocher with dust on sweat from the ocher road with no traffic.

I appreciate that sober survival adventure, sampling earth.

We don't linger in the cities, but we have a good look and walk around, keeping our vehicle in sight.

Majowsky takes my picture in the ruin of Agadir still tumbled seven years after the big earthquake. Before the desert starts, we halt at the souk before Essaouira. We drink mint tea, *hatai*.

Bedouins gathers under the shady roof. I am sitting with a metal tea pot and sip my glass in my white dress printed with climbing roses, surrendered by the Shleus, the Berber blue men, hiding from the sun and the sand in their Indigo kefias scarves.

Agadir, still in ruins from the 1960 Earthquake

We drive across the scorching heat through a grove of prehistorical Argan trees. They have low spikey twisting branches, easy to climb and full of perched goats munching oily yellow berries with a dark hard pit.

This precious oil for the salad, the hairs, the skin, the beauty of the desert dwellers is harder to get than hashish.

In my bikini I climb one Argan tree where we stop with the car. Majowsky takes my picture.

And one hour later we get stranded in Goulimine, because of the puncture of one threadbare smooth tire.

With no more money we request assistance from the Qaid, the village chief, and his friend the chief of police, obliging saviours at our rescue.

We must keep going and go back. The Qaid lends us the modest amount of Dirham we require.

While the tire is patched at the mechanic, the police chief takes us on a desert village tour, by Jeep, all around his domain.

Hassam, chief of police in Rissani, focus strictly on my enchantment. There is a picture taken by Majowsky of this gallant chief officer and me in front of the Sahara desert's wonderful scenic view.

I wear my mini one shoulder slanted dress in green paisley satin silk.

Climbing an Argan tree

Apotheosis of this wonderful day; the sun sat huge and sank into the orange sea of rippling sandy dunes, I ran quickly bare foot into the squishy grains.

We sat in the oasis of Erfoud under the palm shade at the outdoor café, open for us only.

We thirstily savoured almond milk with rose water followed by fresh squeezed orange juice with minced fresh mint; admired the magnificent orange afterglow lingering on the orange infinite Sahara.

Wind swept sandy waves rolls endlessly with nothing else under the desert sky.

After a tagine feast and many gilded glasses of sweet mint tea, some luscious dates, watermelon and cakes shaped like gazelle horns stuffed with almond honey paste.

I received a gift, a white cotton translucent foot length Abaya, a light covering desert robe, a souvenir for me.

Hassan just got it at the Rissani night bazaar at the end of all roads.

I passed the robe over my scanty dress, and subsequently I got immediately soaked with two liters of the finest rose water chief Hassan pored all over me.

I was overwhelmed by the extent and refreshing finesse of this impulsive daring Sahara courting.

This evening bazaar baptism concluded the day.

We were invited to spend the night at Chief Hassan's spacious and comfortable police station.

At the end of the Sahara's orange dunes, I find myself alone with Hassam when night falls.

Majowsky is out of commission. He was offered and ate a majong cookie after dinner with his mint tea and soon sleeps deeply on a low bench in the house entrance, right beside two police assistants on standby playing cards.

I join Hassan in his salon.

Now I prudently warn him about my strict father who trusts me to respect, imperceptible, boundaries.

And the chief of police proceeds to drink whiskey, but it is just fresh squeezed orange juice for me. I want to keep my wits.

I smoke, like a dragon, keeping myself at an honourable distance, waving, my one-foot-long bamboo and ebony cigarette holder like a sword dancer.

I do most of the talking, I keep him fascinated. Everything is cool and proper for hours.

Hassan in the middle of the night, now, propose to marry me, he is a free, modern, young, established man.

Standing in front of Marrakesh

To seal his proposal, he wants to load immediately on the roof rack of the deux chevaux, preliminary engagement gifts.

He starts to seize the low lemonwood table inlaid with mother of pearl, abalone and black ebony. He also grabs a painted camel saddle gracing his Moroccan salon.

I refuse it all. I manage to convince him to sit again.

The night is almost over, he is drunk, and I am getting tired and uneasy waving the fire of my cigarette on the low divan.

When finally, Hassan loses hope of my willing conquest, he stands and rises to pounce on me. I bite his index finger and don't let go, some blood drips under my strong fierce bite.

Hassan threatened by my bite, follows me while I gather my belongings and wake Majowsky from his sound sleep, ordering him back into the driver seat, through my clenched teeth.

We must go, now!

The assistants are told by sobering Hassan, to let us go.

Only when the motor is running do I relieve his index finger from my bite.

And so, we escape my opportunity to be a police queen in the desert.

When we stop for changing the puncturing tire for the patched spare, I lay on the road listening for the sound of pursuit.

But we are free to go, no one is after us...

Now my white Abaya is dry and still smells very good.

Next, we stop in Taroudant; again, we must patch another punctured tire.

Taroudant welcomes us with another gallant police chief to the rescue. He's eager to help us and proud to give us the tour of the ancient city.

I climb on a kneeling camel. When he stands abruptly his two-time motion jerking me up on his hindlegs, high up on his knobby knees.

I ride the one hump camel, holding tight for a long half an hour promenade on the majestic testy beast, rumbling up and down, I am getting slightly nauseous.

We are charmed admiring the camel trader city. We can savour the tranquil pace with no tourists except us real voyageurs. We eat a great Moroccan dinner with mint tea.

This police chief offers me a white embroidered night gown and his sister's enormous ornate carved bed for the night.

What is that white dress Moroccan custom?!

When he offers me to rest for the night in that big bed, I keep all my clothes on.

I am not so surprised when our hosting officer, one hour later, shows up through the window in uniform with his shiny gun at his belt.

Posing with the chief of police in Rissani, at the edge of the Sahara Desert

I suspected his sister is his wife; she looked dejected and worried about me entering her house.

Consequently, I had the whole night to talk the expectant chief's ears off about his admirable Moroccan city providing us with such a civilized generous hospitality

I am relieved to see the sun rise.

The chief is almost asleep still all dressed, with his gun in his belt, when I wake up Majowsky, fresh again after a good night sleep full of majong.

And away we go, my honour safe, and me again so lucky to force respect and keep police chiefs at bay.

Majowsky must purchase new tires in Rabat, before driving back on the long road to France.

On my own I still want to explore the country.

I take a bus to Fez.

The guy beside me is called Akhmet. He invites me to the wedding of his sister.

Before we arrive in Fez we stop and visit the sacred city of Moulay Idris, but I cannot enter the Mausoleum of Moulay Idris.

The Moroccans come to this mountainous city in pilgrimage.

It is said that coming six times during the festival honoring Idris the saint is equivalent to one Hajj to Mecca. Its only open to Muslims.

I distrust religious sectarianism; I want one open divine world with all manifested aspects to welcome me.

We enter Fez through Bab Al Jeloud, the beautiful stucco arch. Fez used to be the Paris of the Arabic world, the grandest big city of North Africa.

When the bus parks we walk to a pisé shack made of pounded clay, to stay with Akhmet's old grandmother for the first night. We sleep there with her and her goats on the beaten earth floor. I experience something familiar with the small barn in which it feels easy and comfortable to live one day at the time at this pace. I realise I am on the same track following the way of Mary and Joseph with baby Jesus, just looking for shelter and food...life flows on.

Akhmet's grandmother looks ancient, strong and wrinkled; she cooks outdoor on a fire of twigs and leaves. She makes us some soft flatbread with the local rancid butter for our breakfast and spurts a fresh warm drink direct from the goat udder to my glass.

Fez city is full of elaborate, ornate stucco palaces with sugar fondant colours and enchanting gardens perfumed with jasmine roses and Daturas during the day. After sunset, the tiny trumpet flowers of the Queen of the Night open their bloom to yield their sweet and intoxicating aroma.

Then we take the city bus to the bride's house and meet the rest of the family.

I assist in the first wedding festivities, and I am delighted to hear them ululate shrilly: "You you you!" repeating endlessly in exuberant staccatos.

They welcome and carry the adorned bride in her festive green and gold buttoned caftan. She wears a parure in gold filigree, with a belt, necklace, stud earrings with emeralds, and a ring from the Fassi jewelers' market in Casablanca. That is part of the traditional dowry requested from the groom for the family.

I am welcome to sleep in the overcrowded house on the carpet with many guests.

In the morning, Akhmet and I escape from the crowded house to smoke some hash in the Fez palace garden. He is a student; he hopes to travel the world, so I give him my address at my parents'.

I don't stay until the final ceremony; the wedding festivities last a whole week. That is enough local culture for me. I take the bus after three days, back to Casablanca and catch another bus directly to Ben Slimane.

My last trip is to Marrakesh with my new friend Fatima, the young nurse at the hospital of Amal. She is happy for me to share her home and we bathe and chitchat in her mother's *Hammam,* a steam bath.

Her mother is the first and the most important of the four wives of her father. We follow her father to visit her brothers and sisters at his three other houses with wives and children. His second wife has a hardabashery shop, the third one a general grocery shop, and the fourth one a fruit shop.

The Marrakesh water vendors

I stay a week with Fatima and her mother. Fatima stiches me a turquoise dress from the remains of the percale she made the new drapes for the hospital with. It has a low waist with a white zip and a white rickrack trim. I put that dress on to go to Marrakech.

We buy our tickets in advance for the morning bus, we get up and walk to the bus stop at a leisurely pace at the exact scheduled departure time, Fatima must have her sandals mended and we stop at the cobblers who repair them.

I am jumping up and down with impatience, but Fatima calms me by explaining the bus driver is her uncle, and he is waiting for us. With that I understand how personal Moroccan culture is.

When we climb in the bus with genuine feelings of going somewhere, Fatima talks with her uncle for most of the voyage and when we arrive in Marrakech her uncle drives us to his son's house, Fatima's cousin, it could be anywhere in a family home where we spend two nights.

I would not know we are in Marrakech if I did not insist to visit the town, Fatima's welcoming family intent on spending our whole trip bonding. We must insist to have a one hour walk around the exciting Jama el fna place and go to visit aguedal orange grove.

Fatima's uncle comes to get us in his bus, and we go back to Ben Slimane after a full day catching up with family at her cousin's.

I dove headfirst into a traditional reality with exotic rules I can't be bothered to grasp. I have no more money to go on traveling in Morocco. I stayed long enough in Ben Slimane.

I loved all of it. My trip to Morocco was my initiation to the orient to which I am indebted and grateful, especially to Wanda my most intelligent, fun, and spirited elder sister and long-time friend.

Now it's time to go back to Paris and publish my book.

I get a ride in the car with two French teachers from Wanda's School leaving back to Biarritz; they will drive me to France.

We roam as fast as possible overland through Spain.

The Spanish stare indifferent to us, we don't count, and they don't speak French.

My creative Spanish gibberish is not good enough to feel welcome in Spain. I only get arrogant stares.

It is another way of life. I try to speak for the two fast talking French guys.

I run through the Prado so quickly in front of Velasques, but the drivers wait for me, impatient to go home.

Spain is just the road on the way back.

I have no time to linger and discover Don Quixote and Carmen's country.

Back in Brussels I complete my book, accepted by the publisher Flammarion.

With Maman, Mamouche and Papa we spend numerous afternoons to get my proofs ready.

"Le voyage Ambigu" is published in 1968. I get interviewed, I am a young author at Flammarion, and it feels almost real!

I camp at Rive Droite near the Champs Elysees at my friend Khlava's.

I share her dove cote room. We speak animatedly drinking wine and smoking cigarettes all night in her attic room on the seventh floor. The lady

Me editing La Voyage Ambigu

from under beat her ceiling, our floor with her broom, hoping we will shut up. We whisper for a while, but again we grow enthusiastic excited and loud, and the insomniac lady bangs again on our floor.

When we go down the steps, mid-morning the lady is sweeping her landing furiously while looking at us with murdering eyes when we greet her politely stealing down her flight of stairs, like prancing deer.

We drink our espresso, beside four celebrating guys, reporters from associated press. They came down from the nearby newsroom. In the Champs Elysees bistro.

They invite us to share their wine. Immediate sympathy flares with a flow of great conversation and red wine. I bond particularly with Bruno.

We have a rendezvous planned for when I return to Paris from Mexico.

I signed my contract, I made my dedications and confidences to the press, and I got my advance royalties and bought my flight ticket from Luxembourg to New York and back.

Papa drives Elsa and me to Luxembourg airport.

I fly for the first time, with Islandic airline, in a Stratacruiser with a Rolls-Royce motor. A big ancient pterodactyl machine.

We roll in it on the tarmac, I feel, and I hear the tearing lifting us from the ground and the heavy climb into the sky.

Then it cruises, moving almost silently for some hours.

We dive again to the ground to refuel and take new passengers in Reykjavik.

I drink with Elsa the worst coffee in the bleak transit canteen. Nobody else got out of the aircraft, we put our feet in Iceland, one new country we touch the ground of on our way.

We fly to New York, over to the big apple of the United States.

I am singing all the way, not sleepy and so excited to fly in the belly of this big monster.

Six-foot-tall Elsa fold quickly falls asleep cramped in her small seat. She is a seasoned traveler who has flown before.

The plan is to proceed overland, as cheap as possible, by greyhound bus to Mexico. Details of it shall be mentioned later.

7

PARIS ISLE SAINT LOUIS ON MY BOAT

Now just returning from Kathmandu Nepal, after a slow and long voyage on the road. I gathered all I deem precious and relevant, before that journey.

I am aiming to tell that true story. My completed initiation, on the overland hippie trail.

Before getting away from it all, I was experiencing my young bohemian life on "Le Mutin", one leaky wooden 22-foot pleasure boat. A relic still afloat, moored for the rest of its time, on "Quai Bourbon", on the Seine River on the left bank in Isle Saint Louis.

The bigger of only two boats legally moored there.

That remote abode floated and bobbed, accessible only by a wooden rowboat locked on a rivet down the steel ladder. I had to unlock and pull the chain to glide to this shelter.

Bruno invited me. I could, if I would like to, stay on one of the two boats for sale, he pointed at them, from the top of the bridge very close to his bachelor mini flat.

Of course, I was enthusiastic and delighted about this free lodging offer.

I choose Le Mutin, leaky and in disrepair but in it I could stand and stretch unconfined in my own space.

Bruno worked night shifts reporting for the newsrooms at the associated press by translating the English fax. He had traveled previously to Japan; his hobby is playing Villa Lobos and Fernando Sor, the two famous beginner classical guitar pieces.

Le Mutin and my rowboat

I became a Parisian resident, moored at Quay Bourbon, with a permit still valid for three years.

I slept locking myself in the cabin, on a narrow couch wide enough for me.

For my comfort Bruno bought an efficient stove and a bright lamp with asbestos mantle. Deodorised, kerosene fuel available at the local hardware store on the island, I can light it myself. It quickly warms the cabin and burns silently with a sweet smell.

On the wooden bar across my bed sits my Remington portable typewriter.

Green eye black kitten, Beranger, slept with me. For that kitten I paid a thousand old French francs at the metro entry of Rungis flower market, double price, since I foolishly insisted it should be a male.

I got a sentiment of security from a sharp bayonet in a metal scabbard, from the French revolution.

I selected that self-defence weapon among cutlass, swords and daggers, from my Russian Bon-papa Illoucha's arms collection in Brussels.

I sleep with my lively black kitten and the passive Michu from Odessa, the ancient ragged mangy teddy bear of my father who traveled with him in the Pelikan submarine from Odessa.

Morning like evening, I glide on my small rowboat jump to the quay with Beranger on a red leash. We go for cat walks to the Latin quarter passing through the court across from Notre Dame De Paris.

Every Sunday we take the metro to Saint Ouen flea market with Bruno and Beranger. I dance in the street of saint Ouen, to the irresistible guitar of Maurice Reinhart, Django's cousin and the other gypsy violin player.

I dance, for those in the square in front of the café des sports.

Bruno holds Beranger.

Maurice Reinhart invites me for dinner. I accept his rendezvous in the Latin Quarter. He shows up wearing a blue suit, a white shirt with golden cuff links, and a red tie. But I cannot be at ease with the genial Manouche, looking like he could be my father.

I am frozen in my inexperience, not relaxed during the dinner, wondering what I am doing here. I refuse to know better the musician man and prepare myself to get away. I run, back to my limbo world, not lingering and not daring to take my chance further into the gypsy world.

Beranger is a very good swimmer, for a cat. who often falls while attempting daring acrobatics from the narrow railing of the Mutin. I drag my cat with the red leash, to #4 Rue le Regrattier, there I shower, cook, dress up, and listen to Bruno practice of Sor and Vila Lobos on Classic guitar. Bruno pays for everything; He is infatuated with me.

Bruno at thirty-five is old for me. I am not attracted physically to my gentle hopeful new best friend. He will stay generous and available for me; in case I get desperate and horny and settle for him when I get older.

But he is not my type, a bit short with nice blue eyes, but not irresistible. I feel somehow devious; I need him for protection and all the comfort I can get. I am just exploiting my opportunity.

Scintillating discussions in my skillful domestic company seems enough contribution. I know to play this waiting game during the patient courting truce. I am stalling with one open mind so ready to take advantage of all offers.

The fact is, I am still searching I need supporters to build myself.

Bruno is my latest bluff worshipper. At this point it would be a real waste of my precious time. I am not compromising while in doubt. That is my way. I have never worked for money.

All my friends seem to be happy to support me, so what is wrong with that. I am free to investigate, I don't have to worry.

Straight from a Persian miniature, a tall, bearded man with a turban dreamily contemplates my boat.

Will we ever meet? Do I fit in a common dream with anyone I notice? I could start my story.

In Morocco, the unconquered kingdom, the sun gate opened wide to the orient, initiating for me that personal voyage. After my enticing detailed reportage, my parents, with Papoum will visit Wanda, Amal, and Natacha in Ben Slimane.

I am back in Paris; from the Mutin I walk from Quay Bourbon to Rue Racine, to the Flammarion author office to sign my books.

It is Bruno who writes a loving delicate presentation on the back-cover page of *Le Voyage Ambigu*. I get my picture taken pulling my chain on my gliding bark.

The old 'Mutin' needs a lot of bailing when it rains.

Bruno uses cement to patch the rotten holes. That's a precarious measure with no safety guarantee.

The river police snoops around the Mutin with me luxuriating on board. They rev their fast engine and come speeding close by, making waves that causes the Mutin to jerk and rock me wildly, gurgling water.

I thrive, stationary afloat for many months. I work on my typewriter, I make tea, and I sleep with Beranger.

The low ceiling boat beside me hosts Momo, who retired after ten years of guerrilla in the French Legion, around southeast Asia ending up in Laos near Sopsien.

At 18 feet long, Momo's boat is sound and does not leak. His war godmother bought it for him, so he can live in peace now.

We converse; I listen to details of Laos and Vietnam guerrilla crimes still entertaining vicious conflicts for vicious interests.

He listens to my hopeful projects. We are so interesting and so different.

We are two privileged marginals; we keep separate from the bums and the wandering homeless hippies.

Since the spring of 1967, the vagrants sleep under the bridge twenty meters from our two boats.

In the sunny afternoon, Momo paddles us in my rowboat all around the isle until he beaches it at the point.

I swim and sunbathe joining the resident swimmers on the sunny slope of the tiny park comprising of a shading weeping willow and a single bench.

I watch Michele Morgan, the legendary Diva, arriving home in her chauffeured Citroën; she catches the light beam of sunset entering the gate of her mansion in isle Saint Louis.

Michelle Morgan gets into her gated mansion in her garden overlooking the point. I see her in slow motion entering her gate, I am surprised to see star light perfect beauty in this mature woman.

Moustaki lives around the corner, near the café des sports where I have morning café au lait croissant. He is a famous Greek in France. He wrote Milord for Edith Piaf, he was her young lover for a while, he wrote many good songs, still well known today for Serge Reggiani.

Moustaki was born in Egypt to Greek parents. We play together on the electric billiard, we become acquainted, he takes me for rides on his bike, he sings me his new songs on his piano. He has a daughter around my age.

After my first trip solo in Morocco, I yearn to travel more. Bruno rents a deux chevaux to go for a long ride through France to his home in the Dauphine near Grenoble.

I meet his sister and his parents. I walk in the pine forest he owns, and I still maintain an attracting distance between us.

With Beranger getting bigger, we drive from the Dauphine to Italy. Equipped with a single burner propane gas stove, a pot, a kettle and two sleeping bags, we camp along the way and visit Italy, stretching Bruno's holiday budget.

I cook in the clearing in front of the bush where we did sleep under a transparent plastic sheet secured to the branches on top.

Beranger explores this Adriatic extension of his Parisian territory, first in Milano with the white lacy marble train station.

We enter Milano, park the car and walk. We unleash Beranger at the park. Beranger run across a big rectangular basin, full of active lime, mistaking it for a big pool of creamy milk. With a wooden plank across, we rescue and rinse him.

Soon after that accidental bath, some of his belly fur falls off and grows back purple.

We are camping in the bushes in one of the seven hills around Rome. If I walk on my own to get milk and bread, pane and latte, without Bruno as bodyguard, Italian men follow me like a cloud of flies. They attack and touch me, pester me, I must furiously battle my way through.

I phone my great Uncle Jack. I previously met him with Maman, his only living niece and closest blood relative.

We had tea and cake a couple of times in Brussels at the Hotel Metropole. Uncle Jack told me to call him from Rome. Jack is a monk of Malta, a genealogist, and a middleman for N.A.T.O arms dealers.

He lives alone, separated from his wife Erica many years ago, but divorce does not exist in the Catholic Italy. Cordial distance is taken with the daughter of the master illusionist Eric Jan Hanussen, the great magus who taught the art of staging and mass control to Benito Mussolini and Adolf Hitler. He married her in 1943, 10 years after her father was killed.

Uncle Jack is willing and happy to host me with my cat, in his tiny bachelor suite near Piazza Navona behind Via Veneto in the elegant Rome.

Bruno is obviously not invited. He tactfully disappears from our family reunion sight while I am getting presented to Uncle Jack's elegant circle of roman aristocracy.

I can refresh, shower with hot water, and dress up in front of his full-size mirror. And get to know my one and only impeccably groomed Grand Uncle.

He put himself and his modest ground level lodging at my disposal. Uncle Jack occupies a bachelor closet refuge in his one everything room.

Everything he owns is here, books on shelves, things on a table, his valuable Aubusson tapestry.

A large wooden wardrobe with a full-size mirrored door, well stocked with several elegant outfits and dry-cleaned costumes and shirts and cravats, scarves, gloves and bows, English gentleman suits, and many shoes shiny and matte.

In two dry cleaner transparent bags I notice, he shows his grand robe and hat of a monk of Malta, plus the uniform with a cape of a Knight of Malta, with a great parade sword, inherited ten years ago from my Grand-Papa Roberto, his elder brother.

Jack sleeps in his single bed in the alcove under the auspicious protection of his grandmother's magnificent portrait.

My trisaieule princess Casimira, born a royal duchess.

Her youthful bursting beauty, in one important gilded carved oval frame with a young elephant trumpeting on top of her duchess crown over dark azure, three diagonal bands red and white, and the shield.

I see her for the first time, entirely glorious, young, beautiful, and imperturbable with her Avant-Garde short haircut.

Princess Casimira - My great great maternal grandmother

I'm introduced to this and the tapestry and a Fabergé egg and photos and records of our uncommon aristocratic family in silver frames.

The first Winspeare originated with the Celts and Vikings in the Isle of Man. They later settled in Yorkshire, although eventually left England following the self-exile of the Jacobin court to get Catholic alliance in Italy. The defeated court plotted to reinstate Roman Catholic Stuart Bourbon as king on the English throne.

With them they took the orphaned David, who was born in London, to Livorno Catholic court in 1704. Later he became a marine officer at the service of the Spanish court and married Anna de Ferrari in 1737. He died a prince of Salento in Naples in 1774.

David Winspeare

His son General Antonio Winspeare was born in Livorno in 1739 and later became engineer and major in the army of Naples. He built the first bridge and road in the kingdom, and married Giuditta Scilliani in 1772, eventually dying in Naples in 1820.

Antonio Winspeare

Davide Winspeare

Antonio's son Davide was born in 1775 in Portici, Naples district and died in 1846 in Naples. He was the most important Neapolitan jurist and was made the first baron in 1814 and transmitted this title to all the descending family members. Revolutionary in the kingdom of Naples, Davide wrote the *History of Feudal Abuses*, under the French rule of Murat, for that important work on social revolution he was made baron.

His brother Francesco Antonio (1778-1870) was a lieutenant general in the army and then war minister for the kingdom of Naples in 1860.

Roberto Winspeare

The youngest brother, Roberto Winspeare, was born in Portici in 1782, he fought on all battlefields from 1800 to 1815, first as an ally of Napoleon, then as an enemy. He was later appointed Colonel and assisted the great duke Michael and was distinguished in the battle of Smolensk and Borodino, commanding the twelfth battery of Sevardino, the same one Tolstoy makes us visit in War and Peace. He boldly fought until the siege of Paris where Roberto lost an arm to a cannonball. He was decorated for merit by the King of Prussia, awarded the Grand Cross of Vladimir, The Grand Cross of Saint Anne and The Commandery of the Black Eagle. After the Napoleonic wars Roberto was now a general; because of his injury he could not fight and was instead a military adviser in the first Crimean war. The family were instrumental to the unification of Italy, defending the Bourbons. When Naples kingdom got incorporated into the united Italy of 1861, he married Raimonda Ricciardi.

Their first son Davide was born in 1826. He graduated early from the Nunziatella military academy in Naples and became close to Tsar Nicholas, who would introduce him as his best friend, before he was a major in the Neapolitan army, a hero in the last stand of the bourbon army against the forces of the new Italy. After the unification of Italy, he chose self-exile and retired and died in Cannes in 1905. All their portraits hang in my parent's home.

Anna de Ferrari
(David's Wife)

***

My great Uncle Jack was born in 1898. He became a skilled genealogist, eventually proving more than 18 noble quarters. He was an ordained monk of Malta and had his two brothers knighted.

This is all his life, what he owns and show me. The historic details of my mother's side, a nostalgic presentation of the abolished nobility of Naples and the two Sicily's. I have been watched growing for many years, by the oil painted eyes portraits of all those ancestors, decorating the walls of the spiral staircase at my parents' house.

Giuditta Scilliani
(Antonio's Wife)

Slowly Uncle Jack is getting old, but not yet retired or destitute. He is a working actor of the roman scene, still proud and hopeful for me.

We set my sleeping bag with clean sheet and a blanket on the parquet floor. I use my bag of clothes for a pillow.

Between the shower and the kitchenette nook, we put a cardboard box lined with the saw dust we asked for at the butcher shop for Beranger's litter. We walked around the back street and his corner shop and Uncle Jack told the butcher who I am and bought veal for diner and got a gift of chicken lungs for my cat.

We keep the sliding door open.

My first hot shower and a good night in relative comfort.

I dress in my black ballet dancer stretchy bodice with a red and green flaring tartan skirt with a tight belt showing my very tiny waist and round appealing contours.

I puff American cigarettes from my ivory cigarette holder, a snake with ebony eyes.

The Winspeare family coat of arms

8

ITALY ON A BUDGET

Uncle Jack introduces me to the abolished aristocracy of my Roman relatives. He is the youngest brother of Grand-Papa Roberto. Jack is the only survivor of the three sons of Princess Maria Antonia, my great grandma, the widow of Baron Ricardo, the gambler who lost our family fortune.

He is an indefatigable socialite who lives by all his contacts.

I meet our successful cousin Comte Malatesta, an industrial entrepreneur belonging to the Italian Communist Party. He speaks French to me; his verbal lavishness knows no boundary.

I am the daughter of Jack's niece Anna Maria, the actual baroness, painter and novelist, the only surviving daughter of the baron Winspeare Carracciolo di Torella's blood line. I am the first daughter, his cute niece, and already a published author. Everyone speaks to me in French.

We meet for lunch in the garden at cousin Malatesta's villa.

Malatesta humbles himself in front of my youthful importance, I feel excessively flattered to be the subject of so much extravagant praise...

With delicious white wine flowing continuously in my glass, under a sunny pergola.

Everyone is super posh, dressed up impeccably. All are grouped around Karla, the Austrian mistress with her porcelain skin and sapphire eyes. Absolutely perfect in her Nina Ricci two-piece blush rose suit.

Family vacation to Lago di Garda in Sermoni, Italy

Karla shows, on the pale pink shells of her ear lobes, two glistening noticeable one carat sapphire studs, and some tamed lustrous coils of her chocolate hair.

Before we leave the house, she put on a brimmed hat. Karla takes me into her room and invites me to dress in her jade Chanel two-piece suit with some fine heels to match, which fit me perfectly with a bit of toilet paper stuffing.

Karla lends me a miniature fine straw hat, to crown my own elaborate perfectly pinned hairdo, like Maman showed me.

So, like that, I fit the merry stylish group on display in the best front seats on the eight rows. It is us, the V.I.Ps at the Villa Borghese, we proceed to watch the "Grand Prix Des Nations".

Uncle jack seems very happy and solicitous with me. I can dream for hours, gazing at all the prancing meres and jumping stallions. This show is fascinating, but so very long. I was not prepared to hold in my bladder so much wine for so many hours.

And I cannot express decently, such a trivial need, in this formal fabulous affair.

I realize after three hours of restraining it, it is no longer possible as the show is slowly dragging on with commentary and salamalecs, to ending.

I stand up and fall in a faint, moaning "ahhhhh", blissfully flooding with my relief, faintly suggested by some darkening green in the Coco Chanel suit.

I am carried away to the car, by two fussing gentlemen, plus one solicitous Uncle Jack to hold my hand. Such is avoided all embarrassment about etiquette and poise, until my departure forever.

***

More gelato via Veneto and a good look at Trevi fountain, so much smaller than I imagined when I saw *The Dolce Vita*. I descend through the catacomb. Inspect the Vatican and many of Rome's basilicas and churches, including Saint Peter where the bailiff scolds me for wearing a mini dress.

With my Roman family I got a taste of Roman life.

After three days sleeping with Beranger on the floor in front of the bathroom at Uncle Jack's I am ready to go away and explore the rest of Italy.

Bruno appears dishevelled, a small French man looking wild from sleeping al fresco in one of the seven hills. He fetches me back to the reality of budget traveling

In Venice with my family

I hug and thank Uncle Jack as we depart, with Beranger, going on to Pompeii in the deux chevaux.

Further in Verona, I descend to lie in the empty stone grave of Juliet. I close my lids and make my wish for a long healthy life and true love.

In Tuscany, we advance across the gentle hills covered in grape vines with cypress up to Firenze to my favourite place in Italy, Piazza de la Signorina.

In his alcove, stands beautiful green Perseus holding Medusa's head on his shield. Benvenuto Cellini's masterpiece is the one I turn around and contemplate for half an hour.

Not to be compared with David white marble, of Michelangelo, I admire in passing, but it's Perseus I fancy.

Pisa's leaning tower, Bolonia, and Ischia, and Capri.

I learn to properly valse to Lara song, the tube hit in Doctor Jivago, with a gallant Old Italian.

Signor Bruno Vecchio teach me how to glide with grace in his firmly guiding arms, 1 become instantly the waltzing queen at the popular ball room.

Arrivederci Italia.

9

PARIS LEFT BANK

We drive back to Paris.

I reintegrate into the floating Mutin with fattening Beranger now pregnant. Turns out it's a female after all.

Once a week I have a rendezvous with Jean Blanzat, my literary mentor. Jean is a big, white, slow, bearish man from the Limoges province who speaks with a small timid voice.

He lives, now in Paris, a notorious author, first lecturer at Gallimard publisher.

He is the one who discovered me and coach me once a week before getting me published. He employs the word "apocalyptic" for my writing. I like that word and so does he.

I drink red wine with him in the bistro for all the writers, closer to Gallimard. We speak of my future; I am invited to his home for dinner to meet his wife.

They have a maid, a simple and nice apartment. Furniture from the Limousin country they are from.

Their only son, a doctor generalist, has died very recently by falling asleep with a lit cigarette in his bed. He was not married; I feel like a fiancée for his ghost.

Between Gallimard and Flammarion editions at the Odeon, I dream of success browsing at the curios and antiques shops. I examine the traditional Chinese antique embroidery; all of the world's antique finery is in Paris window displays.

I wear the original parachute silk dress designed by Maman and stitched by my paternal grandma Moumoune after the war. That dress had a tiny sleeveless top with an immense skirt billowing like a big expanding pale cloud. Most of all the parachute material including aerodynamic geometric patterns already stitched in.

That parachute. a present from one American parachutist who spent some days hidden in a plywood box in the middle of Bon-Papa and Moumoune's big apartment on Brugman avenue in Brussels.

My grandpa bon-papa was also a hero of the resistance. Along with the parachute, the American soldier also gave tins of Quaker oats to my grandparents. We ate porridge from one of the inextinguishable old stashes of canned Quaker Oats which lasted them up to the midfifties.

Now I wear that first quality enduring silk. The dress fit me; I am hovering in it, on top of my high heel shoes like a cumulus cloud. When the full moon lights the night and it is not raining, I walk up to the graveyard, daring to explore on the sharp edge of fear seeking my destiny.

In that parachute dress I try to perceive spirits.

I meditate about the mysteries of life and death and get in touch with who or what come into my thoughts. I close my eyes listen and I look inside, and I watch what is growing getting ready to share my life

Whoever may come across me walking alone at night in my parachute dress under my beautiful black lace parasol, must surely be mystified.

I like that, when I feel immortal.

***

It's a cold lingering winter.

I am getting bored with drinking wine with French authors and journalists in Paris, it is not real.

At the Flore, I drink my café with Jean Edern Hallier, "Le Grand Ecrivain". We have fun trying to impress each other, he walks me to my boat on Quay Bourbon.

He's easily fascinated when I jump from the icy stairs into my rowboat full of ice and glide away pulling my icy chain to enter the privacy of my boat. He invites me for dinner at the Butte aux Cailles for a steak with green pepper corns; together we drink a lot of good wine. And then the day after we go for a ride to his country castle in his Ferrari.

I love the automatic windows sliding at my touch on the button. We drive through the pale cool night two hours away from Paris. It is the clear night of the full moon.

The castle is cold, and no water run from the frozen taps. I am a bit worried alone with this big man, like a possible prey. I help him gather wood for the open fire, and in the park lake I fetch a bucket and fill it up with broken icicles and freezing water. I make tea; we still talk nicely on even terms, like curious strangers.

He has a glass eye since a childhood accident; his wife is the one who bought the Ferrari.

We talk all night, he speaks about echangists and orgiastic partouze; but no, I am not at all interested in a cerebral sexual adventure, speaking with him is how close I get.

After this vain, sleepless, civilized night he drives me back in the morning after one early café au lait and croissant at his village café.

***

The winter gets milder; I still believe I will make my living as one successful Parisian young author.

I visit, about once a week, my old friend Genia who live Rue du Bac in a narrow attic room on the seventh floor with her cat.

She initiates me to her crystal rocks and Venetian glass ludions collection. Like Maman, she also paints commercial art for a living, for textiles and wallpapers.

She drives around Paris on a Solex to sell her work to her clients.

She is older now, but sort of the same, with her turban, like I remember her since my early childhood in Croissy on the Seine near Paris.

We have exalted conversations. We share Italian almond pastry and sardine livers in tin cans she buys down her building at the Italian trattoria.

Genia is a narcoleptic, she falls asleep in the middle of a sentence, only for half a minute, and she wakes up and carries on the conversation we started.

I do share the love of cats with her. She never had a baby. Neither did I but I am still young, and I cannot compare.

We share subtle affinities, and she speak fondly of my mother, who reunited us in Paris

I climb to her seventh-floor attic room Rue du Bac; I support her while she proceeds to gut unfinished attic space to expand her domain on the side slope for storing extra books and neatly labeled personal stacks of papers and drawings.

***

On the weekends, I hitch hike, or take the train from Paris to Brussels. I still have my room at my parents. With my friends at the Estro Harmonico, and Jean-Marie, and Patrick, Philippe, Peter, Robert, Clairette, Khlava, we expect I will soon become rich and famous.

No one I know can help me more.

After I sign my books, I plan to go away for my mega-trip with my advance money from Flammarion.

Because of DH Lawrence's, *Under the Volcano*, and because of Fernando Cortes, one of my ancestors, I am inspired to start the great journey to my destiny hopefully awaiting me in Mexico.

Enthused by that I plan my dream journey I get fired for it speaking to Elsa.

I visit Elsa, like Genia, regularly once a week on the second floor in her grand apartment on boulevard Saint Germain.

Publicity photo for the launch of Le Voyage Ambigu

Her younger new husband makes lots of money selling luxury sales lots.

At 35 years old, Elsa still occasionally models for Nina Ricci collection. Elsa is kept in a spacious elegant apartment, near La Coupole; she takes care of 4-year-old daughter Nathalie and 14-year-old son David, from her previous marriage. Portia, a black female French Pitbull is always tied up in front of the kitchen in the hall.

Since the birth of their daughter, her husband Claude is no longer faithful. Elsa plans to take a break from her unsatisfactory predicament and share my great adventure with all her savings.

Her mother will take good care of little Nathalie, her son, and Portia the bitch.

10

NEW YORK AND MY FIRST JOINT

Papa drives us to Luxembourg.

It's my first airplane flight I am super excited, I sing from Luxembourg to New York all the way to the dosing passengers.

Before landing at Kennedy airport, I reverently notice the Iconic liberty statue guarding Ellis Island. My paternal grandparents and Maman and her mother made that journey on boat, while I fly in one ancient bird to cross the great water of the Atlantic.

The whole week we walk tirelessly to visit New York. The city swings with me, I feel like a new ball bouncing in the middle. I trot fast, leading on my heels, trying to keep up beside 6-foot-tall Elsa, a splendid, classy specimen with blue eyes like a tranquil lake.

We are sticking out of a vulgar colourful crowd...

We grab a cab and reach our free accommodation at Uncle David and Ada's, our Zionist hosts in New York, on eighth avenue near Brooklyn.

We are welcomed to spacious high ceilings, big square rooms, and a tasteless, neutral, rather ugly decor.

We are put up in the study room with two student beds beside a large library, the only sign of their European culture. I wonder why they do conform to this anonymous plastic world.

I must see the Guggenheim Museum and the Museum of Modern Art. I push all closed doors. The museum guards call me "Honey!"

I am shocked at the American direct approach. There is no class distinction between people here.

We walk most streets.

We meet up with my sister Claude, who's working as an au pair for a rich family with 5 kids in New York. She guides us, allowed a day of complaining of being mercilessly exploited by the family she is the babysitter for.

With Claude, we climb stairs and take the lift to the top of the Empire State Building.

Central Park, Rockefeller center, and Saint Paul Cathedral; a disappointing modern miniature version of Notre-Dame.

Walls are colourless and high, food is tasteless. Colours, when displayed, are screaming. Women out on the street with curlers on their heads in stretchy jogging suit comfort, all shod in mass-produced sneakers, or slippers.

Most citizens are dressed in loud primary colours and generic sportswear. Tee shirts, jeans all over, all weird inelegant people. Many are fat, others obese.

This is a cultural shock, but where is the culture?

Big cars spew exhaust fumes on the very few pedestrians walking on the big sidewalks.

The friendly curious peoples call when we pass. We are a remarkable pair, noticed, approached, and talked to. Elsa is a magnificent giant who dwarfs my 5'2" frame, even with my eight-centimeter heels.

I've got on my new navy-blue mini dress with thin white pinstripes I just bought from the Champs Elysees gallery. Underneath, I wear black fishnet tights and black varnished shiny shoes with ankle straps and my black varnished crocodile saddle bag.

Brown eyes rimmed with blue make up, long reddish gold hairs in a ponytail on the side.

We are drawing a lot of attention.

We end up in Greenwich Village, a bohemian enclave with a nice vibration.

We meet some young guys on the terrace at the outdoor café restaurant. They look good, different, more like us; they invite us in their flat with a balcony, around the corner.

They pass a joint to Elsa and blow smoke in the twitching nose of their eager white pet rabbit.

It all seems all right, but I say; not now I want to be ready before I try.

The guys give me a rolled joint of Marijuana to try at home. They say it's called Acapulco Gold.

I light up that joint two days later in the sole company of Elsa in our study room, while Uncle David and Ada are still at work. I lock our door shut, for this religious experience.

I experience a distortion in my feelings. I laugh and giggle at the echo of my thought. My initiation is comfortable and private.

Greenwich Village is one easy place, full of young hip bohemians. It reminds me of isle Saint Louis with younger people.

In Manhattan we want to go browse at Saks and Alexander.

At the metro entrance a black shoeshiner insist to shine my shiny shoes. He lifts me like a doll to his highchair in the subway entrance.

He performs his most choreographed number, then lifts me back on my feet again. He admires himself laughing in my polished shiny shoes on my fish netted feet.

Then he asks me for money. There is no way I will give him any dosh, he abducted me! I humored him.

A big, tall, weird guy watching us gives the shoeshiner money and then proceeds to guide us.

He grabs my arm on his left and Elsa on his right. We manage to ask in English, "what you are doing with us?"

He says this is an American custom and he squeezes and drags us on both sides of him almost lifting my feet.

He understood we want to go to Saks and Alexander; he takes us inside the metro. It is rush hour, very crowded, there are no seats.

As soon as the train starts moving the guy tries to push Elsa through the slowly closing door and keep me in his grip.

The interested passengers squeezed with us on the compartment realize I am getting kidnapped. They take hold of Elsa and push this pervert out the door tearing me from his iron grip.

My first New York metro warning experience. I shall not bite or swallow the scary poisonous side of the big apple.

We got invited for dinner at Cathy's, a school friend of mine, somewhere in the city. We find the anonymous apartment and punch her number in; we take the lift to her tenth-floor suite.

She married a New Yorker, and they have a two-year-old daughter. Cathy is just twenty, no more a girl but a woman getting too plump, showing unexcited lassitude.

She serves us, for dinner, some ready-made little wafer cones full of a tasteless plastic bright yellow cheese and more weird artificial looking food. Iceberg salad with mayonnaise from a jar, rubbery flavourless cherry tomatoes and bland olives on toothpicks.

We wash that down with Coca Cola and Nescafe.

Extra sweet bright coloured cupcakes for dessert.

I find no desirable joie de vivre in this young family.

What's happened with the wholesome Hungarian food? And the joyous playful life we shared in Brussels, with her brother, her Hungarian refugee mother and Pierre Della Faille, her Poet Stepfather?

What happened to Cathy twirling for me, showing off with her six beautiful Hungarian skirts all embroidered on top of each other.

She and I, both voracious readers, stimulated each other's culture together between ages eleven to fifteen during the height of our friendship.

We wrote outrageous thrillers with ferocious vile heroes, to impress each other and our adult audience.

I was well fed in Cathy parents' house.

Now in her modest New Yorker setting with no more excitement in her life, her subdued America seems dull and lonely with her average looking husband and her cute snotty little girl.

When we leave her apartment, I feel numb and bored for Cathy's middle-class house life.

Miles away, in exciting Greenwich Village and Soho, we met young and free playful people full of sparks.

With Elsa we are not impressed with colonel Sanders basted chickens or Mac burgers, greasy tasteless freezer fries, or colourful Jell-O, artificial flavors, sickly sweet jellies.

Not impressed either by the impersonal American homes we enter.

***

At the central Art Deco Greyhound counter, the ticket seller asks, me; "New York City to Mexico City? Are you sure, honey?"

I say, "Yes!"

And I burst into hysterical laughter, hearing myself, responding with a simple correct word, to this absurd new world.

We roll across America; the driver wears a grey cap on with the greyhound logo. He is a pale, sort of grey with grey eyes unseeing me, he wears jeans and chews gum.

It is hard for me not to judge hastily and dismiss as stereotype all the passengers.

I perceive them, worn out and unappealing.

The bus we sit in is full of average mostly fat American males, a few of them obese. I focus, fascinated by an enormous young pinkish pale obese man looking like sliced baloney.

The bus has a toilet inside, like in a train.

At the Philadelphia station, a nice, classy girl enters the bus and sits beside us, her name is Mary. She is going back to Pittsburgh.

We chat animatedly, in French, at the Greyhound diner, where the food is tasteless and artificially coloured.

We learn Mary just graduated from the Sorbonne in French speech and botany. She invites us to come and spend a few nights in her home. With Mary, we step into stylish America and old money.

Her father runs a steel business. He introduces us to this steel city at a time tense with racial riots. Black people are getting more rights; Malcom X and Martin Luther King Jr. are ironing the differences. The employers must patiently endure the strikes.

Elsa and I enjoy this colonial American luxury, the real silverware, solid wood antique furniture, fresh strawberries and whipping cream in fine porcelain, good English tea and buttered scones and homemade jam, and quality hospitality.

We are served by a black cook and housekeeper with curly grey hair. Her whole family is lodged in the house. Her husband is the gardener and the chauffeur, her daughter helps doing the chores. They seem happy to have a good paying job for the moment, afraid to get out of the house and get included in the riots.

We get driven in the polished black Cadillac around Pittsburgh with Mary sitting by her father. We are pampered for two comfortable nights and three days. We discover the sights and the turmoil with cultured American hosts who understand their place in history. At least we discover a glamourous side to the poor hard-working democratic America.

We climb back into our Greyhound to pass similar monotonous towns all the way to Texas.

White painted wooden houses with shingle roofs, and flat roof clap board industrial buildings. Gigantic fields growing wheat or grazing fat cattle and to break the monotony, immense silos, penis shaped.

Our long unexciting Greyhound journey, with different drivers under the same cap and twenty minutes stops in different cities offering the same diner rest, with tasteless food and drinks, nothing too tempting.

Through Louisiana and Texas, we arrive in Laredo, Texas to cross the Mexican border.

At New Laredo we step down from the bus and carry our bundles by a long file of cars. We line up behind a massive crowd of patient travelers, we stand at the border.

Like everyone crossing we get aggressively investigated under suspicious scrutiny.

11

TRAVELLING MEXICO OVERLAND

    This is it! We transfer to the Mexicana bus linking with Greyhound.
    We pass the frontier after dusk. Now we roll in our old Mexicana bus into the warm Mexican night. Until a mechanical problem stops us abruptly on the road. After one hour patiently waiting, another loaded Mexicana bus takes us and a few of the other passengers, they don't take our luggage which we are told will get to us in Mexico City at the Mexicana bus depot near the airport, our terminal destination. We fill some customs papers in the night with the flashlight of the bus driver, before stepping hastily in that next crowded Mexican bus.
    I start to practice in creative lingo, with Latin, Italian and French as a base, Español comes to me way easier than English.

The first major city stop is in colonial Monterey. We enter a big cantina with madras red and white cotton tablecloth covering wooden tables. We like the look of it.

We sit with relief and anticipation in front of the appetizing red and bright green fresh cut crudity offered on each table.

What we think is salad, upon taking a greedy bite, happens to be fiery fresh chilis. A surprise and a shock!

We are, crying coughing and choking, amusing other customers profusely.

The Mexican street food and cantina food are rough with fiery chilis as the only condiment. The main staples are fresh cooked, nutritious and cheaper than the artificial mass-produced diner food in the United States.

Beside the offered garnish of burning chili, we eat corn tortillas and rice, black beans, raw onions and avocados. I notice a lot of turkey birds running amongst a few wiry chickens. When we order a plate of turkey meat it is overcooked, dry and almost rotten.

Fresh orange juice squeezed on the spot is sold in little wagons everywhere.

What they call *"refrescoes"*, soda, Coca-Cola, Fanta, Seven Up, Limca, are sold in rolling stands pushed under the moving shade.

I am feeling the hint of Latin flare.

We travel direct to Mexico City, our base camp being Hotel las Americas, a cheap hotel on Garibaldi Street. We will be staying at least a week.

Around Mexico City there are a lot of Aztec sites to visit. Plus, we must wait for our luggage.

My friend Philippe Dasnoy, a reporter at the R.T.B, gave me the phone number of Carlos Fuentes so I could meet the Mexican author. It would be nice to be received by that interesting Mexican author and get introduced to the authentic side of Mexico.

When I phone Carlos Fuentes' number I refer shyly to my Belgian friend's recent interview and my new author status. I get easily discouraged by his secretary, the Author is not there right now, and if I insist, I could get an appointment in a few days.

Anyways, I am not confident to find the time to ever meet that notorious writer. I only read one of his books, "The Death of Artemio Cruz" and I am sure he did not read my book.

I am not pursuing if it is difficult, anyone I meet must be on my way.

We walk around the hotel and take a bus to visit the important and fantastic Anthropology Museum.

After a week of calling the bus depot daily for our luggage, it's waiting for us at the airport compound of Mexico. I must go and get it, it's one-hour ride on the bus. Elsa is tired and since I speak better Spanish, I go alone.

When I reach the airport, it is already four in the afternoon. It is sweltering, and I have to walk all around the hot ground to find the right office. I finally reach it, sweating and relieved to enter a big office where I can see two officials in uniform arranging little slips of paper on a big desk. They seem concentrated on that task and annoyed by my interruption when I present myself with my own slip of reference.

They look at my paper, then at me, and say, "Mañana!"

I have already eyed our bags laying on the right of the desk! And I point at them!

When I hear the word "Mañana!", I repeat it loud, twice!

And I say "Oy, Ahora!"

They look at me with arrogant disdain and keep at what they are doing.

Then I proceed to flick with my hand the orderly papers that fly slowly like butterflies to land on the floor.

After two flicks of my outrageous hand, the two officers hand me the bags.

I sign the slip of release, say "gratias and adios!"

I leave in a modest triumph satisfied to have proven I am a late conquistador daughter of Mexico.

...

In Mexico City we buy a guidebook in French at the international bookstore.

I get entranced by the visit to Santa Maria de la Guadeloupa, the great white cathedral on top of the hill which contains the shroud of the virgin joining her hands in the greeting of prayer.

That Virgin is the key symbol of Mexico.

Santa Maria Guadalupe in the moon crescent carried by one cherub, stands on the sun protected in the shade of a leaf of maguey the agave plant that yield Pulque.

Inside the cathedral I see mysterious jungle peoples clad in leaves and feathers, performing their devotional dances.

The priest in red lace on his high pulpit vociferates in a loud microphone to the crowd inside and in front of the big church.

Multiple saints: brown, yellow, black and white, stand for their eclectic worshippers in the many altars.

...

From our hotel in Garibaldi, we are not far from the Mariachis center.

With a big, white, bejewelled sombrero and red and white parade costume, comes Pedro.

His guitar and his partner Diego with a trumpet, in matching outfits with sombreros.

Pedro, sit right beside us, and he emits for us piercing and melodious falsettos, clears his voice and releases *"ouilles"* and *"ayes"* pacing them at his tempo, again and again.

They show us how to drink tequila with lime slices and salt on the glass rim and like them we nibble on green chilis, boldly emulating true Mexican Mariachis.

We spend two mornings marching from the temple of the sun to the temple of the moon through the way of the dead, following all grounds of the sacred Aztec sites of Teotihuacán.

At this site countless selected victims were sacrificed, with their heart ripped out of their chest by the priest warrior with one obsidian knife. That was the only way to propitiate Huitzilopochtli, the blue hummingbird warrior sun god of the Aztecs.

The Aztec, or the Nahuatl tribe, built Tenochtitlan, now Mexico City, on the marsh lands given to them for their mercenary war services.

Shiva presenting a marijuana leaf to Montezuma, who gives a peyote button in return. Painting by my friend Marianna Rydwall, artist of sacred art

We glide with our new Mariachi friends. Pedro and Diego paddling the canoe in the Aztec floating garden of Xochimilcho.

The Mexicans built their proud capital of Mexico City on their new land. They made Xochimilcho their getaway pleasure garden.

It is hot and dusty dry, just before the imminent rainy season. Heat exhausted; Elsa sits at the refrescoes stand in the shade of a mango tree.

After I guzzle four bottles of fizzy, cold, over-sweet soft drinks, I run up, bouncing on top of all the pyramids. I am driven to physically understand this invaded culture.

We sit beside our Mariachis friends and down tequilas with two extra Mexican goons who buy everyone's drinks. When everyone is full of the magic brew with salt, lime and green chilies, the goons at our pursuit follow us up to the lobby and we have a hard time shaking them off.

We just manage to run to our room, lock ourselves in and let them tire of waiting for us, and go away.

We are polite with our few words in simple Spanish. With our Parisian way still rooted in the Latin Quarter, how could we truly discover this mega city?

To complete our discovery of Mexico we attend the Sunday *corrida*, a twenty-dollar ticket sold at our hotel. We find our numbered seat in the grand arena, among the crowd of thousands, for this savage show of Spanish gladiator games.

I am horrified from the start, at the bloody spectacle with pompous trumpet music and Paso Doble. Everywhere I look at bloody injury.

The horses in their thick caparison, the Banderilles planters, the Toros, the Picadors, the Toreadors, the Matador, every participant pursue hurt and kill the fierce or meekest beasts.

I feel personally outraged; I have to interfere! I stand up from my seat to step down in the arena. Elsa, with our male escort, pin me down on my wooden seat, and I can't move inside the arena.

The crowd clamour "Ole!"

Until, the corrida circus is over, I watch until the end.

...

City street maintenance crews explode a charge of T.N.T not bothering to warn us passersby. While they unblock the guts of the mega city, we decide to get out of town, to explore the hills under the majestic Popocatepetl volcano.

We leave Mexico City by bus to Tasco, a mountain city with a silver mine.

We enter resorts, parks, and hotel bars led in by polite men interested in buying us and showing us how to drink tequila with salt, chilis and limon.

Tasco has steep streets with silver lines striating all the way down to the plains. There are silver jewellers stalls everywhere.

To get closer to Quetzalcoatl, the plumed serpent god, I buy a silver snake ring.

From here, we share a group taxi to Oaxaca market city.

We are greeted by potter's stands, weaver's stalls, handicrafts, food and fruit stalls. All in the dusty air sweltering for the swarming flies all day under the sun.

Visible poverty infiltrated by sneaky, boozy, corruptible Policemen and bandits. We eat the cheapest food, and we sleep in the cheapest rooms, in a flea and bed bug riddled bed.

Elsa is suffering from this total lack of luxury, but that's all we can afford if we want our trip to last and to be able to see it all.

I am inflexible; we only ride the cheapest bus with the Indigenous Mexican families with goats and live turkeys and chickens.

Giant cactuses line the roads, and lots of sombreros everywhere.

We study our French guide, follow the directions, and make sure we do not miss any marvellous sight.

We are strange foreigners. We do not speak English, but we are no gringas. We are particular European chicks not eager to mingle with other gringo tourists.

I wake Elsa up by sleep walking in the middle of the night. Elsa hears me speak old Quechua lingo, and watches me, metamorphosing into an ancient warrior.

This is not a surprise for me, maybe that is why I came to Mexico, inspired by past family history and karma.

I am disappointed by the obvious U.S.A. colonial supremacy so evident in Mexico, overpowering the Spanish supremacy overpowering the remaining Mayans, the remaining tribal peoples, the Mulattos.

Triumphant mercenary warriors of Tenochtitlan became the Mexicans. They offered to their blood thirsty blue god of the south all the blood and the skulls of the defeated; they erected the Tzompantli skull rack for adorning Huitzilopochtli's shrine.

After the warriors sacrificed their victims, they feasted on their brain cooked with chillies and tomatoes. Mexicans are a mixed people. But it did not happen gently.

Foreign conquest came easily after every remaining tribe had lost at the Pelota game and all their warriors were decimated by human sacrifices.

The Aztec's violent supremacy was overpowered by a small troop of conquistadors erupting on horseback. The other tribes did not trust their barbaric Aztec rulers and saw with the strangers a chance to survive.

Quetzalcoatl reincarnated was expected to save the kingdom of Mexico and enforce peace. History blames it on Fernando Cortes.

We go on to discover the church near saint Miguel Alliende with a vaulted ceiling of stuccoed multiracial baby angels adoring anyone looking at them.

The streets explode in many fiestas in the Zocalo with the Mariachis joyous brass, guitar music and bouncing marimbas, everyone dances.

Fiesta goers throw gifts of food and drinks, someone manages to break the clay piñata, and throw handfuls of clay skulls and figurines filled with mescal drink for many hands to catch.

I dance.

Zapotec land, in Mitla, the underworld resting place within a labyrinth to Monte-Alban. Satiated with enough human blood, the god is still at rest after three thousand years.

In Acapulco we take a break from intense touring, a ten-day rest vacation at the tropical beach, waiting to receive Elsa's extra money.

The Pacific Ocean bathes in the shadow of the Sierra Madre del Sur Mountain. The ocean is warm, deep and blue; luring me to join all its creatures.

After our breakfast of pan dulce and café con leche, we take the bus for one easy ten-kilometer ride, and escape from the gringo touristic bay trap of Acapulco.

In Lido Tortuga, a beach near a small fishing village close to Acapulco, they still fish with a harpoon on a fast boat. The giant old turtles swim fast from the beach, pursued by the fisherman for their abundant sweet grainy meat on Lido Tortuga beach.

Many fishermen have lost a limb or a hand to a shark encounter.

This local cove, with a maze of many moored fishing boats feels remote and private.

In Lido Tortuga we sample the turtle stew with chilli garlic and tomatoes, for two pesos at the beach shack.

Across Lido Tortuga lays Burro Burracho, a tiny island. A local's day excursion by motorboat to buy beers to share with the beer guzzling donkey.

It does not look so far to swim across. I decide to attempt the long swim. I go on steadily for two hours of breaststroke. After that I start feeling soggy and tired, I worry I won't be able to ever reach this beach still looking very far to me.

I float on my back for a rest wondering if I should go on, or go back, until Elsa shows up to my rescue.

I am grateful to climb dripping in that fast boat and grab the helping hand of Elsa and the driver. It would have taken at least two more hours of my swimming.

While only three minutes of motorized speeding suffice to bring us to the island.

We buy a beer for the happy fat donkey and two for the driver. We speed back to Lido Tortuga in the motorboat, and I feel childish and silly as well!

Acapulco's dazzling ocean calls me from every sight. Swimming or looking at the ocean is all I want to do.

Elsa received her American Express money. To celebrate, we charter a motorboat to go fishing. The captain guarantees we will catch a big fish.

He is driving his boat and looks good in his navy-coloured uniform and cap with blond hair and ocean blue eyes.

A strong black guy with bleached blond hair is helping us unravel and control the single fishing line hooked onto the boat.

We are running so fast trailing the lure in the sea foam. It's exhilarating and scaring me, this fast attack cutting the sea in a spray of water with the loud whirring motor matching the deafening surfing sound of the boat.

I am tensely holding onto the reel with the running line. We roam the ocean.

Two hours after we left, one fish is hooked on the bait and Hans the captain and Juanito the mate take over the rod and carefully reel in a tuna. It's an exciting, suspenseful moment!

We pull it on board. The mate weighs the fish on the hook scale, it's more than two kilos. The mate cooks it in the galley recess, and together we eat our tuna fish on board at the dock.

Elsa fascinates Hans the blond German captain in his smart navy suit.

I interest Juanito, the young black mate with bleached blond curly hair in a lined blue and white sailor jersey and navy corsair pants, and a sailor white cap.

Juanito is about my age and strong, but no taller than me. He is dark and sunlit and has got pink palms.

We are interested by our difference and feel comfortable and curious enough to approach a little. I had yet to meet a black guy that close. With him I improve my Spanish and I get more familiar with the Pacific, walking the beach and swimming.

Elsa improves her English with the captain. The four of us hang around the port after they complete their day with tourists on the white and blue fishing charter,

Juanito, guides me to his side of Acapulco, he lives on the laborious side of the tourist economy.

We meet every day in the afternoon at the harbour beach and flirt between the beached boats. I find him appealing and strange. I let him kiss me, he is sweet, playful and we laugh a lot together about our different ways.

I am a bit curious and excited but not as much as Juanito would like. On the beach beside a small boat hiding us, we kiss, and it is okay, then he pulls on my shiny silver Italian bikini bottom, but I pull it back on right away and we both laugh.

We spend our private time in each other's exotic company; he takes me to his modest two room house in a ghetto far away from the holiday flats and guest accommodations by the sea.

It's half an hour walk from his work to his house. He lives with his mother and grandmother. Spanish and black, we talk Spanish, Juanito supports them, and they tell me what a good guy he is.

I am touched, closer to sharing real life and enter Acapulco's heart.

But I stay on the edge, afraid of losing my standard and perched looking for that picture in my head. Not quite ready to lose myself in that interracial Mexico classless pool, not even for a week.

Elsa, like me, explores her limits in Acapulco. We have no gravity, and we are special tourist girls simply floating by like colourful tempting balloons, just drifting lightly.

I won't get for real or loose with the cute black fisherman. Neither will Elsa with her handsome captain, a Nazi's son.

The great Pacific Ocean calls me in, I can't get enough hour's swimming in it. Juanito warns me about the hungry sharks, but I don't care. I dare that midnight swim glistening with the warm ocean under the stars. Juanito howls "Tiburon! Tiburon!"!

Like a wolf he sings at the sea and the sharks keep away for me.

"Tibuuurron! Tibuuuron!"

Hans and Elsa watch us, very interested by our little scene.

Three times we walk across the Quebrada diving site, returning everyday with the crowd to watch the divers in the afterglow.

The high divers jump right after sunset, they follow each other, taking time to cross themselves and dive. They spread their arms like wings then fold them in a perfect arc aiming precisely from the vertiginous Quebrada rock forty meters above the cove below.

Their bodies curve and point like one reaching arrow, they enter the water with a small splash. Some of them close their eyes and all are pale when they resurface, they pass floating full of air behind each other. Walking right beside us.

And we conclude Acapulco visit by watching the Mayan Pacific Ocean with the synchronized swimming ballet rehearsed by U.S.A Olympic team.

Elsa generously splurges with me; I take my share of her necessary luxury. It took no time to spend her extra cash. I have to hoard the traveling money to keep going and complete our tour, we can't stay here much longer.

We say "Adios" to Hans and Juanito with some melancholy.

For the last leg of our trip, we take the slow train out. A long haul to the Yucatan peninsula, the train wheels do not fit exactly the rails, so we get tossed hard above our seat.

Elsa crashed in her seat; she sleeps through it all with her mouth wide open.

Our Mexican neighbour prefers to stand, gripping safely the metal pole since Mexico City, still standing, gripping that pole firmly for the three-day journey on this train.

He helps me grab Elsa's giant legs, to prevent her from smashing her head on the low roof of the compartment.

When we reach Yucatan, I keep climbing to the top of every pyramid.

We rent a group taxi Jeep to reach Palenque jungle. We arrive, in awe at the sacred sink hole in limestone, a round pool with deep clear water reflecting the blue sky and the green shade of the jungle trees. I dive cautiously in the sweet water of Palenque cenote; I've heard how deep it is and that many young girls were sacrificed in it.

I am surprised to meet here, one huffy, heavy woman with enormous swollen legs. She treks and hops all around the jungle with a guide, a detailed map, and a cane.

It's hot; we sweat profusely while exploring the remote ruins.

Going down to the underground shelter that hides the treasured Jaguar, the mysterious dense jungle teams with quetzals and parakeets, with woodpeckers and monkey calls and hummingbirds, with birds of paradise, and orange and black clouds of monarch butterflies.

Here the deafening sound of the jungle calls with many voices.

Crickets chirp and birds sing their distinct songs, and of course there is a pride of lively jaguar hiding nearby. The jungle conceals slithering poisonous snakes, prudent iguanas, and furtive zorros.

There are no more tourists here in this remote jungle destination, except us and Virginia, the Washington D.C. anthropologist on a field trip, the big woman with Elephantiasis in her legs, climbing up and down the rugged terrain.

The Jaguar temple of Palenque with the carved stone shows Pakal the last Mayan king on top of his tomb. He sits on his throne, a Jaguar with jade eyes and carved inscriptions. The site was recently discovered in the green jungle.

We meet Virginia again in the ruins at Tulum beach. We view all the ancient carvings in between all the American hippies who have taken over the ruins as their squat.

The best-preserved ruin is Chichen Itza, the best Pelota game court in the ancient empire. Where the final of the ancient Pelota game used to be, under the sun, with no shade at all!

That is the last of the Seven Wonders of the World.

On the mission to climb every high step, I run up under the heat trickling with sweat racing all the way up, to the high chamber open for the god on top.

As fast as my heart beats, I melt into the river of my own sweat. I race the mystery of the war for sacrifice.

The victims received the guiding sacraments of magic plants: Pulque, Poyomatli, Peyote, Teonanacl and pounded seeds of Datura flowers or Jimson weed, and the vines of Ayawasca.

I read books about that, but I have no experience.

I tasted mescal, drank quite a bit of tequila. I only smoked my first joint of Acapulco gold in New York, and some Sebsi in Morocco.

It's just the beginning of my story.

All is here still echoing in my simple mind. I listen to the names of many substances opening keys to the mysterious world.

Elsa is happy to look at me from a shady refrescoes stand, she is thirstily guzzling Coca-Cola.

Everywhere, except in Palenque, we reach by the cheap bus.

In Veracruz we meet two students at the park. We talk about the youth revolution starting all over the modern world.

They show us around the campus. We look at the wall brightly grotesque painted by Diego Ribera. I don't know anything about Zapata or important contemporary Mexicans. I want to decipher the ancient world to start.

With our Veracruz friends, we take an hour bus ride to the open-air museum of Tuxtla, six carved basalt Olmec's Atlantes buried deep with their giant heads sticking out.

Mesoamerica, three thousand years ago, here they are the giant heads of the Atlantes, like the ones guarding Easter Island.

At the ancient Tula site in the Coatepec region, sits a grand statue of Coatlicue. She is the mother of more than four hundred gods with her fangs, her necklace of hands, hearts and skulls and her skirt of snakes.

Coatlicue was sweeping her shrine, tapping the agave cactus they call Maguey, making Pulque white and thick perfumed with cocoa and volubilis flowers, preparing her offering of sacred drink.

When she found a beautiful feather fallen from the sky in her sweeping, she tucked it in her bosom. That is how she became pregnant with Huitzilopochtli the warrior sun god.

He is born armed and blue wearing a head dress of hummingbird feathers, to attack his sister Coyaulhauki, the moon goddess who had her mother's head sliced off.

And that story of the cosmos goes on, it sounds terrible, but it makes sense amid revolution. She's the Mexican mother goddess and is the same goddess as mother Kali.

And maybe that's why I came to Mexico.

Two big bottles of premixed margaritas drank between the four of us.

We are playing around between the ocean and the beach, doing cartwheels and swimming.

On Vera Cruz empty white beach, we drain every drop of the margaritas.

The boys play guitar, and we sing and dance along the beach repeating the same Beatles song, over and over "When I'm Sixty-Four!"

We end up getting lost walking through the jungle behind the sandy beach after I repel firmly my blond student's conquering assault.

Sobered by fear, we end up searching our way back home in the night looking up at the stars. I lost my sandals to the sea tide in the cove.

I was speeding away bare foot, running from the guy with round big blue eyes, who looks like the blond hero in *Blow Up*.

He got mad when I resisted him, but then, he fell on his knees asking me to forgive him, which I did, and Elsa appeared beside me.

The two students gave up on us, they were gone. They left us in a lurch.

We stayed alone, lost in that jungle night with some moon and star light.

We did not panic, we looked at the stars, the sky showed the light over the city, that was the direction we took to find the asphalt road, our way back straight ahead, through the dissipated margarita fumes.

Elsa in her sandals and me bare foot on the asphalt road, another dodgy adventure turned acceptable.

It was just a couple of miles to our hotel in Vera Cruz city center.

***

We finish our Mexican journey in San Cristobel de Las Casa; a colonial city which was called Tzotzil in pre-Columbus times, nestled in a forest, high up in the Chiapas Mountains.

In the first cheap accommodation at the end of a democratic row of guest houses, the inviting macho host locked himself with us in the dingey room.

We pushed him away, fought him shouting, and pounded him. Managed to fish the key from his plaid shirt pocket we unlocked the door, seized our bags, and ran away to find a decent room close by, but not so cheap.

The troop of Chamulan people dressed in undyed woven wool, march through the mountain's ancient path and leave behind the Spanish conquered domain which they incorporated into their own religious custom, with Catholic baptism as a first rite.

At the Zocalo, colourful tribal people from Zinacantan and other mountain villages sell their crafts. Each tribe got a distinct dress. They sell weavings or fruits, or flowers, or salt, or amber.

They keep private, they only recognise numbers on the dollar bills, or the pesos, and they sell their things to tourists.

Their remaining refuge is higher and further away, inaccessible by any vehicle. We don't dare to follow where they are climbing, in rough hide sandals with rubber soles made from old tires, away from the mountainous city's slow bustle.

They haul big packs on their backs containing all they need, including the small picture of blond Marylyn Monroe, the preferred American movie star torn from magazine pages beside the picture of the Santa Maria de Guadeloupa virgin.

We spend two days in this cool city at the Hacienda hotel. We meet polite Spanish *hidalgos;* it's almost cold at night. We buy some woven shawls.

By the cheap bus, then train somnolent all the way. We retrace our steps.

In Mexico City we buy two sombreros with the help of Diego and Pedro, our Mariachis friends.

We show our crumpled return ticket and take our seat in the Mexicana bus line affiliated to the U.S. Greyhound all the way to New York City.

And well, I have the time to reflect about this voyage after we close and pack the Mexico guidebook away.

I did not travel alone like I planned initially. I entered Mexico, expected by no one in the cheap tourist category. I met a Mexico full of scary ghosts pumping gringos' dollars.

I can almost forget Mexico, it's been alienated too many times, it feels disintegrated. I don't think I will want to return; it did not welcome me like I had imagined.

We did our cultural tour, avoided accidents and traps. I stepped into significant bloody tracks. It is the furthest escapade I could think of, but I am a bit disappointed; it is not the conclusive freedom step I hoped for.

From all the women dressed in black I did not meet any I remember.

The fruits and the fresh orange juice are great. But I did not fall in love with this country, its food, or anyone in it.

In San Cristobal, I noticed a cool bunch of hippies purposeful and grounded. How different they looked from the tourists!

I longed to feel free like this and live day by day without having a return ticket, like we had.

We rolled back to New York. Dosing and riding through the night, twenty-minute rest stops in the diners and refuelling stations. That returning bus journey passed in a blur, unraveling faster on the way back.

I speak more Español now, and the beginnings of English.

We arrived back to New York at the gloomy Greyhound station near Harlem.

We took a chance and walked a shortcut through Harlem to Uncle David and Ada's with our bulging bags, guided by three funky black guys. They threw our two sombreros on their heads and helped us carry our bags and danced us through this forbidden Harlem.

The black people in Harlem, like the white ones, some are fat and some ugly, but like every person in New York, they're lively and aware looking. That same American average, same dress, same curlers on the black lady's head. They wear the same morning dressing gown and slippers in their street turf.

We sing, across the invisible frontier in Brooklyn, the three black guys drop the two sombreros on our heads. Uncle David and Ada are shocked we risked that short cut through Harlem after they warned us not to go there. But I think that was pretty cool.

We never went to their beach house in New Jersey, but I can't imagine I missed much. I have seen white only suburban paradise and it is such a bore.

I don't care for more of that America. I'd rather immerse myself in New York's swing and feel a part of exotic humanity in the Central Park jungle.

With three months in the new world, that course of my quest is over and done with.

I did not like what's new in that ancient, conquered world.

The Icelandic airline strata-cruiser brings us back to Luxembourg.

We are expected. Elsa's fashionable husband, Claude, picks us up in a new Citroën. He appears in love again, eager to reconquer his beautiful tall wife.

He brought with him in his new car my beautiful mama Sia, relieved and happy to recognize her intrepid daughter globetrotting on her way home.

12

LE MUTIN SANK AND I AM LETTING GO OF A PREDICTABLE FUTURE

    Le Mutin is gone, it sank two days after my departure for Mexico during mid-morning after a good rain. Bruno was sleeping after his night shift.
    Momo present, lamented.
    For the benefit of the frogman, diving to search for me, alive or dead.
    Momo pointed to my lynx coat bloating big and white between the waters and waltzing with some floating rotten planks.
    They retrieved a few spoils and a piece of board with the engraved name of the boat.

Bruno keeps it.

I spend some grounding days in Brussels. After that Mexico voyage, I am impatient to find my own place. When I lost my floating space, the race started.

I am restless now; I want to win my place. I am in transition.

My family and friends of the Estro Harmonico listen to my travel report. It's a bring down when I realise, I spent all my advance book money for that trip. I realise also, Le Voyage Ambigu is not going to be a best seller.

I still need to earn some substance before I can be truly free.

I go back to Paris with Bruno in time for his three weeks of paid holidays, I convince him to explore Greece with me.

I move to and fro from Bruno's tiny apartment, where I cook and take showers, to Bertrand's loft, where I sleep.

Both studios sit across from one another on Rue le Regrattier.

It's the beginning of June 1968, and the streets of Paris are still in full revolution turmoil.

Everyone passing is confronted by the riots. Stones fly around at the café terrace when I sit for coffee, taking a chance like a few others.

Right behind my back, revolution steam rolls a wrecking frenzy.

Young people feel suddenly important. They manifested, took occupation at the national assembly and Paris senate.

People get trapped in the street, by the gas masked Police Cordon tear gassing the crowd.

This is the sixties revolution against a sluggish system, the everlasting Vietnam War, the atomic bomb, the racism and the social injustice.

Make love, not war!

Many more slogans and peace ultimatum written, pass me by on the walking banners.

The herd of heroic protesters, manifests on boulevard saint Michel and boulevard saint Germain, they cross the bridge proceeding to the Champs Elysees.

I am sitting on the back seat of Georges Moustaki's Harley Davidson following the sputtering bike of his friend Roger.

We zoom, snaking through traffic and demonstrators, attentive to negotiate our way by maintaining a steady pace through the confusion.

It's a funny revolution going on. I can't believe it concerns me! I am no citizen. I don't have a slot; I'd rather go away.

During my trip to Mexico, Bruno was reporting events at the national assembly and he's still all excited about what could change.

I won my time tirelessly pleading from friend to friend about freedom. I feel lucky to escape so far everyone and everything.

I try to charm all who listen to my inspired words, offering them a virtual glimpse.

It makes me joyous and content to prove in confidence we share the same exact thought exactly in that moment.

13

STEPPING INTO THE REAL THING

I like a great story. It should be something real, but one could laugh at it and have some doubts.

I leave with Bruno by second class train, with a return ticket. Paris to Brindisi, Brindisi to Paris.

I pack a bulging cumbersome travel bag filled with dresses and bikinis; I walk in my new Christian Dior silver boots with a zip on the side.

We leave Paris's South station with fifteen hundred new Francs for three weeks. It is not enough for a holiday but enough for a thrifty gypsy voyage.

We cross the Italian border from the Brindisi station to the ferry by cab.

We embark on the white ferry straight to Corfu, a short passage from the Adriatic to the Aegean Sea. We witness a good omen of jumping dolphins.

On this white island surrounded by turquoise sea and a sunny beach, we plan to spend the first week relaxing.

We find a budget room with two single beds, in a private home.

I unpack my number one bikini, a pale almond green with scalloped petals, tailor-made, the Champs Elyse bathing suit maker adjusted exactly for me.

For my first beach entrance I come out, wrapped in a pareu of aquamarine and white Hibiscus flowers, with Bruno tagging as my escort.

I appear on the beach and peel my wrap, a bit self-conscious beside my unthreatening protector and slightly shy about all the male attention I am garnering.

I wonder about feeling prompt to tease, but not quite free. At the same time, I feel gratefully guarded. With Bruno's gallant escort, I smile wisely to the ladies, befriending Corfu paradise for Greek families.

The first Greek family is curious and smiles back, especially the men and the big boys. Among tamed conservative females in black dress and baggy one-piece dark bathing suit, I stick out, shiny and scandalous.

Easily befriended, we step in, soon invited to a lavish family picnic.

The host pours us glasses of red wine and fills our ears with political discontent, while the busy women cook a feast on a portable hibachi. They grill fish and octopus with a garnish of green peppers, thick sliced onions, eggplants and tomatoes.

We refresh with big slices of sweet watermelon and drink copious amounts of Corfu red wine.

Soon I learn to drive the Vespa with Stephano, the teenaged son who is a bit slow to communicate with me because he doesn't know English or French, but it's not so bad.

He lets me drive and direct me holding nicely my waist without insistence.

Stefano's father has been more daring; he respects me after he triggered a slap by foolishly pinching my butt.

At the age of twenty I am already used to display and guard my Latin bird plumage, just passing trouble, trying to win over the world. I am still available.

Of course, my parents are worried about what's in store for me. They would be reassured if I marry the patient providing Bruno, or any other reliable securely minded candidate.

I presented to them a choice of suitors susceptible to take care of me.

But I believe I don't have to settle so soon, anyway I am not attracted to any of the choice at my disposal. I play and tease, it's a game worth waiting for. I trust, one day, I will know who I am ready for.

That fun week in Corfu ends very soon with a canoe paddle and dive in the cave in the cobalt blue, glittering, bottomless sea. We pay the inflated fee for our week in the private house lodging. We are now seasoned drinkers of Ouzo, Retzina, and Krasi.

Before we walk away from Corfu, we hug each member of Stephano's family saying *"Ephkaristo poli"* (thanks a lot) and *"Antio"* (goodbye).

The ferry toward the Peloponnese takes us back to land.

We hitchhike, enduring interminable hours under glaring hot sun. Infrequent rides through scattered crumbling ruins of ancient extinct cities.

Each rare friendly motorised farmer takes us away from his field in antique vehicles to a more distant field. Between rides we walk sweating on the dusty road with no shade.

I forage for almonds and figs. With my heart beating fast, I run inside a field growing watermelon along the road. I don't see the farmer anywhere and I yank at the resisting stem of a big watermelon far from ripe. I hold onto that stem and twist it until it tore and release the green stolen fruit.

We break it open, hacking it on rocks and chew on a starchy bitter bit of moisture.

We get a ride to our first kafenion, a café/restaurant, on the side of the road. So grateful for the water, we happily sip our gritty Greek coffee.

Calling this coffee Turkish is a faux pas, but I can't resist. The Greek coffee server gets very touchy about mention of Turks, and for that word I get one earful of war history.

We eat psomi, country bread, with voutero butter and Melissa honey and feta and olives. With our Greek coffee we drink lots of water.

We crash in the backpacker's dormitory.

Each step follows historic tracks in the Peloponnese. It is a tedious and exhausting pilgrimage.

All ancient Greece is ruins. A few marble columns still stand or lay tumbled in the dry rocks, all along the blue Mediterranean.

Dry ocher dust and whitewashed little houses with flat roofs dot the dry dusty landscape.

We are trekking in sandals, dehydrating under the mighty sun and the hot cloudless sky, a blinding blue.

This poor place, glorious before Rome, here is all of what remains of that ancient culture I was fascinated by in my history course at school.

Mycenae, Sparta, Olympia, Thebes. I want to see it all, but we've only got two weeks, it's no longer a holiday. Our relentless journey almost complete, we end at the Acropolis and Piraeus.

We complete our Athens visit in two days. We still have a day left before returning to the train in Brindisi, I insist to hitch a last ride to Delphi for the final sight.

I am happy I did.

At the lovely white marble Apollo temple, the Pythia whisper to me: "Do not go back!"

I am impatient to be on my own.

I am going to visit Kriti alone and stay until I spend the hundred and fifty francs and the thirty dollars remaining. Still trusting in my prompt return, Bruno generously leaves all that money to me.

Bruno embarks on the ferry back to Brindisi with his returning train ticket and some metro tickets in his empty wallet. He is going straight back to work the next night in Paris.

I buy my passage, deck class on to Heraklion, the Minoan empire capital of Kriti.

I am off towards the land of ancient gods. To the original cradle of European civilisation, the place of the

Bronze Age goddess with bare breasts who holds a striking snake in each hand.

14

MATALA, HIPPIE COVE

Forever stifled, I must split my old scene. A faint sketch of the adventure with no ties, neither future nor past.

I rake my brain and make my plan.

With ascetic sobriety and humble thrifty ways, I can go on and stretch my stash. I will sustain minimal needs as far as I can roam, to free myself in the Minos' ruined empire.

I disembark in Heraklion. I vibrate fully in new life mode in my pristine white chicken dress. I feel very Parisian for the first time in weeks.

At the wharf, divine Poseidon is waiting for me.

I recognise him with his long trident beard and his long hair. He approaches, greets me and he asks if I am on my way to Matala.

"I don't know yet, let's see. Wait a minute!"

I pull out my map with Matala circled in red pencil by my neighbourhood friend Moustaki. He was the song writer for Edith Piaf and Serge Reggiani, now ready to launch his own singing career with his nonchalant, soft, seducing voice.

In Isle Saint Louis, we recently hung out at the café des sports and I was roaming through Paris on the back of his bike with his other motor bike friend, Roger, an interior architect for small apartments.

"Yes! I want to go to Matala" I say.

"I am from Holland, what is your name?" Volks replies.

"Brigitte, I live in Paris. What about Matala, what's there?"

"A beautiful beach with fantastic private caves carved in the rocks, where everyone can live in, for free..."

"Well, then, of course. I want to go with you!"

We take a comfortable seat at the terrace of the taverna on the main square, in front of the antique dolphin fountain.

I've got a guiding pamphlet about Crete, and they do mention this fountain.

"Give me your bag to carry!" Volks offers.

"Thanks!" I say.

We are getting this ride with a cantaloupe melon seller, welcoming me with one ecstatic smile, we exchange greetings.

Kalimera !
Tikanis !
Kala !
Kala essi !
Oreo!

Yorgo the melon seller orders for us a sumptuous breakfast of Greek coffee, Greek bread, Greek olives, Greek feta, Greek honey and fresh curds.

He pays for breakfast, then the three of us depart in the melon perfumed Volkswagen van.

We are the lucky passengers on a complete tour of Crete hamlets delivering this melon cargo, the final delivery is due in Matala.

Our host Yorgo, jump at the wheel, and attack the rough ride through windy pot-holed ways and sinuous high passes.

For sure it's very hot at the end of June in Crete. It has the same climate as North Africa, not so far away, like written in the prospectus "Kriti".

After two hours of rough driving in heat and dust, that same morning we end up in Paleo Castro, a charming cove with one narrow ocean creek hidden down the mountain.

We find a cane shack to have lunch and a swim in the transparent lukewarm sea. The water is full of smooth pebbles and enormous boulders daunting over a turquoise abyss.

If you dive to the bottom, watch out for urchin's quills. We get out of the blissful water, finally refreshed.

We dry up dancing to the Greek tunes on one radio, motorcycle battery powered.

I know how to dance Sirtaki and Zebekiko, due to my recent Corfu experience and the movie Zorba the Greek with Antony Quinn.

Melon Yorgo attempts to teach us. We try hard to learn more steps.

Volks with his long trident beard, his long red hair and his round rimmed spectacles, is the spitting image of Poseidon, God of the Greek sea.

We drink with no restrictions, taste the various local strains of Ouzo, Retsina, and Krasi.

We smoke a lot of Karelia cigarettes.

I pull the smoke with my long bamboo cigarette holder.

We consume oily fish, and oily potatoes, corned beef, oily green pepper stuffed with rice, cucumber tzatziki, watermelon and of course sweet cantaloupe melons.

Many crazy dances, laughter, jokes and glasses of wine later, gushing with emotions we separate from the patron of each stop.

We are the sole clients. We swear and promise to meet again very soon and then we leave forever climbing through the pot-holed earthy way, driving on toward the next delivery.

At each kafenion, Yorgo unloads some of his melons, and we have a bite and drink more wine and Ouzo. The patron got his stash of fresh melons, and a nice experience with foreign hippies.

Yorgo must add more water in his parched carburetor.

By the late afternoon, hot, tired and dusty, we halt at a water hole, in the middle of a wild rocky pass.

One venerable bearded shepherd is busy watering his many black goats and white sheep.

I emerge first, clad in my white and turquoise Tahitian bikini, closely followed by Volks in a striped multi-coloured bathing suit.

We run away from the van to dive into the rectangular freshwater drinking pool. Under the arrested focused gaze of the old shepherd.

He subsequently proceeds to negotiate to buy me, with Yorgo and Volks, offering them the considerable sum of 3000 drachmas.

This sum seems to me a high stake I find flattering. I decline and explain to this old man, through Yorgo, that I own myself and I am not for sale.

Well refreshed we go away, our slow way.

Next stop is a vineyard with a farm and more sheep and goats. There again, unloading melons.

We eat lamb and drink copious amounts of local Krasi. I am getting tired, even anxious, about ever reaching the goal of distant Matala.

When night falls, men are looming over me, getting too close and too familiar and drunk.

I demand a more distant respectful approach.

Poseidon Volks must be my protecting shield, and wave off the blabbering lecherous drunken host.

We approach the finish line and reach Matala. First stop in town, Yorgo unload the rest of his melons.

Yorgo, rich now, proposes to marry me or to make a generous financial arrangement at my discretion, for exclusive rights on my favors for the time I choose to stay here.

I must answer this open-hearted generous offer, with some diplomacy. I do want to stay free and avoid insulting this new friend.

I am smiling at him, untouched, uninterested and reserved. I escape, making the man feel noble and chivalrous, forcing late respect coupled with frustration.

I am still a cock teaser. Aware of how easy money can be made; but I am no easy girl.

I like to have fun playing the available woman, which I love to stay. I will not commit. I have to be devious to stay free.

Now on the final leg of the journey, the van parks and we get out in Matala cove.

In the opaque night, I perceive the darker shape of the sea.

We walk through abundant sand, towards an obscure cave filled with Dutch people.

Yorgo, our driver, is tired now and wants to sleep with us.

This is not possible; there is no room in this Dutch Hippie cave to accommodate a Greek man. Rejected and pissed off, Yorgo leaves us.

I have no blanket to sleep with. Volks gallantly offers his sleeping bag for my first night.

As soon I slip in it, he cuddles to warm up to me and dives into seduction mode. Doomed to fail.

No one is going to force me.

I am still thriving high on universal platonic relationship. I have no energy for bondage. I am tired, I want to sleep. I don't wish to complicate the novelty of my existence by kissing anyone.

Tonight, Volks is just my latest guide here, who knows about tomorrow?

Volks is tired too, he puts on my long African skirt to keep warm and fall asleep right away beside me. In the middle of the Dutch cave. The horde of seven lay all around me crowding the sandy floor.

I found my place, amongst sleeping bags, backpacks, guitars and drums.

I cannot fall asleep, ants and maybe fleas are biting me. I am too excited reflecting on my exciting first day of freedom.

I fidget fantasying about my unpredictable future. Finally serene I doze in the comfort of Volks sleeping bag.

When I wake up, I leave the cave to get my bearings. I get my first glimpse at a three-hundred-meter amphitheater with a deep soft pale golden sand beach, lapping the turquoise sea and flanked on each side by a cliff.

The pale petrified sandy cliffs, with caves carved like uneven honeycomb stalked on three rows, by the resident lepers' colony. They lived in Matala into the reign of the prince of Knossos two thousand years ago. Then the Romans used the caves as burial crypt.

And now it is the hippies' free accommodation.

The best sunset is right here, famous throughout all of Greece, as is the unpolluted ocean air loaded with divine virtue.

A few kafenion shacks along that beach and behind it, the tiny village.

Two, sparsely appointed grocery shop and a bakery with a big round wood oven where everyone can bake their moussaka or pie for a drachma.

A white cupola orthodox church with a friendly pope, lets me in the door. The restaurant owners are fishing and hunting rabbits and birds to supplement their menus. This whole place is filled by a young seasonal crowd of backpackers.

The bigger part of the travelers is camped on the right cliff in the honeycomb caves. The surplus of them, sleep simply on the beach.

The foreigner season starts in June now, there will be no more vacant caves until the end of August. The other set of caves on the left cliff is reserved for local fishermen, their boats and their gear.

So, my first morning in Matala I open my eyes and rejoice looking at this beach paradise.

In the nature theatre, fully lit by the beams of the swift rising sun, I am about to take my first bath. I am sure it's real only because of my flea bites.

I feel the flow of joy in this morning of creation.

I am, renouncing right away all my recently acquired American standard paradise notions. I imagine many days here in my new freedom.

I still measure my future by the fifteen banknotes I have left.

I get out of Volks sleeping bag and the Dutch cave. I rush to discover this place encrypted in rocks.

I first go down and dive into the turquoise sea.

Five kafenion line the beach, three with music, and the best one with a juke box with all the latest hits.

There is a restaurant in the village for those who may prefer to hear the sea without seeing it. One hotel for the Americans who want a bed and a bathroom.

Emerging from the water I meet Manoli, patron of the first and smallest kafenion nearest to the caves. Manoli invites me for a coffee. At his place I meet a mini tribe of French hippies.

We stay together all day; I soon show off for them.

I do cartwheels and the split right there in the sand, my best spins and cat jumps.

We don't shut up for one moment, it's all coming out in an enthusiastic gushing delirium. Philosophy, and dreams and goals, and essence, existence and passionate contestations.

We explore, together we climb rocks on the side of the village through prickly bush. A steep goat path brings us down on an empty narrow beach with red sand and some ripe figs on a loaded tree.

We meet three stark naked hippies sharing grapes from a paper bag. We stay with them a while.

Then we climb back to Matala before glorious sun set.

That same first day I move away from Volks and the Dutch cave. I give him back his sleeping bag and take back my African dress. I already forgot a possible sleeping bag romance with vexed Volks.

We are friends but distances taken are growing fast even in this small world.

For my second night, I sleep on the beach in my African dress. I share body heat back-to-back with my new French crew.

Money penury is general among us. Whoever has not shall be taken care by who has. Let us not worry.

It is possible to vegetate blissfully one hopeful day at a time. Day by day, time passes.

My future becomes brighter, and the looming prospect of my return is fading.

I am now a part of this homogenous group, we won't leave each other, we will manage to stay.

At about four o' clock in the morning, I wake up soaked in incipient icy dew. I battle energetically with aerobics warmups and then go back to sleep soundly.

In the morning around eight, the sun's heat drives me into the sea.

I wash, I pee and then I take a soft water shower in the toilet of the resto Delphini, where I eat breakfast in French company.

I am a cultivate original, I prefer to be different, it gives me an edge. I make friends easily. I push for action. I won't compromise, all must be still possible...

One week passes. New friends appear.

Michel, a twenty-five-year-old sailor, rents a private room in the village for all of us to share.

Henri and his brother, Jean-Claude, with the guitar and his girlfriend Monique. Plus, Belgian Marc and Dutch Petra and Marieke.

We all move in with Michel in his tiny room. Each new day, a few new friends we just met pile on top. We crowd up three to the narrow bed, all the others manage on the floor with sleeping bags and one busted mattress.

The congenial vibe is exciting, we keep it up drinking loads of the various Greek alcoholic brews. Krasi, ouzo, raki, retzina and beer.

For drugs experiments, some of us absorb forty or fifty Rohilar pills.

Only two pills is the dose as a cough remedy.

This legal drug, when overdosed, provokes hallucinations. Its available in all pharmacies in Heraklion, a sixty-kilometre bus ride away.

Hashish and marijuana are expensive, hard to find, rarely appears.

We are all willing to go on with an exalting psychedelic initiation, more promising than chemical Rohilar, or too much booze.

Being high on psychedelics is still a prerogative of the affluent American hippies who can afford it.

We are segregated, they don't share with us, and they don't speak French.

Generous Michel is a survivor with job experience.

He shelters us, he amuses us. He knows a lot of lewd songs and sailor entertaining stories. A mate recently retired two years ago.

In Heraklion and now Matala he makes his dosh peddling bogus Swiss watches to German tourists.

Soon he will get enough saving to invest in hashish from Istanbul. Istanbul is not far, just one ferry ride from Rodhos.

Henri, my special new mate is cocky and rude, but he enjoys my company. And together we explore the place, in search of what is needed.

I am an eloquent and playful girl, able to fetch a cornucopia from curious Greek tourists. All is shared between us.

Belgian Mark and French Henri are fucking around with Amsterdam Petra and Marieke. Chestnut long straight hair blue eyed Petra ending here her world tour after a year working in a kibbutz. She speaks Hebrew when she is drunk. And Marieke, a cute small girl with brown curly hairs and matching eyes, she likes Rohilar and beg for a beating when she is high.

Michel is gushy about American girls. He hunts for one like the one he once had, everyday hoping the right simple nice one will turn up.

Jean-Claude, older brother of Henri, is with Monique. He entertains us and make us sing for the chorus his Anglo-French repertory.

Each new day is hopeful, and the spirit always seems to keep rising a notch. My financial concerns cease to trouble me. I discover the present is now.

Via mail to Bruno and to my parents I announce my postponed and uncertain return.

I am experimenting survival mode at rock bottom. It satisfies my needs day by day. Here at the belly button of the universe. I exist in each moment.

We sing I join the chorus and sing, vulgar lewd French songs: "acapoum, poum, poum! Acapoum poum poum! For poor horny buggers who fuck and won't pay". We share more French nursery songs and the drinking songs. Improving with practice, the bunch of us enjoy performing.

Blue is the colour of the sky in the morning, when we all rise. We all Share Michel's room until, the new month's rent is due.

At the end of July, we are ready to leave the overcrowded nest to Michel privacy with his latest American girlfriend.

Two French couples leave at the start of August. They offer us the cave of our dreams. With Henri and Petra, we score the biggest cave on the ground floor.

A front main room with a nook for Petra and Henri's double rock bed, and behind is a sleeping cell with my own private carved rock single bed. Under it is a carved recess for my bag.

We forage around for necessities.

Two major, exciting, nocturnal raids suffice to equip our new outdoor kitchen with an iron grate to cook on and pots and pans, plates, glasses and cutlery.

We find many towels abandoned on the beach.

Henri and I trespass into a tourist's vacant home for what we can scrounge. Some fluffy pillows and we discover one massive smooth oak bench, and a grill to cook on the fireplace.

We retrieve and drag that from the accessible window of the villa, distant but not too far. We install the cooking grill and bench on a narrow terrace in front of our cave. From there we survey the entire circus of Matala beach and sunset.

To celebrate we throw a cave warming party.

I cleverly invite Mike, who comes every weekend with presents from his G.I. base. He calls me freckles and he is a bit lonely, he is young like us, but he wears a crew cut, a white tee shirt and jeans. Being a soldier is a burden he must compensate in kind to feel admitted in our happy unengaged hopeful party.

Mike comes in the afternoon early with a cooler full of Coca-Cola, hot dogs, hamburgers, white buns, relish, ketchup, peanut butter, jam, graham crackers and a big bag of marshmallows. Plus, a bottle of Bacardi white rum. All the American's abundant rations are for our potluck party.

I have invited local landlords who are always buying us drinks and food and like to share our fun. With Greek wine and ouzo, a big watermelon, a tin of processed cheese, a box of Laughing cow and biscuits and bread.

For our cave opening party, Xristos, my Cretan admirer, offers me a fluffy warm blanket.

Every evening since I dance at the Delphini, Xristos spend some drachmas on a stack of twelve porcelain plates he throws under my dancing feet.

I don't care about my bleeding feet. I feel no pain stamping and dancing on the braking plates to the Greek music.

Israeli Swiss Marco came here from Switzerland with Aviva born and raised in a kibbutz near Tel Aviv. Our new neighbours soon become my new best friends.

We project to travel to the Amazon Rainforest and photograph the butterflies. I may join in that adventure and write the photo-reportage.

In September, all the vineyard landlords recruit pickers to harvest the grapes. For a day's work we will get a minimum of 60 drachma and more if we fill more baskets. Food and sleeping on site are provided with the job.

It sounds promising. Marco and Aviva volunteer first.

Three scorching days later they are back, they look exhausted. They complain about abominable food, excruciating work, impossible rest and too little pay.

We still want to try.

Henri, Marc, Jean-Claude, Monique, Marieke, Petra and I embark to the vineyard, filling up the open truck bed.

We leave after sunset to arrive in a sandy, unplowed field and spend the night amid local labourers.

We are welcomed to a meal of hard stringy goat and rice stew with no spice with some red crassi to swallow the grub.

We lay right here freezing in our clothes. Bug bit and restless until dawn.

We get up for more stew and wine, and then follow the lead to the grapevines.

To girls they give sickles to cut ripe grapes and to guys they give baskets to load and dump the grapes in a tank.

We are inexperienced, slow at cutting, and slow at loading. We can't compete with the locals, the minimal of sixty drachmas is all we get reluctantly paid for that hard day's work.

We all go back to Matala, that same evening after sunset with the truck going to fetch new pickers.

After three months in Matala, I still have my bill of twenty dollars rolled with my bill of ten stitched up in the hem of my African dress. I live in a timeless present.

Everyone I met here is my friend, restaurant owners, vineyard owners and the whole seasonal resident travelers.

Christos always pays the bill for dinner and drinks for my complete gang of friends.

I sleep well warmed in that fluffy woolen blanket he gave me. I am grateful for the bounty.

I dance with joy proud to entertain local patrons who may never leave their home and discover how big and varied the world is.

Everyone is welcome in our cave to play music and sing.

The boys succeed at catching fish and shrimps with makeshift rods of peeled branches, a nylon line with a safety pin for a hook. We sizzle the small fish on the grill.

I cook nutritious stew, with onion and garlic roasted in olive oil, potatoes and carrots with bay leaf and sage I pick on the hill.

I make pancakes with eggs, whole wheat flour and milk, and French breads with stale Psomi bread soaked in egg beaten with milk.

I steep sage and basil tea. I gather what edibles grow around us, figs, and barbarians' prickly pears.

It's so gratifying to fulfill basic needs playfully, and get by with no money, to banish unnecessary worry and share.

Three French hippies stop in Matala on their way to the south of France. They come all the way overland from Nepal, through India, through Pakistan, Afghanistan, Iran and Turkey.

We invite them to crash in our cave and eat with us. We listen intently, impressed by their intriguing stories while they give us black Afghani smoke to sample.

I write the names of the magic places they passed through; maybe I will go there.

That hashish is the initiating substance! I clearly need to acquire some. I unstitch my hem after four months to retrieve my ten-dollar bill and buy six grams.

That journey overland becomes my goal. All we have in common is nothing to lose.

I already left behind boring security.

All together we are conspiring bird of a feather, savouring this good quality hash, our Psychedelic sacrament, the liberating ingredient, the next step to freedom.

We now prefer this hard-to-get novelty to the Greek wine so easily poured into our empty glass.

Here I decide to renounce alcohol and embrace that different chapter.

I feel selflessly enhanced. I'm open and lovingly concerned with everyone's fascinating self, sharing this good hash.

A joint, or a chillum, unlocked the magic. I want to be radical and sacrifice alcohol for my psychedelic metamorphosis.

Thanks to psychedelics from now on, I renounce alcohol abuse. I don't want to carry on this habitual distraction, already so entrenched.

Unsuspecting addict, I have been proud of holding too much drink and keeping self-control, still not completely numb.

I am lucky to feel I have a choice.

What else should I do, but bounce with this revelation a step further into smoking with my generation?

I will not substitute hash for booze or deny there is individual power playing with the subtle comfort scale of pleasure.

Psychedelic hashish enhances my perspective.

No more inhibited I get in touch with everything alive and therefore connect to others.

So, with the help of this avant-garde hippie returning from India in September 1968 in Matala I am not alone to be seduced and to engage in the psychedelic era with a discreet "bang!"

Our restaurant patron suddenly discovers at the bottom of his cash drawer, some pieces of Turkish hash, and some red Lebanon to share.

We are painting our faces and bodies with water colours. We keep more private in our caves to meditate about the now. We smoke and share Hashish, our exclusive transforming experience.

Henri, while he smokes, feel obliged to keeps very silent, subdued and quiet, Petra emulates him.

Marc says now when he smokes, "I am completely stoned", instead of "I am completely drunk" when he drinks.

Hashish launches me into space and sharpens my senses. It links me with what I perceive, allows me to connect.

The Delphini got a jukebox and a pergola to provide cool shade in the afternoon sun. It's Matala's new stylish hang out with the most entertainment available.

Yorgo, who runs the Delphini, appreciates my dancing full power display to the delirious drinking music night after night. He also appreciates the guitar skills and melodious voices of Jean-Claude and Monique. Yorgo proposes us to perform at his night club on the road near Heraklion.

We are engaged as foreign attraction, and staff, to entertain the customers. Yorgo leaves us in charge of running the club after he deposes us and show us what to do at the *Auto Club*.

On the small stage, every forty-five minutes Monique with Jean-Claude will sing and play guitar, then I will dance, our show only lasts ten minutes.

Between our live shows, we put on pop music cassettes.

That gives us thirty-five minutes to serve and entertain the clients. Prepare the drinks, clean up and wash the glasses. We chat and dance with single clients.

For all this we get a fix rate of 30 drachmas per night, plus 10 percent commission on the drinks, plus tips.

We receive free lodging at Yorgo's mother's guest house and free food at Nico's, Yorgo's brother's food bar. Nico will drive us after we eat our evening meal and come to pick us up. He will count the money and pay us every night.

This splendid irresistible offer makes us proud to be paid to perform our show business. We pack and leave our cave to the safe keeping of our friends.

We sit for a minute in Yorgo's car with our gear, but we must get out and help push.

Yorgo drives and his brother Nico pushes running with us to start the old blue car parked on the incline.

Our first stop in Heraklion is Yorgo's mother's guest house. In a separate room with two single beds and a sink, we deposit our bags and put our toiletry on the sink tablet.

For the whole guest house, employees and patrons, there is a single shared bathroom with a shower two floors down.

Yorgo presents the three of us to his mother, a pinched mouth severe lady dressed in black.

We go to dine downstairs across the street at Nico's restaurant. Yorgo's brother doles us a portioned sample of the foods bathed in olive oil. Each one on display in a rectangular metal container.

We eat the oily food, then go back up and dress in our show-biz costumes. We go in the car to the Club.

Our big plan is to make enough money to travel overland on the hippie trail up to Kathmandu, Nepal's capital at the roof of the world, still very far away!

I got my first mandatory shot against cholera and yellow fever at the Heraklion dispensary. The male nurse injected my arm then stamped my vaccination booklet.

The Auto Club comprises of a square dark room with a mini stage. Behind the stage, a dark kitchenette with a single propane burner, a wood counter and a tiny bar fridge.

Not very impressive, but conveniently located to start the car running on top of a small hill on the road to Knossos, three kilometers away from Heraklion.

From 9pm until 3am, every single night we are on display, hard at work. I dance solo, but also with Jose Garcia, my flamenco partner.

Monique and Jean-Claude sing songs and strum the guitar.

We prepare and serve drinks; we wash the glass and dance with the single clients who buy us drinks between performances.

We mix crushed ice with Nescafe and sugar with a slice of lemon, for us, plus an added peg of Bacardi white rum for paying customers.

The Auto Club is not so popular.

We work hard for our pay; we only make about fifty drachmas per night for hardcore, sleepless nights and putting up with horny bachelors.

After a single week Jean-Claude and Monique quit. I stay sole in charge.

So, I wash the glasses in cold water, and brew the drinks whisking a teaspoon of Nescafe powder with crushed ice and sugar and a slice of lemon on top.

I add the booze, I serve the beers, and I dance the slow with all the regular customers. Between my first number of the Gershwin favorite "One American in Paris" I finish with a classic solo ballet, on nutcracker final, and jump in the split French cancan style, always a hit.

Between pop music tunes a twist, a Charleston, a rock around the clock plus a professional Flamenco performance with Jose Garcia who also play guitar and is a maestro dancer who knows how to toss me in the air and make me do acrobatics I didn't know I can do.

Then a jazz blues suggesting number mellowing at the end of the night.

I feel okay alone in my guest room, the promiscuity of amorous Jean-Claude and Monique made me cringe. That week felt long. We fast became irritated by lack of personal privacy confined in that bare ugly room.

After 3 a.m. all the clients leave. The work is over. I still have to run every night down the slope pushing behind the car to start the engine.

I persist on my own three zealous weeks. I keep performing and serving selflessly. I get rid of a few abusive bullies who think I owe more favours for the drinks they bought me.

My gold Dunhill lighter gets nicked for a token memory by my regular client, with only one arm who loves to dance with me.

My first job for money turns to be a rather sordid experience. It brings me down, for not much profit. I feel lonely and insecure and resent holding the fort alone at the goofy night club.

My Matala friends come to see me perform. After the show Bimbo, Michel, Henri, Petra, Marco and Marieke tag along with me back at Yorgo's mother's pension, and all of them spend the night in my room.

In the morning after ten o'clock, one at the time, the seven of us come down to the bathroom.

Yorgo's mother is pissed off. She demands money for the night and locks my room with all our luggage in to force my gang to pay.

A raucous chorus of mockery is the savage answer at her black mailing tactic

Henri stays with me in the hall, backing me up. We occupy the hall entrance. All the others are waiting in the street.

Yorgo's mother simulates a call to the cops. This unleashes my ire to a devastating unrestrained fury.

I seize up, toss and shatter on the floor, each adorning ornament in the reception area,

Precisely enumerated one red ceramic ashtray, one Ludwig von Beethoven plaster bust with brass veneer, one bohemian crystal vase with plastic yellow tulips.

Every Greek of the house is running about trying to stop me. Finally, the lady patron decides to unlock my door.

I barge in and seize my friend's already packed belongings and sleeping bags and throw them down the staircase. I order Henri to wait for me while I feverishly pack my own things.

At the top of my lungs, I let everyone know I am fed up with being the main attraction, and I am going away.

Right now!

We are all piled up in Bimbo's car. Everything has been collected, stuffed in the car trunk, and tied on the roof rack. We are moving away at a slow pace in the overloaded deux chevaux.

15

RETURN TO MATALA

Bimbo, our hippie doctor drives us to Matala.

We are home again and settle back into our cave waiting for the end of the tourist season.

It's cooling off. Petra is going back mid-September to get her Master's degree in anthropology in Amsterdam. She is the first to leave.

A week later Henri and Mark leave for Israel planning to sell their blood in Haifa where they heard they will get sixty dollars for it.

Mark plans to work in a kibbutz with his uncle, but Henri knows only Mark and hopes to go and work with him. Henri had just enough money for a one-way ticket.

Jean-Claude and Monique managed to get a kilo of hash ready packed in their guitar in Istanbul. Back in Matala, we play a last concert with that guitar, and we sing the chorus before they exit to Paris to make a fortune.

If everyone programs succeed, we will all meet again on the road.

I am already on my way. I don't want to go back.

The kind of life which awaits me in Paris with Bruno, and all the people I already know is full of alienating compromises I must make to survive there. It scares me.

I don't want to return to that, it is nothing I want, and I prefer the unknown. For nearly four months now I manage, without security. I don't care, I am not worried. Not anxious about my future. I breathe freely, on my own, like never before.

I feel free and invincible. I need my dose of personal experience with no return ticket. I don't care!

I am expanding in my hashish bubble, but it will burst if I go back to Paris.

Michel saved enough to go get his kilo of red opium in Istanbul. His nice American girlfriend will wait here for him.

Sylvie is the latest. A nice girl from Boston, who appeared after completing a French immersion summer course, at the Sorbonne in Saint Germain des Pres.

We immediately become close friends. I want to speak more English, and she wants to speak more French, we teach each other.

Michel left Matala with a bit of hash planning to sell it in Heraklion for a good price. When two young straight guys ask him if he knows where they can score some hash, Michel offers to sell his two ten-gram slabs of good quality black Afghani. They are plain clothed narcotic police. He gets arrested.

The police officers confiscate his money and his two slabs.

Then they search for more criminal evidence in his hotel room to find, and confiscate as well, all his Swiss watches.

Michel is waiting in jail, hoping to avoid the maximum sentence of five year. Maybe a lawyer could help him but who will pay?

Yorgo at the Delphini did understand and forgive my tumultuous escape from his mother.

We are still friends. He heard what happened to Michel from his cousin the cop. Paranoia seizes us after this warning.

Matala's only two cops search Michel's room at Sylvie's for nothing.

I am now the only tenant in my cave. I still got my six grams of black Afghani I bought for ten bucks from the French hippies.

Yorgo tries to convince me to go back to perform at the Auto Club, he will increase the basic salary to 100 drachmas a day plus my tips, plus 10 per cent on the drinks. He adds a 10% incentive on selling packets of 10 premade joints with good Moroccan hash for a thousand drachmas. Or one single joint for hundred drachmas.

An excellent offer, but I got all disturbed about Michel. I refuse to risk my freedom. I don't want a risky job, I am not greedy, and I have never been ruled by money. I am learning how to survive day by day, my way. I want to play my own scenario.

There is no solitude here. Matala swarms with friendly travelers. I am staying right here. I like to meet all the hippies coming from everywhere.

Sunset time.

On my way to the Delphini, a very fair guy walks into me in the company of a younger guy with curly red hair, practically invisible in his shadow.

The striking apparition of perfection; beautiful, long, straight blond hair, green eyes, bare arms and sun-tanned skin. This ethereal androgynous creature got a golden brocade vest on over worn trousers, well-cut and beige.

That is 21-year-old Danish Walter

Entering Matala with seventeen-year-old Paul in his shadow, very curly red hair, rusted eyes, a traveling freshly landing doing his dodging before he may be called to the army. He comes from Washington D.C. U.S.A, in a tee shirt and jeans.

Tagging beside this Danish prince charming who intrigues me. I compliment him on his costume. He got his top at the theater costume sale in Copenhagen where he is from.

I can't believe how good looking and engaging Walter is. I get in the middle of the two guys, and I listen to Walter's voice speaking musical French to me.

I lead them at the front seat before the setting sun. It takes just a few warming seconds to be the best of new friends.

Paul is not saying too much, but he is part of this new situation. Paul got his frizzy red hairs like a balloon around his smooth pale face and shaven neck, Jimmy Hendrix style.

Paul does not have any bristles to shave yet. He is discovering the exciting old world all the way from America.

The two new guys are nice, and I especially focus on green eyed, blond hair Walter. He takes a direct and clear approach in the musical French he speaks with me.

He switches to English with American Paul, Italian with Manuelo, one other, just landed Roman beautiful guy with soft curly brown hair and dark eyes.

We wait until the sun lightshow is over. We drink Krasi red wine and smoke Marlboro American army ration cigarettes.

Immediate sympathy floods us, and we bask blissfully in good vibrations. The just arrived guys need a place.

Paul and Manuelo can have the cave right beside mine, and Walter, which is the one I'd like to know better, can stay with me.

Walter sparks immediately my fancy, an obvious hippie prince with who I want to play, in my new life story.

There is no time to waste. I want to merge in that superficial bliss.

I recognise the selected brothers I was waiting for. I had been waiting for the right people, killing time, labelling everyone in my growing book.

All my friends so far have been limiting, not entirely hopeful, off going somewhere, trying to grab my attention. Obstructing my infinite perspectives.

I just met company to follow, with me, one unpredictable dream.

I am no longer the younger one, I am about to take my place in the race for time. At least all these new people disponible in my generation have opened their eyes to the present.

I propose a joint in my cave, I still have the good Afghani shit. All night we are talking about our new happening world. About Mao Zedong and the revolution. About all the world's mystery, we need to change for the better.

We can spread peace, end all wars, partake of all resources, open all frontiers, tolerate and evolve, fit in, open cultures with peace and love.

Everybody wants to be together. That is us.

We all eventually fall asleep right where we are. On the sandy, cave floor. We express cumulating exaltation and are now intimate friends for life.

We all wake up early, Paul and Manuel go claim the next cave, and Walter stays in mine as we both wish.

In the late morning everyone is eager to share breakfast and help me prepare it on the iron grill.

Whole wheat pancakes and French toast made with my stash of stale bread soaked in milk and eggs.

Three delightful English musicians in their thirties play their trumpet, a guitar and a mouth harp on the beach at the sunset. Afterwards, we clap in appreciation. They serenade us and make us laugh, and we invite them to join us in the cave.

In our cave, every evening starts with a jam session, before sunset and after sunset we jam together, again until late night.

We play and sing after dinner.

Walter sits cross legged on the stone couch, he gets the beat going by banging on two metal cups and everyone follows. There is guitar, trumpet, horn, flute and voices and spoons and metal pots and saucers, glass bottles, sticks and stones.

We improvise the story of the day with a very long song each night.

Life it is not only about music. But music is a big part of our life, a satisfying occupation we share together.

I am putting to work all the boys who like to share the food. Manuelo is taking care of the fire; Bruno is gathering the wood and cleaning up the dishes in the sea. Paul carries the shopping. Walter fills up the jerry can full of drinking and cooking water at the Delphini tap.

I put it together everyone, helps prep the ingredients.

Morning breakfast after the beach one pancake each with copious amount of French toast and freshly gathered local infusion.

After sunset big stews and candle lit dinner before our night super jam.

After shopping in Matala, I pick all the flowers I can reach. Pink and white vanilla flagrant Oleander, purple asters, spikes of green canes, and wild bay leaf branches, rose and white oregano and purple sage from the hill behind the caves.

I recycle my wilting herbs decor by brewing teas. Except for the poisonous oleander, and the purple stars with yellow heart of Atropa belladonna shiny green vines.

On the wall in between fresh garlands hangs a giant poster of Bob Dylan. A present from L.A Joe and Wendy in the upper cave.

Joe and Wendy own a battery-operated player and a stack of long-playing records.

They've got the music we dream of. The Doors, The Creams, Jimmy Hendrix, the Beatles Bob Dylan and Ravi Shankar. Plus, a marble chillum they bring down to our cave.

With fresh whole wheat flour, bread yeast, raisins, fresh butter, fresh milk, cinnamon, eggs, Matala honey and a spoon of the baker yeast I prepare my Belgian grandmother Moumoune's Vervier cake. I mix it raw in the cave and bring it to the baker oven for one drachma.

I love to invite friends to share my good cuisine

With my new inseparable friends and Sylvie's coaching I practice my English. And I continue to learn to improvise music, two important subjects.

It requires continuous attention to understand, but if I listen, it makes sense. I repeat the musical phrases and take part in the conversation.

Most crucial word resembles each other, with their own accent, French and Latin, Italian, Spanish and of course English, Dutch and German.

I start to communicate in English.

Nobody really understands Joe and Wendy's Californian slang, but it's groovy, and that's what we learn and mostly repeat what they say.

Who needs too many words when blasting that great rock and roll music?

In the next cave live Marco and Aviva. We are no longer best friends, since I upset Marco by blurting inconsiderate sincerity.

I don't trust anyone. I can take no one seriously, not even myself, and I don't believe anyone is consistent.

That hit Marco as a personal blow. He turned red, personally offended by my careless statement. When I burst into foolish laughter at his mounting fury, he feels mocked and slaps me.

I have to retaliate. We roll into the sandy dust of the cave floor; I bite him, and I scratch him. It's one exciting physical, short fight.

I lost my opportunity to discover and write about the butterfly fauna and special flora in Amazonia. There goes the trip to South America.

Never mind, we still speak, say hello and share some occasional pancake feast, there is no lasting hard feelings. But there is no more hope for partnership.

In September, the season ends, we hang out longer in the cave to smoke hashish with passing cool freaks.

The hippies traveling back, bring the good news, and the good stuff. I note in my tiny book the names of places to stop and meet my growing tribe on the road.

We still spend time out in kafenions, especially the Delphini with the potable water tap, the outdoor shower and the jukebox with the latest rock and roll hits and irresistible Greek dancing tunes.

Yorgo employs hippies, I cook and dance for him with my beautiful friends. We are the fascinating fun barbarians attracting affluent Greek customers.

The smallest kafenion nearest to our cave belong to Manoli. It is bursting full of young local business.

The Greek party dudes called *Mangas*; show off by dancing with a wooden chair or a wooden table between clenched strong jaws.

They play hard and enjoy throwing a ripe uncut watermelon well aimed to explode on each other hard head. They show off, especially on Sunday picnics.

Xenophon, next to the Delphini kafenion, has the contestable repute to serve the best spaghetti to his steady flow of customers. Also, in a great location just like all his concurrent neighbors.

The beach kafenion circuit ends with Costa. The oldest, fattest and quietest patron. Costa, welcomes and cherishes his Hippies. He gives unlimited credit, nourish and satisfy our appetite with enormous plates of interesting, tasty titbits.

On Saturday and Sunday, G.I. Mike with a friend, comes from his nearby base to mingle and share all extra rations. He offers me a carton full of Marlboros.

Greek tourists climb our cliff sportively to sneak into our caves with camera ready to snap.

O.K., but not for free.

A bottle of Krasi or Retzina if we agree! Or a muscular Hippie will bar their insolent way, snatch the camera, tear out the film.

With face and body art on our naked flesh, each of us take the paint brush to put the final strokes, tourists must pay for immortalising this impermanent art display.

We are increasingly beautiful, perfecting the image of the growing heroes we choose to be. We are making progress toward the mysterious approach across exalted cultures.

We have escaped from the world's cities where we had no space of our own. We dive in, trusting we will find our place when we know a bit more. We experience, we perceive, we don't want to know anything about patient suffering. All of us insolent and happy

I am fascinated by Walter's immediacy, everything right away. I am not personally wanted, just a nectar flower to a butterfly.

That one is not for me. My sexual self is still dormant. I thrive, still patiently waiting to be woken by a kiss. All of me wanted forever.

I admire him, like Narcisse his own reflection. I keep him close by but at a small distance. I am not the one who will cross the line.

I still englobe Walter in my universal loving interest for these beautiful strangers I like to understand.

I believe love will be coming just for me. I am watching, keeping inhibited and cerebral about sex.

I now relish refined preliminary contact giving me lots of time to enter womanhood. I would rather stay waiting a little more and be sure it's not a mistake to choose and be chosen. For now, dancing is enough, sleeping, eating, talking, laughing and thinking about kissing, it's all enough.

I am seduced by this international Hippie happening, no one has wrinkles or any concept of the ravage of time. We feel forever, so different from the rest of the world.

We have all the time. We are impatient to embrace a firmly clinging possibility. We discard creeds, politics, war, segregation, religions. It's all pushy faceless authority.

Words, to avoid and laugh about, we don't need it.

We want the world made newly, special for all of us. A new easy opening way with no threatening restrictions.

A traveling couple walks by us. I notice they hold two children about one and two years old. Each on a sling on their back, they carry lovingly their heavy chubby babies. The young parents are starting to look older, a bit eroded by time and survival struggle, like ancient art.

On the third and last layer of caves is big boned, plump, powerful American girl named Sherry. She entrusts some American dollar bills for me to exchange for Drachmas at the black market in Heraklion.

The blond German, Kurt, with long hair and blue eyes is installed with her. I saw him arriving. He walked fast from the bus depot in Heraklion, he kept his speed walking the sixty kilometer it took him, ten hours, to reach us for sunset at the Delphini in Matala. I was impressed by his determination and stamina. He obviously prefers trooping for a free hippie life to the mandatory German army.

Lucky Kurt landed in Sherry's American cave; she can afford to go with him overland to India. Kurt speaks in German with Walter about their approaching departure.

Joe's twenty fifth birthday party calls for a major celebration. Joe and Wendy's cave is small, we will host it in our double cave and prepare a memorable party together.

Wendy spends two entire days cooking. I elaborate a three-layered Mayan pyramid chocolate cake with a chocolate buttercream icing. Topped with maraschino cherries and a dusty packet of twenty-five real birthday candles, items I discovered on my business day in Heraklion.

One impressive stack of favorite records collected from everyone's cave. Every resident Hippie with a record player contributes a favorite record to the party.

Ample wine, hashish, savoury food, two packs of white candles, three petrol lamps with glass hoods. A complete set of eight new batteries for the record player. A pile of dry wood for the bonfire and last-minute cooking.

Before the party start, I wash laundry at the tap of the Delphini, when I see two robust looking Greek men retrieving our borrowed oak bench and march back with it to the tourist house it came from.

I can see Paul and Walter attending to the fire in front of the cave, they do nothing to interfere with the two guys repossessing the bench. When I come back with the laundry, we improvise a new sitting arrangement with all cushions on bamboos canes.

To celebrate Joe's first quarter century, we connect. Acknowledging the age where youth mature. "Great!" that is all they can say, and all there is to say in L.A. California. And that we understand.

Joe's happy birthday is totally groovy.

***

The English musicians play on the beach. Buck, the leader, plays stark naked only on the weekends to tease tourists.

Buck sips raki and plays his melodious trumpet, his three mates casual in bathing trunks, beat a drum, blows harp and a horn.

The hat protecting Buck's bald skull is the only garment he's got on for the weekend. At the end of the show,

Buck with flourish, throws the hat to the tourist audience gathered, and they put money in it, innit?

Buck works a day job in one industrial complex near Manchester. He has got a real job and bills to pay. He is not a snob and a kid like all of us, he is at least thirty.

German Kurt cooks for us naked. He lights his farts through the cave entrance, and it makes a flash of light.

Sanitary police inspect our caves on the weekend, so we escape to the red beach. We get naked and paint ourselves, we return all painted to parade for money on Matala beach on Saturday and Sunday. Nobody stays home in the caves.

October starts with crafty opportunist pseudo hippies departing, selling their caves and gear to latecomers.

We disapprove of merchandising what every one of us got for free. We disapprove of speculation, negotiations, and money business.

Money is nothing. We just need a place to sleep, something to eat and drink, and some extra luck to catch the flying carpet on the road. And share hashish, a sacred essential component we pass around and all use.

We look for more hashish. It helps with the feeling of peace and love.

I help my Greek friend Mimi by introducing him to the new girls he notices. Mimi sends me on errands in Heraklion, once a week.

I change dollars into Greek money, get Rohilar, and stuff from Mimi's associates, buy special food supply and check the post-box for everyone's mail.

I survive my thrilling tale unfolding on my way

I send my rushed report about Mexico to the *Figaro Litteraire*. I hope it will pay for my way to India.

The hippie commune starts dispersing, it's getting colder.

October 16th is the twenty-second birthday of Walter. For this I bake a four layers chocolate cake, Mayan pyramid, with the creamed butter and chocolate icing, the remaining tin of Maraschino cherries, and twenty-two birthday candles.

We grill enough beef steaks on the fire, and jacket potatoes in the ambers.

A carved giant watermelon full of fruit salad with whipped cream, like Wendy made for Joe birthday. Everything plus.

We dance perched on the perilous rocks daring to chance our rhythm on the restricted precinct in front of the cave. We sing heartfully the happy birthday song and Walter blows his twenty-two candles. We sing with the Beatles: "love, love, is all we need", while I perform my inspired fire dancing with a lit birthday candle on each of my ten extra-long fingernails.

We share a joint of marijuana *churrus,* triple pressed pollen from Morocco.

We dive in the chilling sea by the moon light. Everyone is delighted. Walter is stoned and excited holding on to me for familiar grounding comfort.

I still don't know if he prefers girls or guys. Maybe he likes both? But he has me charmed and I don't really care.

We generate a joyous light fondness purring for each other, I get affectionate cuddles kisses and hugs, and that is what I am ready for.

We all will be going to India and will hopefully soon meet again.

Walter will go for Christmas in London where he plans to take L.S.D. Before that he is going back to Copenhagen for money, then we will meet again soon, but I don't know when.

I interest him with my Parisian artful life, my cooking skills, and my reserved exploding upbringing.

I enjoy the lightness of the pair we make. We practice some accurate elegant spitting in faraway corner. While I plan my own program with him playing a part of the picture.

The shared piggy bank is empty. Everyone must scrounge for themselves to get away somewhere. Manuel moves in with Sylvie.

Sylvie and I teach each other language. Exchange phrases.

Paul and Walter are the latest arrival of Hippies butterflies. They blew in last minute of the ending season, boosting my interest. Welcome to visit on all floors, invited to partake in everything, until the end of Matala hospitality.

Bruno finds a Japanese girl.

My reportage is refused with a standard note.

Fortunately, Bruno is sending me three hundred dollars for my trip to India at the American Express in Heraklion. In the meantime, I have credit at Yorgo's, Costa's and Mimi's kafenions. I help them, they help me. The season is unraveling.

Manuelo leaves his cave and follow Sylvie, his meal ticket, in Michel's ex-private room in the village.

I talk a lot more American English, Sylvie improves the hesitant French she just learned at the Sorbonne spring program. I speak with simple American words.

Sylvie is interested in my writing. Coaching each other develops our friendship.

Sylvie romance with Manuelo fizzles out. Manuelo leaves her room back to the cave all alone.

Sylvie meets Mimi and they become a happy couple. This grants us cigarettes, hash, food and free access to a private comfortable bathroom with a full-size mirror in a small apartment.

Henri is already back, he never set foot in Israel.

Not allowed to leave the vessel that brought him to the port of entry at Haifa without a return ticket. Henri came right back, penniless like a stowaway with crushed, hopes on that same ferry. He appears in the afternoon brandishing one ancient charcoal steam iron, a present for me. He is eager to move right back in.

Obviously disappointed with all the changes.

I only share my cave with Walter but prefer privacy to evolve this interesting platonic relation in my cave.

I had just painted on the ceiling a spiralling vortex, dark blue and red rimmed with one open eye in the centre. Henri my ex-adopted friend has been exchanged for a new preferred brother and must find himself a cave.

Henri is welcome to participate and share the grub. He moves in with Marco and Aviva. When Henri sleeps with Sylvie, Mimi gets upset.

Sylvie breaks up with Mimi and she gets a job at the mineral water pop factory, the sole industry of Matala.

One entire day from nine to five, with only twenty-minute break for lunch, she washes and fills and cork with a blue glass ball and metal hook, hundreds of soda bottles.

After five that evening, she comes in exhausted, and hands me all her salary. A romantic gesture.

So, my now best girlfriend was planning to discover Spain, but I am going to India. She wants to go with me.

In the cave we are jamming. I inhaled deeply. With just one big puff now I hallucinate. All of us metamorphosed into monkeys, each play discordant music and silly games, we beat our chests and pots and pans, and we swing all over.

It makes no sense at all. It's freaking me out. I leave the cave and search for what's real. I am not sure, if I am alive or a ghost.

Manuelo, Mimi and Henri, too many males trailing behind Sylvie, she decides to leave her room and wait for me in Heraklion's youth hostel.

I will soon join her to collect my three hundred dollars at the American Express.

November storms in, wind and rain beat the cliff and inundates the cave.

Walter attempts to cement a stone wall with plaster of Paris to protect us. The next gust beats it, and it crumbles and washes away. We get soaked and almost drown.

Time is up, storms roll in with the tide. The migration is on.

We were three hundred in June, July and August, now only fourteen remains to celebrate a last full moon party.

Mid-November 1968. The sun still shining and warm. We all still clad in bathing costumes and swimming. At four thirty the sun sets, and it cools fast. Nasty weather starts right after sunset. We gather tightly on top of the cave hill.

We hold hands sharing the wonder at the splendiferous sunset punctuated by the beat of a petulant stormy tide and a mounting vociferous thunder.

Sagittarius full moon. We wrap up warmly.

It is Big Sherry's birthday. Our last blast happening on the flat ground on top behind the last row of caves. Point of view for all the beach and Matala village.

In a circle, we drink hot chocolate milk and feast on a last batch of French toast and pancakes. We pass around the marble chillum.

We play our role. The last party for the fourteen of us.

Big beautiful American apple pie Sherry, the birthday girl, the shemale God.

German Kurt's blond Saint Thomas the evangelist. Dark fiery Bruno Lucifer. Joe and Wendy, Jupiter and Junon, Manuel John the Baptist. Henri Peter Pan.

Marco and Aviva Joseph and Mary before Jesus.

Pale and strong Manuelo Mussolini. Miya co Madame Butterfly

Ethereal Walter's archangel Michael. Curly Paul Pan. Nature's first God. I am Salome.

Sun set and the full moon rise. Wind blows, thunder strikes, and clouds build-up. No rain falls but thunder and lightning give us sound and light. We act and play charade until the moon is gone.

A night full of clouds moving fast, is now dark and everyone go to rest in their caves. After a five-month immersion I am at least a seasoned Hippie pillar dealing with local tourism.

After Sherry's birthday all is falling apart.

Next evening after the full moon, Aviva is harassed by two Greeks who think she is walking alone after sunset. Out of their view, very close behind, Henri and Marco are following her. Henri and Marco pounce on the back of the assaulters and fight them, in this battle, one Greek fell in the nearby well and drown.

Crete is the original place of vendetta, before Corsica another big island of unforgiving survivors.

This tragic accident will unleash the rampant custom of retaliation. This sinister drama looms on us as a menacing shadow

That same morning, before we have breakfast, the police interrogate everyone to conclude it is one unfortunate accident.

Marco and Aviva must leave and escape immediately under police protection. They pack their things and embark on the afternoon bus.

Marco gives me his last piece of red Lebanese hash as a departure present.

No more tourists, no more food, and no more friends, the harsh wind is blowing us away.

Walter is ready to leave with Paul. I am waiting for my money; it should come any day now.

The next step of freedom is departure.

Joe and Wendy must go, called back to the States in L.A for Joe's art show.

Hopefully they will be lucky and make enough dosh to go on the road to India, they dread to leave their cave, they know full well America's promise land, is only for the fittest. They will linger here as long as possible.

Kurt and Sherry are on their way to India. Kurt advises me to hide myself behind a veil to pass safely overland to India, especially through Muslim country.

I know I won't do that after I passed safely through Muslim, Christian and Pagan countries. I avoided the role of victim on several previous occasions, I plan to keep that up.

I have nothing to fear, my main anxiety is about going back to the West to my consumer Paris and Brussels society. Going nowhere could so easily gobble me up.

Next morning Walter and Paul get a lift in a car to Heraklion. From there they will take the ferry to Athens.

Paul will go to Lebanon and Walter to Copenhagen.

I walk with them along the beach, I stay silent. We reach up to the car. There is an expected departure kiss.

I burst out laughing, in tears. I feel sad about my little prince going away and gone.

I don't know my own heart, who knows if we will ever meet again and play again in this world. Or what kind of infatuation is that.

All day long I'll cry childish tears.

Henri is there to comfort me. He moves right back into my cave. But with him, I have lost the light feeling.

Henri wants to come with me and my expected money to India. Henri is baggage I don't need. I get irritated by his testing company. We are bickering and sulking. We will not travel together.

Since Walter has gone with Paul, I am disenchanted, not truly understood or appreciated. I feel again, much better on my own.

I accept to be the mule to score some hash. I sit on the back of old Yorgo's T.V.S. We slowly grind our way to Heraklion.

We reach the bridge, approach the city and slowly start to merge into the traffic; we get lightly hit by a truck on Yorgo left side.

I fly over the handlebar and land, in slow motion, almost softly on the pavement with a bloody left leg and a deep cut on my right hand.

This accident shakes me awake.

I escaped lightly, but now I feel fragile. I will not follow anyone blindly. I must lead, on my way.

So, there I leave old Yorgo and the back seat of his T.V.S on foot and I take a bus to the American Express. My money is here!

They only give Drachmas for my three hundred dollars. I will be able to change Drachmas for Dollars, only in Athens and for a fee.

Waiting for my cash I meet two vivacious girls from New York.

One is Chinese and named Sharon and other half black and half French with afro hair and green eyes. She is called Nicole, born in Haiti.

Both girls are on their way to visit Matala before traveling to Athens. Both have the boring clean look of middle-class tourists.

We take the bus to Matala, together.

I pay my debts. I introduce Nicole and Sharon to Mimi, and we smoke a chillum.

I am ready to leave.

I kiss Henri and Manuelo goodbye. I donate my wool blanket, kitchen stuff and my painted cave to Henri.

I give my white satin dress with the white rooster feather cuffs and a low cleavage to Wendy to get married in in Los Angeles after the show.

Wendy clasp on my ankle one silver bells anklet from India.

After five months, it's the last instant in Matala.

It is getting dark at five o'clock, the happy hour. A very bad time to hitch hike.

I start walking along the road away from the village.

I carry one heavy bursting bag, filled up with all my dresses, bikinis, sandals and silver boots. After less than one hour, I am hot, and dusk turns dark.

I am tired.

I rest my back on the truck of a chestnut tree on the side of the road sitting on my travel bag.

Night falls, I roll a joint, considering sleeping right here.

I just finish my smoke when a car stops in front of me.

At the wheel is my friend Manoli, the patron of the smallest kafenion, the one with the Greek Mangas who like to dance with a solid table clenched between his jaws, and the unchallenged champion of watermelon fights.

I am very happy to get that lift to Heraklion.

Manoli is going to Athens. We can embark on the same boat and share a room at the cheap hotel he knows.

In Heraklion we are sitting to a pleasant congenial dinner. But at night, Manoli sneaks into my bed and harass me for three hours before giving up on seducing me.

Sure, I am free and available, but emotionally cautious.

I am still growing up on guard and locked. So that night is a deadly blow to our friendship.

Early morning, I move to the cheaper youth hostel in the safety of the dormitory.

I share my table at the canteen with Joan returning from India.

Through her long journey she abused herself, injected opium, morphine and methadone. She got abused and she got ripped off. She got hepatitis and she is going home to recover.

Traveling alone is dangerous and even with another girl it still is dangerous. That girl I don't know how old she is, and I don't want to ask her that silly question, but she looks worn and dusty, a scary shadow of youth.

At the port Big Sherry and Kurt embark on the ferry to Istanbul. We are delighted to meet up by chance on our way to India.

We will meet again very soon.

That evening at the youth hostel I decide to cure my cold and experiment with forty pills of Rohilar. I swallow them one by one sipping my hot milk.

I sit in the canteen beside a fifty-year-old guy, fresh from a Christian camp commune in the red neck part of the states.

That guy, full of evangelical zest, is fishing for new recruits.

I am listening, attentive to my feelings inside and the guy beside me.

After a while the Rohilar kicks in and I am surprised to suddenly find easily my eloquent speech in English. Surprised by my own fluency.

I explain how and why I am not interested in cults and communes, and aim to discover my own personal destiny, free of ties.

I go to sleep in the dormitory. I wake up early, feeling fine, my cold seems better.

I embark to Athens with my heavy bag. I walk to the removable deck, the last on board at 9:29.

At exactly 9:30 the crew starts pulling the access deck one last running Hippie jump over in a perilous leap and land safely on board. Here comes Tennessee Rob, we already met yesterday at the youth hostel.

Rob, like me, got the cheapest deck class ticket. We are shivering along warmed by each other proximity and laughing together amicably as close as possible for the long cold night.

Waiting for the warming sunrise's glorious relief.

I am in between worlds. Gazing at the distant shape of Athens city while the mist rise and dissipates.

I hear clearly the voice of Bruno. all the way from Paris, calling anxiously, distinctly my name. Like Joan of Arc, I hear the voices and I answer softly between my teeth "fuck off".

Before long we touch land.

Rob and I debark and keep walking until we reach Plaka, the green village-like section of old Athens, under the Parthenon.

We walk down a garden where we smoke a last joint together, and Rob goes away, and I stay for a heart-to-heart conversation with a small talkative green frog.

In my cosmic plan I am not only relating to humans, but any creature also I encounter leads me on and help coordinates what I must do.

Sylvia got impatient waiting for me in Heraklion and just left for Matala to get me. It's a *chasse croise*.

Now is my turn to wait for her in Athens. The tourist season is over, there are no more cheap beds on the roof like in the season.

Two American Hippies join me in the frog garden, and we share a joint.

I can crash in their cheap hotel room. It's the same hotel where Sharon and Nicole are.

Sharon, Nicole and I, we rush together to the flea market. We feel bubbly and full of sauce. Marching through Plaka we are creating a tricolour mayhem through the streets.

At the flea market I fall in love with a felt shepherd vest with rounded edges, black and white asymmetric patterns.

I bargain hard and pay, it feels warm and beautiful over my black and white Norwegian warm sweater and long African batik skirt.

We reach Acropolis with a trail of men at our pursuit. We march in the middle of the street jeering at them.

"Malaka! Malaka! Wanker! Wanker!"

Some useful Greek word I learned from my Cretan friends and teach to my new American girl friends.

One yellow, one black, one white, we are female warriors defeating unruly Greek phalanx, mischievous victorious angels.

In this moment, we are planning to travel together to India.

Sylvie is back on schedule two days later. We are happy and relieved, together again.

Sylvie must unload her drachmas, and me mine. We exchange the drachmas for dollars at the black market.

We are ready, on the road, hitch hiking to Thessalonika where Sylvie plans to sell her blood for eighteen bucks.

I am not going to sell my blood. I won't shed my blood for money, I hate needles, and anyway I have got money now!

16

OLD GULHANI AND THE TURKS

We stand beside my travel bag, dressed up with our warmest clothes.

I've got on my silver boots, Norwegian black and white sweater, my new shepherd felt vest over my African skirt, over a lined grey and black flannel pants.

Sylvie wears her blue and turquoise parka from Boston superstore over Jeans and keeps her backpack on.

We are getting soaked by the insidious pouring sleet at the crossroads, looking with hope towards Turkey.

We don't have to wait for long, the first truck stops and embark us. We drive three days with the same driver, dozing alternately in the truck.

We tell our life story to amuse Dimitrios, our driver. Each of us sings our favourite songs: Sylvie American nursery rhymes, Dimitrios Greek romantic songs, and my French repertoire.

Our voices pitched to overwhelm the loud vibrating beat of the engine running distances on the bad road.

Dimitrios halts to refuel oil and, gas, refresh water and, wipe the windshields clean of sleet. He checks the brakes and the tires between each long slow haul.

The storyteller's crew, driver and Hippie ladies, extract from the cabin jumps to the ground to walk on earth.

We relieve ourselves in disgusting latrines and consume greasy sustaining food, with tea and water.

Fifteen minutes later, back in our truck seats we roll again all the way to Thessalonika.

Dimitrios leaves us on the third evening in front of a sinister youth hostel. We pay for a bunk bed in the dormitory. So many travelers to meet hitchhikers, van drivers, bus riders to Istanbul. Some hippies coming back from the east with their stories to tell. Most are here to sell blood tomorrow.

Sylvie goes right to bed.

I am awake, meeting with gathered voyageurs in the dim lit lobby.

One English boy, back from Afghanistan shares a chillum of primo Hash from Mazarisharif. The single puff I take knocks me out.

I am disintegrating in a molten core. I can no longer follow details of the story. The pipe owner coming from Istanbul, was staying at the Old Gulhani hotel in the rooftop tent. That name rings a bell, that's the place to stay I had written in my notes.

There he took his first fix with the help of a friendly junkie. He was soon hooked to the red opium. Very pure and still costing eighty dollars a kilo.

Last summer, it was the last day of a weeklong holiday in Sussex country. He was enjoying fixing in his hotel room with a view on the lake. It was a rare, sunny day, in the afternoon his girlfriend insisted on going canoeing.

"I was feeling good and did not feel like moving." he says.

She freaked out, screaming: "That's it! You are hooked! You are finished!"

"For eight days you did not move from the bloody room, you need to clean up and go on a cure!"

"I panicked; I went out in my shirt on the lake paddling with her and caught a bad cold!" he says.

His story triggers my anxiety; I immediately go upstairs to my bunk. Paranoid and stoned.

In the dormitory, one girl is screaming with unbearable pain in her leg. The manager calls the hospital. One ambulance with a piercing siren comes for her.

I climb on top on my bunk bed. Shaking like a leaf. I call sleepy Sylvie to my rescue; she massages my back give me water to drink and calms me down to sleep.

Early morning, a special bus takes the blood sellers to the same hospital the manager called for the girl.

Sylvie climbs aboard with eighteen others. She is back just one hour later, they immediately tested everybody, and her blood is spoiled by previous hepatitis. They won't buy it.

There is nothing we want to see in Thessalonika, we take the next bus to the outskirts, and stand on the road for hours vainly hoping for a ride.

Soaked and wind battered, we finally capitulate, walk back to the bus stop and purchase a bus ticket to the Turkish border.

At the custom office we fill out forms and chat with two guys traveling back from New Delhi.

It took them ten days and cost them forty dollars to reach here. They took the cheap bus, the group taxis and third-class train; they are on the way to Athens, where we came from.

In the Turkish bus, we smoke our first Turkish fag and check the Turkish scene.

Male passengers with turbans around crocheted cap and veiled females.

We breathe a satisfying whiff of this new foreign air.

We converse with our Turkish neighbour on the third seat. He regales us with a thermos cup of strong black tea.

Cold air blows through cracks in the disjointed old bus. As we cross mountainous deserts, we sniffle and cough quite a lot.

All Turkish male children have a big shaven head. I am observing the people, the mountains, and the road. I try to count all the trees along the side of the road, until the final stop in Istanbul.

Still with our Turkish fellow. We embark in a group taxi with half a dozen voyagers, the driver's helper throws the mass of luggage on the rack on top.

The first stop is the Old Gulhani hotel.

This favorite Hippie relay is behind the blue mosque in old Istanbul.

It's a marvellous sight at sunset. We climb up stairs right after sundown.
What a coincidence! Sharon and Nicole are here. We run into them going downstairs and out the door. Their room is not far, in another hotel, but the big scene is right here, we will meet again tomorrow.
In the lobby we register at the desk. I want a place in the tent on the roof for three liras per night.
Sylvie, without a sleeping bag, takes a bed in a shared room with two others for six liras.
We climb the stairs up to the tent. A big shack on the hotel's flat roof with corrugated galvanised metal walls and a big tarp roof, all lined with cardboard. It opens with a wood rimmed metal door.
The patron pushes the door and I follow in my silver boots tinkling with silver bells.
At least fifty, maybe a hundred hippies sit or lean on floor mats around a big smoky woodstove. Many shining eyes turn to me, indistinct in the dim light of a single lightbulb hanging from the middle of the bare corrugated roofing.
A candlelight halo shows young people and luggage. A phantasmagoric collaboration 3-D picture resurrecting Rembrandt and Vandenbosh.
The young assembly smokes hash, plays guitar, sings softly, shoot up, take pills, eat, drink, and talk.
Not one bed or chair in view, only a diversity of sleeping bags edged with luggage against mostly leaning bodies. All fuzzy with smoke.
Not much noise, but a murmur. Echoing, circling around the smoking stove.

From this general confidence, cavernous cough erupts, and sonorous words rise in many languages.

The thick, acrid smoke fills my lungs when the doors open.

I mark my spot, drop my bags, while unrolling my sleeping bag. I ask my new neighbour nicely, not to move my stuff.

I am all set. Sylvie and I follow the patron out the door.

Planted in awe, in the middle of the blue mosque plaza, our four eyes take in the sights. Right, center and left, up the blue sky and down to earth. Up a sky softly scraped by the round and blue minaret with a gold rising moon crescent shining against some passing clouds.

The milling crowd of faithful encircle the mosque, buzzing, coming and going.

A long hair dark hippie behind a Turk approaches us to whisper in our ear some mysterious engaging words about scoring opportunity.

It starts to rain. We are curious of the city; we don't know anything about it. We follow this first lead through the labyrinth of narrow streets.

We have no idea where we are when we step into the opening door of a seedy hotel. I can hear my mother's voice screeching in my mind.

"Turks, drugs, white slavery, watch out! This land is full of fanatics!"

We climb stairs behind a long, greasy, haired guy called Mike. He's half Chinese and half Turk, striking like an apparition. We follow into the room.

We can see and sample and buy the best quality hashish and opium.

"What would we like?"

That's it, straight into the thriller. We can see for ourselves the quantity of illegal produce.

This is a serious dope business, not for us curious girls, our initial sightseeing visit, complete with a rush of paranoia.

The Turk behind Mike is nervous. He jumps at the knock on the door. Two rain-soaked American guys enter cautiously into the room. They have to straighten a bad deal with their friend Mike.

They paid good money to the Turk for two kilos of dark green leathery pulp. They are exchanging the produce, as it is not the primo hash as sold for top dollar.

With keeping a positive attitude, Mike requests just a bit of extra cash, and they leave the room happy with two kilos of the best quality hash.

The guilty Turk babble about American police and losing everything and rotting in jail. Mike scolds him sharply, he shall never swindle his good customers or there will be no more help. Plus, all he fears will come true.

So, we all smoke a chillum of this best produce and Mike offers a small rounded black slab of hash to Sylvie.

Now the lucky Turk starts sweet talking Sylvie. I am feeling restless, I want to go back and settle at the Old Gulhani.

First Mike must attend to some urgent business. He promises to get us back to the blue mosque in half an hour.

Mike leaves the room. I am anxiously waiting on my chair.

One minute later the hotel patron comes to sit very close to me. For the next half an hour I have to express repelling bullshit in my new improving pidgin English.

"Don't touch, I don't want your money, fuck off, I am not available."

He gives up and goes down to the lobby.

I wait impatient for Mike to show us the way back. while Sylvie is talking to the Turk. She accepts kisses and agrees for a date tomorrow.

Mike never returns, the Turk brings us back to the blue mosque.

Sylvie buys a flowery sleeping bag at the bazaar and move beside me in the enthralling tent at the Old Gulhani. We unroll our bedding right across from two freaking guys, holding each other, and foaming at the mouth.

They beg for help in French:

"Please watch us, we lost the plot. We took eighty pills of Rexetin each; we can't cope, could someone watch us?"

I say "okay! I am French; I will watch you until you are okay."

"Ah! That is so cool, you are French, you take care of us, and never mind if we rave, I am completely disconnected, so stoned. I don't even know what I say, and my friend is too stoned, like me. It's too much! We lost the plot, we can't cope, and we don't know where we are!"

The poor guy continues his stoned babbling.

"We bother everyone, yes, yes, I bother you! But please, stay here and watch if we are still alive! It feels way better with you here, you are very kind. I am so grateful for your care; we are too stoned. What is your name? I am Renault and he is Yves."

"I am Brigitte..."

"You will see, here nobody sleeps! You sleep here?"

"Yes."

"Well, you will see! It's really impossible to sleep here!"

With this warning I make myself a comfortable nest near Renault and Yves; they keep babbling all night with a fading intensity.

Renault has a ring on every finger, a linden green, filthy lace shirt over a pair of crinkled, dirty pink velvet pants. Shoulder length, dirty blond hair full of lice, and no front teeth. This made him speak funny.

Renault let me know his two front teeth were knocked out with hostility against Hippies in the Pakistani train near Lahore.

Finally relaxed, he lays with blond Yves on a sheep skin coat.

Yves wears thread bare tweed pants and a shrunken raspberry cashmere sweater torn at both elbows, which stick out.

They don't stop drooling, looking at me with murky green eyes. They make me think of a realistic Louis the Fifteenth marquis. Together they went all the way to Nepal.

At dawn, exhausted, they finally shut up for a while and I fall asleep. When I wake up, limp Yves languid and posh tells me his story.

Somewhere, hidden away from him is his super model English wife called Jenny.

They were always together. When she was working, he was waiting for her in a posh hotel. After her modeling session in New York, they went on their big cross-country trip in a white Jag, with a full bottle of acid. Lots of suitcases loaded with high-end gear and lots of dosh.

They got hypnotised by some friendly strangers out of the blue in a suburb of Los Angeles and sat as they were told, parked in their white Jag and waving two realistic gun replicas.

They received more money. They understood nothing.

They kept dropping acid, they got so high and so lazy, and they could no longer drive. They paid to get carried piggyback by their paid chauffeur to the lift and to their hotel room. They took airplane rides throughout the free world, dropping acid.

Jenny was always dressed up in wrinkle-free polyester clothes with white lacquer on all her nails.

Back and forth from New York, they could no longer cope by themselves. They took a cruise with the white Jag and their things to the Havre in France.

Very slowly from the Havre, they drove to India. When they reached Nepal, a needy friend took all their dosh.

They only had their Jag, with twenty bucks and their acid bottle to manage. What to do?

Jenny sold the car cheaply and flew to Italy with the acid bottle still quite full. One of these day Jenny will be back and then they will drop acid again.

You know, without acid, life is all flat, it all crumbles to ruin!

Sylvie is ready to try L.S.D. and morphine.

I don't want to. There are more than enough complex sensations, and new perils in my new freedom. I am already cautious with hashish and opium smoking.

I don't want to lose the plot and lose my self-control in this strange inviting culture I am exploring.

I want to know myself and find my place, I want to love and be loved, I want to be worthy of life and keep my edge. I got a concrete sense of what I am ready for.

I must hear my voices like Joan of Arc.

All in due time, when I understand I must take a risk or get stuck.

I witness, with many other, the twenty-two-year-old German girl taking her usual opium fix followed by an experimental fix of Rohilar.

With a sigh, she turned blue and expired immediately in the tent, among us, just like that.

Her death brought a police visit.

Three days of sinister questions, about that dead girl I never knew, fading now, gone from life, so soon forgotten.

Hashish smoking with soft, attentive tender people. I bask in the moment, fully present, unconcerned and tranquil about any next move.

Fearless and limitless, suspended like a flight in time.

I feel the necessity to be impeccably clean in this confusing chaos.

Sylvie and I explore old Istanbul.

From the Old Gulhani, we follow, meandering behind our new friends to the pudding shop at dead end of Sultan Akhmet. It is the residing hippie turf for all of us.

We take our seat each day at the pudding shop, close to the juke box. We are eating our puddings and cakes, drinking tea, chocolate and coffee.

I dance between the formica tables, to "Respect", the new favorite song by Aretha Franklin playing over and over on the jukebox.

Brotherhood, Sisterhood, peace, love, tolerance and all that.

My English is still very basic, and I don't entirely grasp the lyrics, but it sounds fabulous with her voice.

Outside the pudding shop is the pharmacy, where a doctor sells and injects any requested pharmaceutical.

Nearby again, post restante, it's everyone address.

We eat at Yenner cubbyhole restaurant under a tiny pergola with a grape vine in the alley behind the pudding shop.

We get served by Yenner, a small man with formidable black sideburns, a thick handlebar moustache, thick dark brows and a black topi. Yenner looks through me with x-ray eyes, and then serves me a delicious stew for very little money.

From the first look, his welcoming eyes shine on me. He is beaming. With some super amorous restraint, he jumps on me, grabs and reaches for any spot he may kiss. High as a kite on speed. He jokes expressively, he jumps on me, like on all his exclusive favourite customers.

For me" "frrree tea, frrree cake, and two frree Rohilar pills for my cold." He exaggerates compliments for the way I dress.

Exclaims at the top of his lungs in French for me:
"Orrriginal, Trrres orrriginal!"

Outside old Istanbul and the bazaar circuit, very few hippies stray further in the city maze

Most are stoned and junked out, stuck here on their own with their addiction, and suspicious of prowling snitch and plain clothed police.

Getting out of the tent, may take days to achieve.

After many trippy sleepless nights, a good rest may trigger a zest for adventure and lead one out.

Inside the tent, the big proportion of dirty junkies' spreads around a contagious malaise, fearful paranoia keeps most in.

Each of us, the healthy exceptions. We must bravely plunge out, for fresh air and promenade, a crowd bath, sightseeing or shopping.

When we come back to that nest, awaited like the Messiah, bringing pills, powders, food, drinks, sweets and letters.

Inside Old Gulhani, everyone clings to anyone, we are connected compassionate brothers and sisters first, and all the rest is secondary.

All pairs, the yield of two distinct individuals, unable to cope alone.

Couples seem to enjoy a slightly healthier life. They have built together a regular routine in their private room and look after each other.

It is hard to avoid new drug experiences because many tempting brothers and sisters' addicts are eager to push speed, various qualities of opium forms, morphine, and smack.

The first time is always a gift. That includes the psychedelic novelty of Acid.

A trip, like death so far avoided, a shrouded myth. I got out of any comfort zone. I want to understand what I am doing here.

Henri said "partir c'est mourir un peu!": Going away is dying a little! That saying is not so dumb.

Istanbul's city spell wraps us with the Old Gulhani and the blue mosque. We need to get out and get to know the city.

Sylvie and I bold enough to explore and determined to get necessary things done. We walk to the vaccination center, far away on the Asian side of the hanging bridge over the Bosporus.

On the bridge with the bustling crowd, we eat fish kebabs.

We find the vaccination center and submit like indignant sheep to the stabbing mandatory injection against yellow fever and cholera. That painful formality suffered, is now, again, recorded and stamped in our vaccination booklets.

This conforming to the rule for crossing the borders makes us progress a step further on our way to India.

Back at the Gulhani, everyone calls him Rasputin, but his name is Didier. He has dark waves of hair on his shoulders and piercing dark eyes. He is airy and very decorous in his antique silk Kimono, hand painted black with a fiery dragon with two heads.

Didier and his girlfriend travel overland and oversea. Back and forth to Southeast Asia. The couple resides in a private Gulhani room since September.

Didier's nickname of Rasputin he won by mesmerizing gullible audiences. Didier pushes addiction. We have many ideological altercations. Debating mystic death pursuit. Mystic is not a numbing, but an awakening.

A habitual junkie, how can he advocate freedom or be a convincing philosopher? Rasputin likes to talk and always can.

We explore our opposition, but he weakens with duplicity while I harass him with a sincere feeling that this new friend does not bother with scruples or respect for innocence.

Rasputin can easily become anyone's treacherous enemy. So, what about Maryan his Swedish girlfriend? Ageless and pale, all fading, her blond hair pale, her eyes transparent barely blue, wrapped in dull pastel.

Shifting her warm loose robes and shawls.

She does not care to hide her tits or ass while she moves around.

She starts shaking with Malaria attacks and only Morphine injected can steady her. She got enough to pay the bills and support Rasputin; he takes care of her. For two years they've travel together by train, by boat in comfort, no chance taken with hitchhiking, they are a couple.

Right here in this hotel, my healthy glowing self befriends troubling peoples. All various shades of characters thrive in this shadowy heaven. For them I shine all my colours.

We peek at each other, and plead for time and pray for some respect, never ever to judge.

Sylvie is having a fling with one English guy, and she disappears for several days, while I get familiar with my two Japanese neighbours in the tent.

Two smart looking guys, Kaso and Kosi.

When they move and speak to me, Kaso long and straight lustrous black hairs and Kosi wavy one, swing down the middle of their backs.

They have made a Japanese enclave with tatamis, expressing clearly their ceremonious culture.

In the tent's general chaos, this minimalist orderly nest, is my initiation to Japanese customs.

I enter their threshold next to mine without shoes and sit with folded legs and back straight on the dustless tatamis. Every morning Kosi sweeps it perfectly with a soft, Japanese, hand sized broom.

We smoke minute tight joints prepared by Kosi and listen to Kaso soft Samurai song; he improvises lyrics while strumming his guitar.

Kaso's show is for me, he is interested in my appeasing contemplative essence.

I spend night after night soothing exhausted sleepless trippers.

I am eager and willing to heal and tame and nourish and cool any burning phoenix.

Kaso only fixes opium three times per twenty-four hours. I pay benevolent and serene attention and try to understand if it is a problem.

I even stich one artistic patch over the hole of Kaso's only pair of velvet trousers.

Occasionally I sleep peacefully between Kaso and Kosi. Three stray, cool cats, fur feeling.

Everyone's peace and rest interrupted by the loud and nervous pack of Austrian junkies.

They scream in fear, and yell in panic at the police daily visit. They borrow and, hoard everyone's things and return nothing to anyone.

From those ten Austrian boys I got the wrong first impression about give and take in Austrian culture.

I missed my chance to go to the Mozart festival in Salzburg when I was invited for a week of stylish musical delight by a proposing mature man who courted me in style at the Estro Harmonico. I was lured for a little but felt threatened in my integrity and decided to pass.

Groups tend to stick with their compatriots, they also replicate their borders.

Beside the Austrians, the Germans stay cool.

The Italians in contrast, warm, caring exuberant and generous with what they have.

Beside the Italians, the Yugoslavs, a bunch of tall and friendly thugs all colourful in primary colours, bejeweled with plastic rings and necklaces and dressed up in polyester clothes.

My favourite Yugoslav boy is called Stani.

Each time we cross each other's path, Stani fall on his knees with two hands on his heart and at the top of his lungs declares to me for everyone to hear: "My love, I love you, I adore you, and do you want to make love with me?!"

That makes me smile, and when anyone opens the tent door, he screams "fermez la fucking door!" I don't know if it's him who has written in big red letter, on the inside door. That same sentence: "fermez la fucking door."

More than hundred and hard to count.

Half of us in the tent, on the roof, encaged by the grated roof yard. With two cold, water taps opposite where to bathe in the wind.

For comforting us a minuscule plywood kitchenette where the patron fries eggs, warms milk and brews hot tea.

Under this main theater stage and down the private rooms, the staircase led to a lonely metal bathtub cleverly placed on a metal grate over the hotel woodstove.

Each special bath costs the modest fee of two liras. I am the only one who takes full advantage of this extravagant luxury.

The patron sends his brother to light the fire and fill the metal tub with cold water. That stove alight warms the water in one hour, sending heat through metal ducts in the private hotel room.

First, I cry as it still spews acrid smoke when I step in the warm water. I don't mind crying a bit and then luxuriate in the warming tub. And after I pay two liras three times, I bathe for free. Every day the patron sends his brother to light the stove and fill the tub.

I love that ingenious funky bathroom. I sing alone in it. I can hear my unlimited French repertory echoing up through the air ducts, for everyone to hear my enthusiastic lyrics. I get out of this tub, fresh, clean and joyous.

Very often the police scrutinize my papers, suspicious of my healthy fresh look. I keep cool when the police enter the tent refuge waving guns and kicking out suspects.

Who knows exactly why or what...?

Istanbul is to me paranoia city, with cops and fundamentalists bigots, wandering snitches, dealers, hippies, junkies, everyone avoiding a controlling system.

No one passes unnoticed in front of the police station. Rolling eyes are following everyone at all times. A military police regime trusts no one. Any passerby is a suspect, just observed while passing through.

Sylvie's English lover is gone she is back beside me in the tent.

She is babbling in French, again, debating the merits of morphine and L.S.D. It irritates me. I don't believe I am ready for more experiments. I won't be pushed to swallow all what comes my way just because it's free.

Right now, I am experimenting with hash, I even smoked some opium. That opium brought me down and made me anxious. I suffer from a deep cough, like everyone else in the tent.

***

We decide to visit the water reservoir of old Istanbul with Naim, a young learned scholar. Currently translating in English and Turkish language, the fish section in the illustrated French encyclopedia of the Larousse in ten volumes.

We met him at Yenner, with Naim as our benevolent guide we discover the depth and importance of the Turkish culture.

The Byzantine Basilica of Hagia Sophia was occupied by the Islam conquest, but the occupants preserved most of the Christian artwork and simply scraped the Christian cross, overlapping a second axis to indicate Mecca.

Naim says the huge fractal stones lining the Mosque are the result of ancient atomic fusion, a polished faceless glory, natural wonder of antediluvian creation.

Here and now, I do feel like a microscopic particle evolving from an Atlantean source, basking now in this drying aquatic air.

We levitate through the blue mosque, listening to Naim's proud Turkish history. So, he says, the Turks invented love and chivalry.

After that tour we go for refreshment at the Pudding shop, for a tea and chocolate custard.

At the pharmacist near the Pudding shop we get our second shot against yellow fever, hepatitis. and cholera. The pharmacist insists on shooting the needle in my bum.

I am reluctant, but do capitulate, unveiling a very small surface of this very fascinating part of my anatomy. When it's over, I ask Sylvie:

"Where did he make your shot?"

And she says,

"In my arm!"

I knew it!

I notice that, in this Muslim country, my ass in a pair of pants, attracts far too much attention.

It is getting pinched, bumped, lightly touched by approaching, too close, male's passerby.

I got a narrow boyish but curvaceous and fleshy ass.

It takes me a short while to realise, my grey flannel pants with black stripes without a skirt on top, provokes unwanted action.

I retaliate, kicking aggressor's ass with a swift silver tinkling boot. All shameless culprits flee for the great amusement of more distant passerby.

Naim, our learned guide, brings us to the old palace of Suleiman the magnificent, sultan of the Ottoman Empire, now the Topkapi museum.

He takes us through endless rooms piled with the world most complete collection of hand painted Chinese porcelain. We are told how to discern the rarity amongst the Ming plates with six headed dragons, or five heads, or four heads.

Rooms of jewels. Precious strands of beads piled up in heap. Scintillating, translucent or opaque.

Precious metal, or filigree, damask work, twisted hills of white pearls. The star jewel and most famous diamond lie on this sober lining of silvery grey velvet.

A frozen firework galaxy of diamonds, the big one in the middle is a pear shaped eighty-nine carat sparkling rock surrounded by his forty-nine perfect brilliant satellites all set in silver for the queen.

It is named Kasikci Elmasi or the Spoonmaker diamond. Naim said it was given to the queen of France Marie Antoinette. Before she lost her head, a royalist officer took it away from her with her box of jewels in Varennes.

The Kasikci Elmasi Diamond

The diamond was then given to Laetitia, the mother of Bonaparte, by her triumphant son who was emperor Napoleon for ten years. Laetitia sent the diamond back to Turkey in exchange for the release of her captive lover.

I give it my complete attention. Minutes of intense scrutiny at this luminous marvel, I project in my Ali Baba virtual treasure cave.

In same that treasure room lays a dagger with three big emeralds, a present made for the Shah who was assassinated before he got this gift. Sultan Suleiman the Magnificent decided to keep it for himself.

I soak in Naim's detailed Turkish history. Naim guides our promenade through the water reservoir under old Istanbul. We step down incalculable stairs, at the bottom of a cavernous watery labyrinth in the filtered phosphorescent light.

I start to count numerable gigantic marble columns planted in marshy slits. I forget how many and give up counting, so many columns support the ancient roof of this vast water vault.

Naim, our new best Turkish friend, invites us for dinner at his house. Naim leads us with ruses to avoid police tail. Unlawful dealings with foreign girls that would surely compromise his brilliant scholar future.

Naim's room is a dove cot, on the third floor of his parents' house. He's got his privacy with lock and key.

That room is crammed full of reinvented technology. He made his own radio, tape-recorder, earphone, telephone, a soldering post, electricity. Everything functions. We are impressed.

Naim mother serves us a Turkish feast with a refreshing drink of apple tea. Naim is absolutely fascinated by us, two cultured hippie girls. We thank and reassure his curious Muslim mother, also a bit worried.

We feel at home in the Gulhani looney den. A quiet and peaceful refuge from the normal frightening world. A safe hiding.

Soon it's my first time in Istanbul's bazaar labyrinth. With Sylvie I look at harem rings, hundreds of them lined up in the windows of many jewelers. It is a dazzling monotonous display of the same design, zooming on I check all the glittery rings in one shop window after the other.

A Turk follows us and proposes us, to help him rob a bank. We must just distract the cashier for fifty-fifty. I am a bit curious to hear more details about all this. But Yves is with us, he has experience, he tells me to forget it, ignore that guy, and let him go! For sure this man is a cop fishing for criminal activities.

I buy a puzzle ring in nine carat gold for three dollars, and I look carefully how the merchant effortlessly show me how to undo it and do it again. I may never be able to do that.

In the leather section I purchase a soft leather bag for sixty liras, a suitable replacement for the torn shopping bag holding my stuff since Matala.

I buy a Russian fur lined leather cap with ear flaps and fur lined leather gloves, a necessary protection against the bitter cold.

Endless browsing makes us tired of gazing at the bazaar mirage. We refresh at the pudding shop.

I dance again by myself on respect in front of the juke box.

Then we go to Yenner's and with Yenner we share a very smooth and tasty smoke of his narghile.

It's cold. I've got on my Norwegian sweater over cashmere, my flannel pants under my African skirt, my felt shepherd vest my boots with socks, my hat and gloves.

I put all that on for the brisk walk in the windy cold winter city. And at night in the tent, I put it all on with the furry flaps over my ears and I sleep with it all on in my sleeping bag except for my boots.

Nobody undresses to sleep. Many only remove their shoes. Many sleep with shoes on.

My Japanese guitarist friends and sleeping bag neighbours, Kaso and Kosi, have regular girlfriends often sharing their sleeping bag in the tent.

For Kaso, Danish Katia who fixes quantities of opium and pukes regularly on people she doesn't like.

Kosi's girl, Austrian Eva fixes morphine, and mostly feels bad.

Way less girls than guys, the proportion may be one to ten. Therefore, any girl feels rare and precious.

The Hippie girls are not concerned about reputation. Sex is a comforting need not as important as food and shelter. I am easily a sister but nobody's girl. With the girl ratio of one for ten guys.

I still expect romantic true love and need to meet the prince exclusively for me. I am aware that I may need to let go of this out-of-date notion.

In the meantime, all my male friends' girlfriends distrust me. While I still flutter on my high cloud, when they suffer real frustrations.

Yenner whispers in my ear about a local youth infatuated with me. For two weeks the guy is waiting to get a chance to meet me, spending hours outside Yenner's door to see if I am coming, and he pleaded to Yenner himself to help him to meet me.

He did not master the audacity to address me directly. I have been warned.

On a rainy morning I can see the guy behind Yenner, expecting me. He sees I see him; he presents himself as Achmed, and shyly invites me for a coffee at the Hilton. I feel magnanimous and compassionate for this poor ordinary guy, who feels very lucky to meet me.

I say "okay, let's go!" and follow him.

This Istanbul Hilton is a decrepit rat hole, American *ersatz* with no charm and not one sign of luxury.

So, I drink that coffee and chit chat.

Achmed gets quickly confident and cling now firmly at my disposal.

Achmed propose to lead me through the bazaar where he has many shop keepers' friends who will give me rock bottom prices for the items I may fancy.

I guess it is an opportunity to spend some time knowing more about what we have in common.

Why not? Since I still want to buy that harem ring with blue opals, and the price will be adjusted to what I want to pay. Achmed's best friend owns a first-class jewel shop.

Tomorrow we have a date in the afternoon.

I, alone, would get quickly lost in that endless maze. For Achmed, it has no secrets, so I follow the lead. With no clue of where I am.

From one of his friend's shops to the next.

I try a black leather pants and matching cape, several sheep fur lined jackets, many rings.

I only can afford to buy my harem ring for ten dollars. It has five rows of filigree nine carat gold with five tiny blue opals cabochon on each row.

I pay after bargaining hard for my chosen ring. I may come back with Achmed tomorrow, *Inch Allah*.

All that window shopping and trying on clothes, exhausted me. We refresh at a stand, eat kebabs and drink apple tea.

Achmed, propose we go smoking some good hash in the privacy of his den before we call it a day.

It's been a long tiring day; my patient guide and I could use a good smoke. I am a bit hesitant at the mention of privacy.

I say okay, only five minutes, for a joint.

So, we get into his building near the bazaar. He opens his door with a key. His small room right on the street level with everything.

Right away, he locks us in mumbling about police.

There is only a chair, a narrow bed, a sink, a kerosene stove and a closet.

I sit on the chair and immediately Achmed lights his ready joint, takes a puff, pass it to me, turns all red and jump on me.

I kick him hard. I scream loud! My piercing scream scares him.

Not even two minutes have passed, and he turns again his key and opens the door. I pass through his den door deaf to his abject apologies.

Achmed brings me back to Yenner's door.

No harm done, *gule gule*, Stupid boy, you will never get my address!

Istanbul's time is ticking, and a month passed at the Old Gulhani. It's hard to move away from all the needy friends

We no longer wait for the promised daily car ride out of here. We miss it every day. We are free to go.

Not waiting six months for money, like Kaso and Kosi.

Or like Mary-Jane, we are not pregnant, not tired, not older and uglier, sickly and famished.

Mary-Jane begs successfully providing for her new family, her talented guitar playing genial boyfriend Frederico, and a growing expectant belly. She earns plenty from charitable compassionate voyageurs.

The couple stays in a private room, nicely decorated, with carpets and a wolf blanket.

Responsibly, they take antibiotics to cure their S.T.Ds and will hopefully deliver a normal, healthy baby.

Kaso starts to climb along his beam part of the roof tent.

Up there perched like an ape he watches the total assembly and plays a frenetic guitar. Together we sing his lines "evelybody goes to Afghanistan, hashish, hashish...evelybody gooooo"; because the Japanese guys don't pronounce any R's.

For a full day and one night, Kaso stopped fixing. His bizarre way a form of cold turkey, and he cannot sleep.

To sleep he would have to double his previous opium doses. To cleanup he needs a minimum of seventy-two hours cold turkey.

Kaso and Kosi are restless Samurais who won't be in Goa for Christmas or in Kathmandu for Easter. And we are sad, and they are sad.

We are going away, from each other's horizon, maybe forever.

I regret, not taking my Old Gulhani friends with us. If I could, we would go away in a slow gypsy caravan with a brave patient horse to pull us, like in the wagon of the Romani travelers of my childhood.

The Romani gypsy also were strange. With my father they smothered hedgehogs in clay then baked them in the bonfire. Then, they ate them! I never had a taste of that and never wanted to have a fix either.

I feel emotionally saturated.

Adios Kaso, Kosi, Renault, Yves, Rasputin, Mary-Jane, Stani, Eva, Mary, Jane, Yenner, and Naim.

Old Gulhani's patron, and Istanbul.

With Sylvie we part like we came. Sylvie got us two bus tickets for tomorrow night. But today we are still here, stalling between two worlds.

We may return, *Inch Allah*, and pass again through Istanbul at the Old Gulhani. And maybe, probably, everyone will still be here.

So, night falls and we go, our hearts still torn. Sheepishly we grab our sleeping bags and our traveling bags.

Making room in the tent.

We flee from this addicting glue, like a reluctant lucky bee escapes from a honey pot.

This is our last rest stop in Europe. Bye bye, my Istanbul.

I cross the Bosporus in a flight of seagulls. That's it, I am in Asia.

In the bus toward Persia, Sylvie claims I do not love her the same as she loves me.

I am taking for granted with some indifference, her patient devoted love. I don't really know how I should answer her. Should I be sorry? And do I care?

17

TEHERAN AND THE SHAMSHUN HOTEL

We purchased two seats for a direct ride to the border in a so called "deluxe bus". Our sincere hope for a smooth ride soon deceived by entering an old wreck of a bus barely functioning.

We precipitate ourselves, hopping down from seven succeeding wrecked unheated buses, big and small, all filled to the brim with soldiers, goats, sheep, chickens, ducks and geese, labourers, veiled mothers and grandmothers with babies and children.

A recurrent, nightmarishly tedious ride.

We can't even get out to eat a meal. We are traveling during Ramadan. From dawn to dusk, no food or drink allowed.

All fervent Islam passengers could not tolerate to see us drink or eat during their holy fast.

Each of our succeeding drivers feed us discretely. They pull the dark curtains down when all the Muslim passengers get out for bladder relief, ritual ablutions, and prayers.

We are two cold, hungry and thirsty infidel birds, hidden in the penumbra. Kind and considerate bus drivers feed us and bring us chai and water. Not sinning against the Sharia law which exempts infidel like us.

We stay hidden and insulated, in our sleeping bags all the way from one glacial bus to the next.

We peek through our covers, watching the landscape, and we pass the perfect volcano with snow on top, Mount Ararat in the clearing sky with a halo of little dancing clouds.

We stop for a full day in grey cold foggy Erzurum. We shake ankylosis with a brisk walk in the picturesque city center.

We are in the middle of a plateau hedged by magnificent frozen glaciers. A large marketplace with many stalls selling wools, embroidery, carpets, tea, fruits and kebabs, sheep and goat hides.

I bargain and purchase embroidered wool socks. I immediately put my warm beautiful socks on, snug fitting inside my silver boots.

To visit Erzurum, we walk around all day the winter white city.

We are invigorated after sundown and a Ramadan feast, and we climb across the seventh final night bus taking us straight to the border.

From Turkey we walk with our bags across to Iran. From here we plan to hitch hike.

On the curb of the Iranian road. A Swiss French guy has been patiently waiting for three days and two nights.

He looks defeated. Unshaven, crumpled, dirty and too tired to be hopeful. No one would take him in their car for free.

With synchronised compassion we propose him to come along with us, optimistic and confident girls. We pose at the curb, almost immediately, one Iranian truck driver breaks for us with a long screeching halt. He invites us to climb in the big truck for a ride all the way to Teheran.

The driver, named Farouk, speaks good English.

I immediately get comfortable in the best small bench behind the driver where the co-driver should refresh waiting his turn for the non-stop ride.

Sylvie and, our new friend, Swiss French Rene, are squished beside the driver on the front seat, still very thankful to be sitting for the long ride.

We roll on, day and night on a pot-holed slippery icy road.

We go on rolling, at a steady snail pace, through frosted splendid fairy land with snow tornadoes. All looks surreal in the truck's high beam's searching light.

It is an endlessly challenging trip, a gruesome draining progress we must bear with.

While Sylvie and Rene chat animatedly about their country's customs, I somnolate in comfort on my bench.

When they are slowing down and fall silent, I take over keeping Farouk awake, I sing a song with all my heart and captivate Farouk's attention.

I watch the road in the middle of this wild country with the wild sky on top. Sylvie is too sleepy to stay alert and dose beside Rene already crashed and snoring.

Sylvie and Rene wake up, achy unrefreshed, expressing jealousy about the most comfortable place I chose. But that place has got my name on it. I've got a most enduring entertaining spirit requested for the longer haul. Farouk has chosen me to be the co-driver, he is happy for me to rest comfortably at my turn.

When I wake up, I keep him alert ask him questions, reveal my personal opinions, sing or listen to his song.

Farouk is athletic and strong, a jolly fellow, looking good and mighty, making steady progress.

We stop every five hours for fuel, food and chai, bladder relief and a bit of walking at the trucker's relays.

We always get Kebabs with a pile of white rice garnished with raw green onions, fresh mint twigs and parsley. It is served with a piece of flat unleavened bread, a long doughy scarf. I find it tasteless like fresh cardboard. They bake it on a charcoal fire, two-meter-long and forty-centimeter-wide, they cut it into strips for the customers.

I find the food unappealing. I hope to find something better in Teheran. Farouk always pays for us.

Approaching slow but steady, we enter the outskirts of Teheran.

We get ready to leave the comfort zone of Farouk's truck. All awake, we look at sparse building with flat roof now gathering more density. Sylvie and Rene, with hasty comments, call it horrible.

I don't think so.

The empty wild scape fills up with yellow flat roof factories, surrounded by high mountains, snow topped, in the soft filtering light.

I see the beautiful Persian miniature. Fast increasing buildings, no more wild space. We reach Teheran heart. Mission accomplished, thanks to our tired driver.

"Bye and thanks!"

Farouk let us down on foot at the first truck stop in the capital.

We carry our bags to the city center. We search for the Bagdad hotel and eventually find it. We get a room for three, each of us will have to pay twenty-five rials per day.

Rene was robbed, he has nothing.

Rene will have a nice long shower and a bed tonight and then leave without paying for it.

We are the only foreigners. The Bagdad hotel consists of a few rooms build around a courtyard.

We stretch and relax with a joint and pass it to Rene, not yet a smoker.

Rene takes his first toke.

At first impression Teheran city is not special, but we have to stay here a while to get our Indian visa.

Rene got his diploma in Oriental language at the Paris Sorbonne. He is fluent in Cambodian written language and would like to practice Cambodian conversation.

After his toke, Rene turns anxious. So far from everything he left, he is lost. Sylvie and I we are doubtful he will succeed to ever reach Cambodia.

I boost Rene with confident optimism, to feel free like us, well on our way to India.

We hurry to the immigration office for our Indian visas. We fill papers in triplicate and pay the fee.

Because of Ramadan we will have to be patient for quite a few days. We enter Teheran's favorite hippie restaurant, the Ameer Kebir.

We sit with Rasputin and Mary-Jean. In good form, well on their way, like us. We share an exciting meal, in synchronised exaltation, everything is possible.

At the Ameer Kebir, hippies and businessmen are trading between Kuwait and Teheran, dates, dry fruits, carpets and gold.

And beside these commodities, foreign girls and drugs.

We are in the thick of Ramadan. Even with the relaxed modern rules of the Shah; walking without a veil in the street is a big challenge. Each male feel entitled to prey on any infidel woman.

All frustrated hunting males are ready to pounce, and tackle, and grab with disrespect. We are impudent shameless tease not accounted by Allah, and Ali, his prophet. All is permitted.

I am braving their menace, armed with two long sticks. I whip the air firmly opening my way, to the post office, the bazaar, the visa office.

I have cut two long supple whipping sticks from a weeping willow tree in Teheran Park. I whip my rhythmic way through crowding males.

That's the way I manages to pass unmolested.

Back at the Ameer Kebir, a, long-time resident hippie tells us it is even worse for women when the Ramadan is over.

We manage to circulate well with my sticks in the Teheran of the Shah Reza Pahlavi where some modern Iranian women are wearing decent dresses and no veil.

Iranian traditional custom is unhappy about the American influence. They start boycotting the modern ways of the Shah, still in power. No religious people in this country call it progress.

The capital museum is not impressive, Teheran bazaar disappoints me compared to Istanbul. On the main square some peddlers sell curios on the pavement.

I approach and stop in front of a grey beard *mullah* selling things on a cloth. I check what lies in front of him.

Here I stand with a willow stick in each hand dressed in my Norwegian sweater and Greek felt vest. Underneath, my red lace teddy with a zipper in the middle going down over a creamy, frilly, billowing lace crinoline petty coat. It is mid-calf, grazing my silver boots with silver bells and showing the embroidered top of my new, warming, goat socks.

I am adorned with necklaces, rings, and bracelets and my crocodile shoulder bag with essential traveling papers.

My fur hat with flaps and a white knitted woolen shawl, all my added layers keep me just warm enough.

I float under all silent attention and almighty blessing. My golden silky hair under the hat is flying loose on my shoulders.

It is a sunny, crisp day in mid-winter. I stand alone in front of a beautiful old mullah.

I bargain for the mother of pearl Muslim prayer beads, a misbaha rosary.

I am delighted, to acquire this sacred object from this holy man. It surely will boost my divine mission to the unknown.

One more necklace around my neck.

On this square I feel the ancient city glow, which takes me in lazily in its flow. I am part of the revolution in this challenging city. I must keep aware of consequences, while teasing bigots.

So, walking with Sylvie, without my willow sticks, we are crossing the widest avenue at the red light, in Teheran center.

A sneaky guy manages to pinch my butt. I trip in my narrow long dress when I kick my foot in his butt. I fall hard pounding my coccyx on the bitumen.

My head is spinning, it hurts, I am not sure I can move.

One passerby comes to my rescue, a doctor. He helps me stand up and lean on him and Sylvie, he gives me a pain killer shot in his office, right on this road. I feel okay now, I can walk.

We follow the doctor into a modern style coffee shop and discover civilised friendship in Teheran. Tomorrow for lunch the doctor will present us to his artist girlfriend Amira, who speaks French.

His name is Reza like the Shah, he walks us back at our Bagdad hotel.

At the hotel we hang out with two students.

Barham, a young and cute version of my favorite French star thug, Lino Ventura, so is his cousin Omar.

They invite Sylvie and me for dinner this evening.

We eat together, but because I don't like the bland Iranian food since my first day in Teheran, I only eat oranges and drink hot milk.

I pronounce correctly, "yahk garam tchir" one hot milk, and buy good oranges at the market stands.

I reject kebabs, flat bread and green onions, twigs of mint and parsley. Only hot milk and oranges for me. I feel very fine and nourished like this.

After the dinner Omar and Reza paid for, they try harassing us. Our new friendship is over. We drop them.

We debate cultural faith and respective philosophy with a curious Persian Mullah in the courtyard of the hotel, with the manager as our interpreter.

Our friend the doctor, is not only a doctor, but a businessman who wants to emigrate to America.

He fears the political situation is no longer stable in Iran. The Shah's modern days of power are coming to an end. It will be supplanted by many anti-American Islamic rules.

Doctor Reza wants out of Iran into U.S.A and for that he proposes to marry Sylvie. If Sylvie agrees to a paper wedding, she will get paid twenty thousand American dollars.

Reza says it should take only a few weeks to seal the deal, wedding included. When the paperwork starts, we will go touring nice resorts of Iran and get married in his favorite one.

I can marry his best friend for the same price, who would prefer a European passport.

Sylvie and me, we look at each other and get excited about owning so much money on our way to India. We have to debate the proposal.

So, we are killing time waiting for the visas, spending many hours with lady Amira, who speaks some French, and composes jingles on her piano.

Amira displays abstract art on her middle-class walls. Big splashes of primary colours.

I am not impressed by her work, but she is warm, feminine and kind. She has a seven-year-old son with Doctor Reza. Amira reads our fortune in coffee grinds.

I get bored with this scenario. I won't get involved in a marriage scam for money.

If Sylvie believes it's her big chance, she can proceed alone with it.

One day before the end of Ramadan, Sylvie puts on a mini dress revealing her white legs. This starts a riot, and we just avoid stone lynching, when the doctor whisks us away promptly into one of his patients shop.

The brave shop keeper shuts all doors and pulls on a metal blind, and we hide there, until his wife and his daughter lend us long traditional dress and shador.

Like that we escape lynching, a favorite sport for the faithful, especially during Ramadan.

There is delay for the wedding more paperwork and time required.

For that much money Sylvie is willing to be patient longer and makes some concessions.

I have lost interest in the doctor and lady Amira, and I go around on my own, whipping my way with my willow sticks.

I visit Rene in his new hotel paid for by his new Indian friends at the Ameer Kebir.

I meet Raja, Channi, Prabu, and Saxena. Four modern Punjabis from Sikh families, and Arvind their Brahmin friend. They have been traveling together for two years.

With western business these young modern Sikhs have escaped from their formal religious traditions.

They cut their oiled black hairs and endorsed the image of James Bond.

They wear jeans and nice shirts. No more unshaven arm pits, uncut hairs, unshaven beards, dagger in the belt, turban with a wooden comb on their head

They all kept a stainless-steel bangle on their right wrist. A last token of the youngest uniting religion, between non fanatic Muslims and fortune warriors whose caste destined them to be merchants, agriculturists, soldiers, and taxi drivers.

We are meeting, crossing over boundaries. We are the world's middle class successful point of view.

We are the new hippie girls opening to the east, while they deal with the west and protect Rene, a hopeful scholar.

We all become friends. We appreciate our mutual reflection what image we have chosen to be.

We get together, dress up to go dancing and rock and roll at the Hilton center at the club Chattanooga.

Our new Indian friends are driving. We all fit in the large Cadillac with telephone and television inside.

We enjoy the rides in their flashy car, before they drive it and sell it in Munich.

They are smuggling luxury cars from here to there, that's how they have so much spare money.

***

Christmas in Teheran.

Sylvie and I move to the Shamshun hotel, not far away from the Bagdad hotel.

Raja and Prabu are staying in a very pleasant penthouse, on top of the hotel, with many windows and a balcony overlooking a school courtyard.

The Shamshun has a reasonable rate and good service. Arvind, Saxena and Channi, stay close by in a boarding room with Rene.

Sylvie and I share the cheapest small room with two single beds, a night table with just enough room underneath for our bags.

We spend the days with all our Indians friends and Rene, in the penthouse. As soon we move in, it's party time at the hotel Shamshun. We got hash and our Indian friends get a bottle of Iranian vodka.

We know better than drinking that stuff. We stick to chai for Sylvie and warm milk and oranges for me.

The Indians guys are guzzling the rot gut and getting drunk, silly and delirious.

Sylvie is letting go of her wedding business with Doctor Reza. To finalise that deal she would need to stay at least three more months here instead of three weeks.

And the doctor intentions evolved, day by day, less clear about business.

Sylvie and I don't think our own programs are considered; we stay away from the pushy doctor. We like our new company at the Shamshun. The Indian visas will be ready in another ten days.

The Shamshun basement has got a hammam.

Every single day I go down there to sweat and make my ablutions. Four floors down, in the privacy of an echoing, steaming, chamber. I sing and listen to the reverbing song back to me.

The hammam, a bottom chamber with a metal lid ceiling, a drab cell steaming hot.

Channi and Raja are tickling my self-esteem. Handsome and graceful Indians they fit in the picture I imagine.

I am enjoying all that fuss with flattering young males competing hotly about me.

I keep cool, I observe. Raja bullies younger Channi, triggering my choice. I don't care, but I feel more protective and less worried about Channi. I focus on both of them in the mirror of the wash basin.

They have lightly bronzed complexion, fine elegant bone structure, very nicely cut glossy dark hair. Beautiful dark and limpid deer eyes with long curved thick velvet lashes. Blue imported Levis jeans.

Through their mirror reflection, their zodiac image suddenly shifts into my world. Channi put on a most beautiful red blood silk shirt. I watch that shirt, with him on display. He is unraveling completely drunk after his fifth of the bottle of Iranian vodka.

In the lobby, he falls in front of me, on wobbly knees. Flaunting his puppy desire to be wanted, he gets sick and pukes on the floor.

I find him cute in this state. It makes me think I would like to be wanted too. I minister and attempt to help with drunken Raja, and drunken Prabu. It's nighttime, so no servant will help us

I got on a translucent blush satin pyjama that keeps me remote like a nurse. Channi in his sorry state is transported in Raja's bed I enter the bed to take delicate care of him.

Rene is heartbroken, like Raja, Prabu and Saxena, all part of the team putting him sprawled in bed.

Rene has already asked me to marry him, because he straightens when I scold him and laugh off his anxiety attacks, we also joke in French dialect rolling our R's.

Rene sees me mothering someone else. But it is just temporary!

A far-fetched impossible cultural transfer. A brownie notch in my gearing to become a woman.

Channi of course, could also marry me. I could follow and protect him, backing west all the way to Munich.

In the unlikely case we prove compatible.

Channi with his eyes on me, understands a weakening in his favour. I would not go out in the world on my own. I imagine I could become an Indian lady. But maybe not. I am still learning how to be free.

This may be a true occasion to embrace the mysterious culture calling me.

Anyways, Channi with Rene and Arvind decide that following morning to also move into the Shamshun hotel, we all live together. I am ready to give a taste of my heritage to my new Indian friends.

I prepare fervently to celebrate in style, that first Christmas party away from my parents' home.

So, I splurge and purchase at the bazaar:

- One bottle of Moet and Chandon brut de brut.
- One, small Sony record player, electric or battery operated.
- Five new long-playing records of my favorite rock and roll and folk songs

· Red roses, and red candles, tinsel garlands and a golden big cardboard star.

To make my Christmas tablecloth I paint green foliage garlands and red flowers on a white bedsheet.

And, in the Shamshun kitchen, I make a giant chocolate cake with pistachio nuts and chocolate icing.

I transform the big room, with the help of Sylvie. We make use of my colourful dresses as drapes and knotted frills on the windows.

I make a festive lamp shade with my red lace teddy on the bare bulb hanging over the Christmas table.

This inspired version of ritual tradition succeeds to make one unforgettable Christmas experience.

We all feel the sacred renewing spirit landing, with peace, joy, harmony. Especially with the spiritual initiation of French champagne!

And I toast, in communion from afar, my missed parents. We blow a fresh wind of revolution. All paying guests on the floor are constantly gaping at our window, generally opened. The penthouse with the balcony looms over the schoolyard of a boy's school.

If by chance we girls go out on the balcony at recess time, we cause a riot. All schoolboys scream, whistle, and applaud our apparition.

The Indian boys are soon going the other way to Europe in their Cadillac.

I do not get any closer to Channi, my fancy fizzles. But we had a good time meeting each other. We learned to appreciate truly these diverse brothers and sisters. We are ready to make the world an open party for everyone. We exchange each other's address and telephone numbers. Channi invite us to enter India, promising us comfort at his parent's hospitable house.

We will be most welcome in New Delhi.

We are sad to let each other go.

Arvind also gives me his parent's address. He will be back in New Delhi in the spring, sooner than the others. He is a Brahman, not a Sikh, and he is not involved with selling or driving the car.

He is promoting his family marble art in the Hindu expat communities of Iran and Turkey.

Prabu, Raja, Saxena, Channi and Arvind vacate the Shamshun.

As soon the Indian masters are gone, the bus boy refuses to serve Sylvie, Rene and me.

I am not tolerating this change of attitude. I remove the narrow leather belt from my waist, and with it, I whip twice the insolent boy.

Right away with sudden respect he serves us tea.

Rene and Sylvie are impressed, while the bus boy does his job again.

Three days later we get our visas and leave Teheran, with Rene. I felt compelled to buy Rene's visa and ticket to Afghanistan, instead of buying myself a turquoise necklace in Mashhad.

18

KABOUL

In Mashhad, we rush to get our visas stamped at the immigration office immediately.

Right away we climb in a direct bus for Afghanistan. The bus slowly going, tackles one never ending kilometer after the next.

We are grinding the wheels through the deserted extremity of Iran, probing every pothole and stone of the slow road. We reach the border long after the sun is set.

The unusual frontier at the end of a bad road, in a deserted land, at night. Our only light the torch of the customs officer.

I hurry with Sylvie to get our visas stamped at the customs office, we want to leave this same evening before the curfew.

We hope!

All shadow people, foreign and strange get moving soon drowned in pitch darkness. The friendly officers stamp our visa and offer us our first Afghani chillum.

They direct us to a waiting Jeep already overloaded with voyageurs, we squeeze in and start to move on our way to Erhat.

Rene did not hurry like us. He will have to wait until tomorrow for his visa stamp. We will meet in Erhat at the next stop.

We slowly roll away from the border, in the increasing cold of a glacial night, crammed tightly with ten other passengers and luggage.

Two very long hours later, the Jeep halts to refuel in front of a mud house.

We drink hot green tea with sugar coated almonds, and we're invited to smoke a chillum with a hunchback Afghani dwarf. He's all dressed up and decorated in a well-fitting magnificent black uniform with gold stripes. Many golden medals dangle from his barrel chest.

That little guy with a big head is scrutinising us with intense curiosity. He believes, or hopes, we may be two traveling whores.

He would like to spend more time with us, and he proposes a sum of money through the American guy who speaks Afghani.

We politely decline his offer, and we finish our tea, getting slightly nervous.

We climb back into the Jeep.

Rumours of bandit's attacks on voyagers in this desert plateau feeds our increasing paranoia with us smoking so much more of the abundant hashish freely provided.

Everybody is stoned, night and day, starting with the customs officer.

Why can't I feel safe and trust all these wild, noble looking, strange men? We worry for nothing, and the Jeep depose us in front of the hotel in Erhat.

We share a room with four beds, with a German hippie photographer and the American who speaks Afghani.

We order green tea and hash and the bus boy bring us Nuqi with the tea, that's what they call the roasted almonds white sugar coated, and a flat supple three-inch disk of black hash.

We relax in the comfort of the warm sawdust stove. We spread out and crank up to the max the music of The Creams on my little Sony machine.

I am still on my diet of oranges and warm milk, but they have here spinach cooked in mutton fat and a nice juicy flat bread catered with the room service.

The bathroom is basic with only cold water. The outdoor toilet is a scary shitty dark hole under tin roof with a tin door.

Nevertheless, we freshen up and Sylvie and I, rest soundly until next morning.

Early risers, we choose, a two-seat wooden pony carriage opened to the crisp light of a cold blue sky.

The driver wears a big pink turban and a shaven face, a lavender finely embroidered kamiz and sky-blue Aladdin pants.

He gauds lightly the little horse, pulling us and trotting, jingling with joyous bells and decorated with blue glass beads and red and pink pompoms.

We trot across the flat city, looking at the mud houses with flat roof, barely distinct from the ground, apart from painted doors.

All men walk or ride on a horse. They dress in pastel colours, wear rolled woolen hats and dark and green lined caftans. Some wear pale-coloured turbans and sheepskin vest over embroidered fine shirts. Their baggy loose riding pants taper at the ankle.

Few women walk around, entirely hidden under finely pleated silky burkas, hiding curious brown eyes under a tight silk visor grate.

This is the most mysterious veil of the orient.

After two hours of trotting around town, we come back, and that same afternoon, we meet Rene just arriving from the border.

We enter a taxi with Rene and the American guy who speaks Afghani and seems to know everything. He takes us to the biggest hashish pipe in the whole world.

In one indistinct two-story mud house, we enter through a maroon door. A tilted pipe bowl rests on the ground. It fills most of the room. Down a steep narrow staircase, one man is carefully leveling a shovel of hashish with strips of tobacco in the red-hot bowl.

Upstairs at the mouthpiece a line of smokers, take in turn, a carefully measured puff. There is a low table with a dozen of stoned customers at rest. They drink green tea and nibble sweet Nuqi and pound cake.

Sylvie and I are impressed by the show of billowing smoke, just breathing is enough to get blasted.

We just have tea and cake, and we don't take a turn at the pipe, but our American guide and Rene do, and they get so stoned they can't move for quite a while. We must wait until they recover, sipping our tea and keeping cool, under the curious eyes of amused Afghani smokers.

The taxi takes the four of us back to the hotel, we rest another night in Erhat. This desert town, barren and rugged with Afghani horsemen armed with guns. We are going nowhere, not lingering, waiting for the next bus to Kandahar in the hotel room with the German photographer.

That nervous German guy fears to be robbed. He sleeps with a loaded gun under his pillow, springs suddenly awake screams "*achtung!*"

Pull his gun from under his pillow look at it, put it back and go back to sleep. This guy is definitely not a hippie, and we are not traveling with him any longer. He is still sleeping in the early morning when we climb on the bus to Kandahar

Another tedious ride with frequent stops. Everyone on that desert road is waiting for the ride on that bus.

We reach Kandahar just before dark and go to sleep in a small hotel at the end of the road. All we do in Kandahar is change money early morning at the black market. We rush back to the bus departing in the early morning to Kabul.

In Kabul we plan to stay for a full month, I heard it is the place to fulfill my dream of a tailor made unique puchinka coat.

That will take time... and will cost money. I am no longer thinking to help Rene.

A first vision of Kabul in her immaculate blanket of snow.

All the pastel painted wooden houses, garlanded with bright colour. Strands of dyed wool, hang to dry. on the climbing hill strewn up in the blue sky.

Columns of smoke everywhere, spew from each house's sawdust fire.

The city unfurls, cross a small bridge over the river into the heart of the denser agglomeration.

We choose our simple room, pale green, number sixteen at the Bamian hotel just across from the police station.

Kabul yields its perfume, sweet and smoky in the crisp snowy air. I rush out to explore a big outdoor market for wool, embroidered Karakul goat and lamb furs. The fur market spreads across the river all around the foot hill.

So many fur vendors sit on goat and sheep furs on the ground in this open-air market, eventually more established tiny shops with merchants hidden inside.

I peek in, entering every shop to speak with every shopkeeper.

"Salaam Alec Um"

I am accepting many glasses of green tea at each shop. Merchants show me, hidden under the pile of furs the firearms they have for sale.

Each shop belongs to a family who has many things to offer. I search until I select the right shop for me.

Mother, father, sister will dye the silk thread and embroider the skins in the colours I choose.

Father will cut, uncle will stich. sons and daughters raise the karakul goats. Cut the heads, tan the skins, ate their meat, and now brew for me the best green tea.

I select nine skins of fine soft grey, tight curly karakul.

The family team make my long-embroidered coat, with a matching hat with ear flaps and a pair of gloves.

All the skins to be embroidered in a flowers and foliage pattern in gold purple and rose silk thread. The soft grey fur will be on the inside.

I haggle for the price and pay right away for the skins. I will pay the rest when the work is done.

That coat will last forever. I will pay all together sixty dollars for it, a major chunk of my money for India.

Rene exits our room to move to the dormitory with three new friends, including a dark guy from Martinique. They all only speak French.

Just underneath our room I hear music. I pursue downstairs the growing sound.

I knock at the door and make friends with Lou and Kelly, two Americans hippies from Haley, looking prosperous and eager to share.

Lou, Kelly, and me we are the only one who have records and a record player. Both our rooms are always full of visitors. Life gets exciting with a record player at the Bamian hotel.

I am intrigued by transactions between merchants, dealers, buyers, and policemen. All is about hashish, the number one cash crop of this country.

To enforce the legit custom of respect showed with *Baksheesh*. Corruption is a bigoted ignorant word for the people who know nothing about conducting business. Baksheesh is the only chance to get some reward.

The police station, just in front of the Bamian hotel.

The window is open to air out the smoke and watch what's happening on streets below.

Hippies, Kabulis and policemen, we all eat together at the roof top restaurant. The Afghani menu is served for breakfast, lunch and dinner. No Afghani visitors are allowed in our hippie hotel, apart from the staff.

The restaurant is busy all day from morning to night. Everyone conducts business transactions and meets there.

Down the street, not too far, is one American style canteen, where we eat mashed potatoes, bland American food, and apple pie.

This place exists for the American base personal and other road builders of the American, Russian and Chinese trading road.

This project in the making prepares the imminent future.

Due to the spicy local food and lack of sanitary conditions, many of us suffer dysentery, fevers and stomach ailments.

This canteen is the North American refuge. I heard of it since Istanbul. It reminds me of the greyhound rest stop, with the tasteless defrosted mash potatoes and stale Crisco crust American apple pie. The food is kept hot, in a warming display all day, for a handful of nostalgic home sick travelers.

Freezing cold, crystal snow is all around us, we put all our warmer clothes and boots to walk around the city.

We apply for a road slip at the Pakistani embassy. There are many boutiques with bric-à-brac bazaar nearby.

Antique tribal silver with Cornelia jewelry, ornate daggers with filigree, swords, guns, Kalashnikovs...silk and velvet embroidered clothing, all fabulous and affordable.

We make friend with the shopkeeper, his son and his nephew.

They speak fluent English, and we feel welcome and appreciated. We visit them at the shop every morning after checking if our Pakistan visa slip is ready.

I wander every day by myself, to spend one hour or two, drinking chai with the makers of my puchinka.

I sit on the pile of fur, for chit chat and green tea with a nibble on warm pound cake, dry fruits and green sweet melon.

I watch the embroidery growing and flowering on the separate parts of my karakul coat. I enjoy the daily visit, I belong here, part of their scene.

At the shop I meet a Kabuli doctor who speaks French. He invites me to his family home.

Everyone is excited to meet me. The first things we do, after we drink a glass of green tea, is to play Arachin, their favourite winter game.

We all sit around the sawdust stove in a circle, only our upper bodies visible, the rest of everybody is hidden under blankets and a token, called the Arachin, is passing from hand to hand.

When the song calls it, it falls in someone lap. Every player is calling "Arachin". In turn, each one that does not have it on his lap answers. Whoever finishes with it on their lap is the winner.

Inside the house women are free and pretty in colourful dresses. Talkative and friendly and very curious about my foreign ways. They are not shy with questions.

I eat their food, play their games and laugh at their jokes. I feel easily welcome and integrated in the doctor's family.

How exciting it is for them to listen, incredulous, and for me to tell my story. We have fun comparing and sharing our different customs.

Together we imagine my fairy tale in this beautiful Kabul winter during this memorable month.

With Sylvie, I check the black market. The post office for letters and the immigration office for our road permit.

At my friends' shop, I pull down untidy chaotic piles of tumbling splendor that I check nonchalantly. Nothing is neat, all is lavish and wild.

Kabul city lay like a gem lit by the sun, in her mantle of velvet snow.

White snow all around me, stretches to the hills, between the many painted wooden houses with flat roofs, all garlanded with vivid colourful strands of curing dyed wool.

The Kabul River crosses the entire city center. Both its banks covered with woolen carpet and fruits stands. Passing by smiling merchants who invite us to stop roaming and check their goods.

There is no car traffic, no traffic lights, no rush. The whole city circulates on foot. A few horses with bells pulling open carriage and a few taxis. All, easy, tranquil, and rural.

This Afghani capital the main spreading village. Big wooden houses painted green and mud houses. Plus, some new American style building oddly standing in the mist of this small-scale décor.

At the antique shop Sylvie and I meet our young friends. They study commerce at Kabul University. They act as our guides in the new Kabul.

They follow the modern trend, project more international commerce and discard the religious blindfold.

Their father, the shop owner, gives me a silver ring with a small emerald and more silver bells to attach to the zip of my silver boots.

Everyone seems to know where we want to go, the taxi drives us to the shop without bothering to ask where we like to go.

I finally bargain for a purple silk dress with matching baggy pants, all covered in glorious real gold and real silver embroidery. I have been admiring it, looking at it again and again, hanging from the ceiling for more than three weeks. I get it for a good price.

But the magnificent woolen socks with colour knitted pattern and gold thread, I bargained for everyday vanished from the street.

I buy a black pleated silken niqab burka, with a dense embroidered criss-crossing mesh, visor to look through. That will hide me, like it hides all the seeking brown and black peeking eyes of Afghani woman. I can't wait to be totally hidden and incognito.

Before I put it on, I will show it at the doctor's house and to my friends at the embroidery fur shop.

We meet Lou and Kelly in the staircase, and they invite Sylvie and me in their room to listen to the new album of Jimmy Hendrix, "Are You Experienced?". We take our first line of pure crystal pharmaceutical cocaine. That sniff religiously snorted through a rolled tight hundred-dollar bill provokes a sensational immediate rush.

A full power sudden alienation. I feel invincible, a great fearless animal, is it me?

I can feel it fizzle too soon., and right away I understand after a second snort, it is one costly addictive trap I can do without.

Happiness, mystical and a life with glorious free choice away from any addiction is what I shall pursue.

But with Lou and Kelly we spend hours smoking a very nice carved long opium pipe. Reclining on low mattress covered in brocade, also experiencing silent blessed torpor.

We listen to the beautiful meaningful music.

In the many pharmacies of Kabul, you can purchase anything you need, or want.

Special vitamins like unadulterated morphine, opium, heroin, amphetamines, and pure crystal cocaine. No one requires a doctor's prescription.

We lie on beds or sit cross legged.

All of us made some effort to be most beautiful, showing up for each other in our choice of bazaar finery.

Details of hair and shoes make each of us very original and beautiful in our own way.

We ask each other about the origin of all our enchanting costumes. We admire and praise each other. Mostly, we talk about the food we miss and the food we will get and what feels good.

We compare experiences, our journeys, a lesson with no complaints and nothing to hide. All of us seeking good vibes.

We walk across the Kabul River bridge to the university campus with our two student friends from the shop.

There is snow all around, we are dressed in all our warmest clothing. I've got on my red tights and my goat wool socks in my silver boots under my African long batik skirt with a loose zipper. On top, I have on my paisley cashmere blouse, my Swedish sweater, and my black and white Greek felt vest, my grey furry hat and gloves.

We reach the middle of the bridge chit chattering animatedly in the bright sunny cold day.

Suddenly, my skirt drops on my boots, and I appear in my red tights revealing arse and legs, not quite naked. This is funny, I can't stop laughing and amusing many Afghanis passing by.

Allah! An unforgettable joke my zipper story. With a safety pin from Sylvie all is correct again.

We visit the progressive campus of the new generation of Kabuli. We drink green tea and meet many other commerce students, answering their questions before everyone's curiosity is exhausted.

To complete my Afghani immersion, I endorse my brand new black jilbab burqa and under that mysterious shroud I go shopping in my silver boots with bells.

Many Afghani men follow me. Walking closer to me they speak to me in their language.

From the way I walk, and maybe seeing my boots they are mystified and obviously interested and whisper many strange words to me.

This takes two hours walking in the city and going in and out of little shops, before I get tired in my disguise.

I feel strangely more intimate and grounded. I got used to be followed all the way.

I conclude my promenade incognito, on my way home at the hotel still under my veil.

I buy fresh baked pound cake, dry fruits and bring it to the party room at Lou and Kelly's where everyone is getting high.

While I unwrap the cake, someone knock at the door. It's the police, for me. There is zero tolerance for Afghani woman getting involved with the hippies.

I am not one Afghani woman, Kelly and Lou are telling me to get out of the room and face alone the police I just attracted. I stall and stay inside, reluctant and scared stupid.

Therefore, I trigger immediate irruption of four police officers in uniform who don't waste any time.

They search us, they confiscate pipes and chillums and passports.

It is too late, when I meekly follow them down the stairs and across the road to their office. I am suspect for my impersonation of an Afghani woman getting into a foreign hotel after sundown.

All that unacceptable behaviour suggests I am a prostitute or a spy. How can I explain myself?

I apologise for my daring fantasy. It's just an experience, they believe me. A childish play, they laugh at it. They forgive me and send me back to the hotel without any of what they took from our room.

For the pipes, chillums and passports they want twenty dollars. Twenty dollars is more than I have left to reach India. Lou and Kelly are gracious and fork the money over to settle the matter. Everyone recuperates their missing items. I lost face. Sylvie severely blames a sorry foolish me.

She pressures me to pay Lou and Kelly back, but I am almost broke now and she must lend me the ten bucks I hand them with my apologies accepted.

Sylvie is now cross with me. I should grow up. We are no longer sharing the same dream. But still, we are almost ready to leave Kabul together.

My puchinka with the hat and gloves is ready and I have kept thirty dollars aside to pay for that extravaganza and then be broke.

I am cozy with my hill friends at the shop where the last touch is stitched on my puchinka.

The doctor is a very special modern Muslim with only one wife, four daughters and two sons. A very considerate modern gentleman. He understands woman feelings and tries to change at home what is backward in the customs.

In his home I have experienced pleasant open happy woman hospitality. I am invited for the last feast in my honor which I will go to in my Afghani purple dress and my completed puchinka.

I try it on at the shop. It is absolutely marvelous and perfect. I thank profusely the proud makers of it, I pay them, and I show myself in it, I curtsy like the hippie snow queen I became.

Finely crowned with my fully embroidered hat and coat and protected against any weather with the matching gloves on. I see in the full-size mirror my lucky blessed radiant, happy amazing self-reflection.

I climb the snowy, well trampled path one last time and enter the house where I become perfect center among all the family girls beautifully dressed for this last party.

I could stay with my friends and their cousins and servants and start another life. All is possible. I could adapt to this culture, live that life. But I only think that for a second, while I sing and dance with them a last time.

I made my grandmother's Moumoune cake for the party. We share a wonderful joyous feast. Afterwards, I leave their house with a pang of melancholy. Swearing to be back and next time I will stay longer.

I have no more money, but instead. I acquired sumptuous regalia to perform my role and great music. My friend Sylvie will pay for me, until we reach India.

We plan to stay at Channi's address in New Delhi.

I sort of count on and demand more money from those who still want to support me. Both Bruno and my parents still believe in me. They may send me money so I can pay my debt to Sylvie and go on.

The cold crisp air, the dazzling light with the snow flashy sparkles, the smell of acrid smoke all around.

The whiffs of spices waft around all the houses and in the bazaar. The appetizing aroma of spiced greens cooked with mutton grease.

The green tea with Nuqi, the dried fruits, the pomegranates, the sweet green juicy melons and the fresh pound cake sold still warm.

Smoking with the smokers at the restaurant filled with noble looking men with rolled woolen Pashto hats, fine crocheted hats with turbans of many styles. Gujer, Uzbeks, Kurds, Farsi and so many other tribes.

I see a few women moving purposefully, caged in their burkas. One of them hold a live colourful bird in a cage on her head.

We leave now, Salam Alaikum, peace be unto you.

Rene stays here, engaged to teach French in a high school, he feels grounded. He lost his anxiety, here he is appreciated for his education. We don't have to worry about him.

We start hitch hiking. The first truck driver takes us away over the Khyber Pass.

We stop and refresh in low creeks with boulders all around us, we take brief breaks and walk a bit. We climb back in a bus to drive across the Afghan desert no faster than the many men we see roaming on their horses.

Hashish is sold in one kilo tin can, on offer to sample. But it is more difficult to get booze here.

19

LAHORE, NEW DELHI

We left frozen Kabul with our warm clothing on. In my new puchinka with my hat and gloves on, I am cozy and sleep through the night ride.

Three hundred kilometers further, I wake up in the subtropical warm morning of Jalalabad. What a sudden change from the deep winter we thought would go on and on.

During the night rolling on, without noticing, we changed worlds.

At the first stop, there is a sugarcane wagon on wheels.

We guzzle thirstily the frothy sugar cane juice squeezed with fresh lime, ginger and ice cubes, two glasses each.

I look at the long canes rinsed with a flourish of cold water, hand folded stuffed with half cut limes and ginger root getting squished under the crushing wheel.

I listen to the noise, tinkling joyous with little brass bells when the rolling hand cranked press yields a first juice. The squished canes are then pushed back for a second squeeze, then a third one, all frothy with split fibres filtering more juice, adding into a pot through the fine mesh colander.

It is now hot. Before we take a bus to the border; I peel and pack my furs and wools. I remove my silver boots and my woolen socks and put my sandals on.

We keep rolling through a green lush country up to a small shelter into the countryside.

That is the Afghani Pakistani border. We are welcome!

On each side a tricolour black, red and green Afghani flag with a white emblem. And a green Pakistani flag with a white emblem. Between those two distinct flags is the no man's land chai shop.

Pakistani chai is the same as Indian chai. A sugary tea made with milk and spices, with ginger, cardamom, black pepper, cinnamon, and clove.

We savour it and nibble on spicy titbits and smoke a chillum cordially invited to the company of the customs officers.

The only sign of difference in country, another flag on each side of the open door. No official decorum. No feeling of tension between one frontier to the other, it is one village to the next.

This anticlimactic passage formality is stamped in our passport. It is hard to believe we had to wait so long for the permit to go through.

I am wondering about war and partition between Muslim peoples and Muslim states.

This is the atomic age, should it be a matter of sects and religious customs?

I am definitely not taking this seriously; I don't trust any of this religious crap. I love to follow that joyous lead, the truce of peace and love, music and rock and roll with no more human sacrifice.

Whatever religion we encounter we pass with a white flag. We enter a party without weapons for sale. That's all we need to work for.

Gods, prophets, and saints, their wise guidance should be remembered. But no one has the right to take upon enforcing blinding rules. I cannot understand, I guess I never will. No one does. Does the police, or the armed forces, knows what's going on?

Who tells people to obey and change all rules of law and order? What is this killer authority?

I am searching for my life. How can I follow contradicting rules? It's all bullshit and bullying to me.

We are the baby boomers. The peace and love generation. We have heard too much about war, now we want something else.

We do not care about patriotic police and evangelic religion.

I think we are the lucky ones. We can fly to stretch our new grown wings. We reach across all boundaries for space.

We are not qualified, not concerned, not responsible, anonymous unknown.

We must roam, this is the only freedom. With no blindfolds, no taboos we call upon faceless inspiration and trust spiritual guidance.

We adore the nameless avatar showing our reflection. Nothing to do with security or charity. We receive. We can take or leave it. We still have choice.

***

We climb in the train to Lahore near the Pakistani border. We reach Lahore, climb in a painted Tonga pulled by a white groomed horse with pompons and bells in his mane.

We trot away and look around for a suitable place to spend a few days. We inspect and reject the stinking dormitory at the youth hostel. We climb again in our Tonga, ringing joyous bells at a trot.

Two Pakistani guys are following us with their open canopy imported car slowed to our pace. They smile and cheers and wave at our pursuit.

We halt our trot in the middle of a colonial city square at the crossing of wide avenues under the soothing shade of flagrant yellow acacias and purple jacaranda trees.

All the side avenues have rows of white painted houses with pillars and wide sidewalks. Traffic is low, and slow. Everyone takes the time to look around. Our followers have engaging smiles. They greet us and offer to be our guides in their city.

Both of us feel okay about that and we climb aboard the white car with all our things.

We ask our happy chauffeurs to lead us to a cheap and best place to spend a week in Lahore.

They stop us in front of the Hotel Colonial just across from the zoo. That place looks luxurious to us.

But our new guides Farid and Azad take charge to negotiate the affordable price we are delighted with. They show us all they are proud of around here. We are lodged in the heart of everything we want to see.

Nearby Lahore, two palaces with walls and vault covered in calibrated miniature round mirrors. Looking at the hallucinating self-reflecting walls and ceiling, we can see our amazed selves, repeated a thousand-fold.

This is the Moghul achievement during Akbar Empire. A third mirrored palace exists in Moghul Rajasthan. But here to be dazzled we don't have to go far, and it feels good to bask in luxurious comfort and be shown around in style.

We eat breakfast under a white pergola on a white dressed table over a freshly mown lawn planted with almond trees and gardenia in flagrant bloom. We have poached eggs, warm toast with butter and marmalade, fresh squeezed orange juice, and raisin porridge with pieces of fresh cut banana.

The waiters dressed in crisp white uniform wear turban hats fletched with fan gold and black. They fuss about us, serving us breakfast under the large white umbrella.

We are pampered, classy, elegant memsahib here.

Our room is lovely. Airy and light with French doors opening out to the garden courtyard.

Our Moghul style beds in carved dark walnut wood, is dressed in rectangular cotton mosquito nets. Our beds become a separate refuge, private and desirable.

In our room, there is one receding wood wardrobe for our things, two night-tables, four brocaded easy chairs and a low coffee table in front.

We have one attached bathroom and a warm water shower just for us. We are lavished on by our two new friends.

So, Lahore from the start is a ritzy experience.

First, we go to the zoo in a green and wooded park where the animals are free to roam safely in walled areas with ample space.

Lions and tigers, elephants and antelopes, rhinoceros and crocodiles, alligators, snakes, mongooses, and monkeys and many compatible bird specimens in cages bigger than houses.

Around the open gardens with pond, iridescent peacocks, swans and guinea fowls prance free. It's only us at the zoo, the animals are just as interested meeting us.

Farid and Azad take us for lunch in downtown Lahore at a trendy restaurant with fine linen and spicy food. We drink fresh pomegranate juice, the ultimate refreshing drink in this no alcohol culture.

We check the museums and mosques. Between sightseeing we go back and forth to Hotel Colonial with our friends who treat us with French champagne mimosas and whatever we would like to try.

Money is no object, a mean they can afford to enjoy and a fuel for relaxed good company.

They do not seem to mind if we are reluctant to engage in more intimate games. We are happy with this cultural exchange. We tell our fascinating stories and our ambitious dreams. We put on our best appropriate outfits which show how exotic we are wherever we go.

We are a pair of foreign white princesses, me the European and Sylvie the American.

Every evening after dinner, we go dancing and drinking and smoking with Azad and Farid in the colonial private club at the Shalimar.

Our week in Lahore passes like a dream. We feel good and precious after riding on that flying carpet driven by our Aladdin escort. Two modern playboys who picked us up.

No fear and no drama, we are shown great hospitality and respect at their expense until we go easily away, merging in a gracious colourful crowd.

Women like children dressed in lots of gold and glitter and bright joyous colours. All around us everyone shines, with silks, jewels and fresh flowers all lit up by the sun.

Everywhere we look it's a feast for the eyes. Each person, each beast, each vehicle, all beautifully adorned.

Like, the white elegant bullocks with their saffron painted horns and necklace of jingling brass bells. The Tanga's horses with pompoms, tassels and bells. The artful miniature of flowers and scenery painted on the garlanded trucks. Everything owned is lively and proudly honoured. I never saw anything like that before.

I heard about Gandhi and the partition too long ago for me, but not long for the previous larger Hindustan. We are, included in it, now smiling and feeling free.

Hindustan used to comprise of Afghanistan, Pakistan, Cashmere, India, and Nepal. The subcontinent of many cultures brewing tolerance with religious faith.

There are many Muslims sects, many Christians sects, Jews, Jains, Hindus and even now, some man-eating cannibals.

Everyone we meet speaks English. The Ramadan is over and forgotten. We lucked out. We liked this oasis of grace and take the bus to the charming border at Islamabad.

This is the prettiest frontier on our way. There are flowers growing on the windowsills and flags and colourful garlanded people wearing fresh marigold malas. Ladies wear bright saris with Jasmin wreaths in their hair. Everyone mills about.

Two Pakistanis coolies with pink turban take our load and stand patiently beside us waiting our turn. One customs officer brings us a comfy chair.

Obvious respect is shown to us young traveling foreign girls without a man. We are enjoying playing that princess role, we are dressed for the part.

I wear my antique purple brocade silk Afghani suit under my new embroidered long puchinka insulating me against the heat like it was insulating me against the cold before.

American Sylvie beside me looks more sober but very smart in her blue jeans with her jean jacket and one sky blue embroidered lovely shawl; she bought in Kabul at our friend's shop.

So, to share this unexpected comfort of the border, further advantage must be taken in this open sky waiting lounge.

I pull out my music and play the Beatles album, Sergeant Pepper, to my new audience. Right away, a mesmerised compact crowd surrender to us. Entranced by the spectacle and this new sound.

The Pakistanis customs officers take charge of clearing this rapid swelling crowd away from us with the help of bamboo lathis.

They escort us with our coolies trailing right behind, we march through the Indian part of the border. The coolies drop their load at the end of the no man's land.

No Pakistani will go through, there is war between these two separated families. Indian coolies with red turbans grab our load of baggage to India.

Here we sit in a first minibus for many hours, shaken and crammed with other tired, dusty voyagers. Eventually, we reach the holy city temple in Amritsar.

We get out and spring into the marketplace lined with shops. We are greeted by the assaulting smells of India: spices and flowers, urine and sweat, tobacco, earth, fruit, incense, and coloured powders.

The market is right in front of the golden temple reflected double bathing in its pond with fountains and water ways. This vision is beyond all that I have seen before.

We follow the pilgrims. We leave our shoes were everyone else does, where our bags are guarded.

The rectangular ornate temple entirely gilded with thick layers of pure gold leaf on its white marble. Absolute glory, bathed in the sunlight.

Everyone is a pilgrim humbled in that splendor. Each carries their offering of a small clay lamp burning oil or clarified butter. Each launches their lamp, adding to the fleet of small boats all swirling orderly on the holy pond. They are full of cut flowers, candied sugar, coconut flesh, pieces of banana, and vermillion powder.

In the holy sanctum, when we reach, we see two turbaned, long bearded priests sorting offering and giving blessings.

Sacred mantras from the Gurmat Sidhant, the Sikhs bible written by the revered guru Nanak, the founder and author of Sikhism the youngest faith of Hindustan. It is a modern compromise between Islam and Sufism addressed specially to the Ksashtria, the warrior merchant caste.

We humbly follow devotees to the end, until we reach again the shoe room and behind it penetrate in the guest sanctuary, every blessed visitor is welcome to spend a night.

We rest, we meditate, we refresh. We receive *Prashad*.

Real nutritious sacred food. In our purified hands, a lump of very delicious suji halva, warm sweet and rich, just a mouthful of roasted semolina cooked with sugar and clarified butter served directly from the big, hot skillet. It's paired with a refreshing gulp from a tiny ladle of a sweet aromatic spiced water. The initiatic food of soma and the elixir of Amrit.

We sit, legs folded in a row on the marble floor to get handed a plate made of dried leaves woven by their stems.

Everyone holds their hand in the prayer gesture and look expectantly at the passing attendants with a pot and a ladle.

They dole a measure of dhal bat, some white rice, pungent spicy vegetables called sobji, soupy spicy lentils called dhal, a dab of pungent tangy pickle called achar, a dab of sweet milky rice called khir, and a chapatti, a fresh flatbread served warm. A drink of buttermilk in a paper goblet plus water poured from a cool steel jug into stainless steel glasses.

This place is the Langar, where everyday thousands of guests are fed. Devotees have donated all ingredients. Devotees are cooking and cleaning, donating money, doing selfless service, called seva, to be part of the human cause.

The written rule proposes that everyone give ten per cent of their earnings towards religious welfare and charity. This is in lieu of social security and taxation, a voluntary established system.

After this feast, just before sunset everyone bathes in the pond, a deep rectangular pool accessible by shallow steps. Everyone keeps all their clothes on, but it is possible to swim, and we do.

Sylvie and I lay a bit, dripping water on the white marble watching the red sun setting on the plain, before we substitute wet garments for dry ones.

All that is done by thousands of peoples at once.

Then we queue for the evening's Darshan blessing. The high priest reads, from the Gurmat Sidhant. The enormous book of the Sikh faith, bound in silver, lay on a high silver lectern.

The high priest in a white turban and robe displays a rotund belly. He climbs three silver stairs, unlocks the book with a silver key and opens it. He reads the page of the day, then locks the book.

Then we go to sleep, like all the other pilgrims, lying on the cleaned-up marble floor in the langar, where we ate before.

Free hospitality is part of the Sikh teaching. Everyone is welcome for three days. If you want to stay longer, someone here will put you on the charity work.

"Where are you from? What is your purpose? What can you do?"

We spend a day, a night and after a morning we have completed twenty-four hours experience at the golden temple.

We claim our shoes, our bags and we are again at the train station. We buy our second-class ticket at the foreign counter for New Delhi.

From Amritsar station I phone the house of Channi's parents, the Singh home. The master of the house himself answers me, we are very welcome to move into their home when we arrive.

It is a long and pleasant journey through plains and fields with many busy peoples and animals to look at through the window on the steam train.

I love the noisy rhythmic pace and the sooty smell of that train. The steam whistle blows a modulate steamy song, like a dragon getting ready to fly higher. My heart is touched by that sound I hear and love to listen to the fainting end each time.

We go slowly and we get chai and samosas, peanuts boiled in the shell, pakoras and more chai.

"Garam chai, chai!"

Loud claims from many vendors jumping on board by the open doors and windows when the train stops at the many stations. They sell everything. When the train begins to move again, they quickly jump out before the train gathers too much speed.

We arrive in New Delhi station, not far from the Singh house on Hailey Road behind Connaught place. We show the address to our turbaned Sikh driver sporting a rolled pinched beard and waxed whiskers. The cab slowly turns onto Hailey Road, our driver carefully inspecting the numbers on the residences.

I notice a fat Sikh with a maroon turban and a rolled beard and a waxed moustache eying us from the threshold of what could be the home.

I am thinking, it must be Channi's father, but it is Channi's oldest brother, only twenty-five years old. Surindar, hides inexperience under traditional, uncut hair.

Surindar whisks us in, immediately we pass through the house into a large walled garden. We are invited to refresh and sit at the table under the shade of a tree.

Father, and mother, simultaneously joins their hands in greetings with the Punjabi Sikh greeting formula *"Sat seria kal ji!"*

We are welcome to a first meal of freshly cooked warm roti, served dabbed with ghee.

From the outdoor kitchen the ladies of the house cook the roti on a fulminating sputtering kerosene pump stove, in a concave black iron skillet with a wood handle, called a *tawa*.

With warm roti we get a thick dhal curried sauce, and a homemade scrumptious tangy achar of mango and chili, a vegetable sobji, and a refreshing raita made with yogurt finely chopped cucumber, spring onions and fresh coriander.

I follow immediately the house ladies, mother and daughter in law, to the kitchen. I love to learn how to cook like them.

Everyone guzzles clear water with the meal, we finish by taking a digestive pinch of sweetened aromatic seeds of fennel, sesame and poppy seed with areca nut called *soupari*. We finish with a cup of sweet chai.

It's a homecoming party. The family want all the recent news we bring from Channi and his friends, the adventurous boys emancipated from traditional dress code.

They are proud of their youngest son, looking like a Bollywood star.

Ours host is curious about what brings us here.

We sit between Surindar and Tony, the jovial middle brother. Tony, just married, live here with his new young bride, they have the luxury of a private room. Tony proudly shows us the house.

The three men of the house are wearing different coloured cotton turbans. The master of the house a cream coloured one, Tony a small paisley print with pinks and blues. They tie and knot their beard, and wax and roll their never cut mustaches with Fixo.

The three men sport western pants with cotton shirts, without ties, and without cufflinks with woolen sleeveless vest for the cool evenings.

We are honoured guests of a merchant's family. They dabble in many ventures: import export, trading, travel, cars, textiles and whatever comes their way.

Their house is all ground level with a garden.

A stuffy living room decorated with two taxidermized tiger heads showing indignant fangs at being killed in their prime.

Beside the tiger heads sit long guns, swords, and a framed picture of the patriarch shaking hands with the actual president of India and other prominent dignitaries.

The floor is covered with a thick woolen red-carpet cushioning everyone's bare foot. Two red upholstered sofas comfortable and bulky, a low table for tea and drinks.

I am admiring, sincerely enthusiast about the relative novelty of this bourgeois décor.

We are welcome to sleep on the two sofas in the living room, Surindar sleeps here as well, on the thin mattress he unrolls at night and put in the middle of the thick carpet.

The father and mother's room adjacent to the living room and everyone pass through it to go to the one bathroom and lavatory.

They circulate from one room to the other without any concern for privacy. Personal space is not part of this lifestyle. Pass by and visit. Sit on your bed for a chat or share an evening snack in your company.

No boundaries, you can lay if you so feel, while someone is sitting at your foot, telling the company about the day's events.

Channi's parents are laid back and tolerant. They make us feel most welcome. The household of family and servants is always open to visiting friends.

Family, guests, servants, everyone is here. Except the married daughter, a professional lawyer, we will meet on Sunday.

The cook, Chanapatasai, and the janitor, Chokidar, live and sleep in the pantry beside the kitchen with Billy the black and white housecat.

The Dhobi come from outside every day, she washes the laundry, sweep and washes the floors and wipe the dust in the house.

The Mali prunes the trees, rake and sweep the leaves and maintain the ground of the wild green spacious garden.

The daily supplies enter through the back garden gate, inspected and paid for by Benji, the mistress of the house.

Every day, the torcaliwalla, delivers fresh fruits and vegetables. The doodwalla brings milk and curd and ghee. Even flour, legumes and eggs are delivered personally by a grocer to the house.

The telephone and a radio set on the corner table in the living room are the modern link to the evolving world. There is no television.

On the 26th of January, republic day, chairs are placed on the sidewalk to watch the parade.

Each state of India parades their groomed troops and flag to the sound of music and fireworks.

It's a long crowd bath of national pride, with cheers!

The ladies at home get dolled up to enjoy a shopping outing. They choose their gold and glass bangles, new silk saris for special occasions. We go for a movie and buy milk sweets.

For everyday dress, new style Punjabis suits with assorted two-meter scarfs, salwar kamiz with dupattas.

Tony is the one who drives the family car, a black Ambassador. He proposes to guide us in Delhi. He will have the time because he has recently dropped his new wife off for a month of traditional visits with her family.

We pass the hot part of the day, comfortable in the garden shade.

Tony, the young leading man of the house, washes his long hair. He dries them spreading them in the sun tilting his head on the back of the wooden chair. Enjoying a sunbathe, he relaxes deeply with closed eyes.

We sit and lounge in chairs around the rectangular dining table where all meals are taken except the evening one after sunset.

Every single day, new visitors invade the hospitable house. Most of them hand a pretty, wrapped box full of addictive milk sweets to the greeting ladies. Everyone munches on them all day. The sweets are called Burfis and Ladoos.

The visitors are very curious about us, educated foreign traveling girls, and personal friends of the sons traveling abroad.

They speculate wildly about us until they come to find out for themselves. We accept many invitations, driven by Tony to other opulent dwellings of New Delhi.

We meet affluent members in the movie business, handicraft art, petroleum and industrial products, textiles, real estate, civil servants, and politicians.

With Tony we visit Delhi Zoo, another vast garden with captured wild creatures, looking well fed and protected.

We check the red fort in Old Delhi, the Moghul fortress on top of the bazaar near Chandi chowk.

We end the tour at the family's favorite Gurdwara temple with mother Biben and wife Bidgi all dressed up and excited for their sociable devotion party.

I am a little tired of traveling. I am ready to savour a family rest. One day at the time and not thinking about the future. My address is here, I savour the truce, feeling content home.

On a clean piece of plywood, I find in the garden I start painting a bright flowery lady carrying bananas on her head.

It takes me days to complete my naïve surreal piece of art, a present to our host. I spend many days, happy with this family life in the garden. At night I dance for them to my chosen tunes on my electrophone. The lot of potbellied Sardar gustily guzzles whiskey.

With Tony and Surindar we go to clubs and dance. Surindar still a burdened bachelor. Especially hopeful, obviously dreaming to experiment with our unrestricted freedom.

He stays timid. But attempt closer contact occasionally. We restrain him.

The family receives Channi's ceremonious letter, informing anyone present about his business prospects. Surindar reads, loud and clear, spelling each word for us all.

This letter ends up with greetings to his mother, father, brothers, sister, and sister-in-law, and present guests. We are bonding with this family. I try to be agreeable and stimulating.

I prepare a steamed pudding and beef stew for them to sample European flavour. Sikhs are meat eaters, from the Ksashtria warrior caste.

To my surprised observation, in this opulent house, meat or eggs are rarely eaten. Maybe once or twice a month and for a special occasion on their calendar. No one seems to crave meat as a daily necessity, like we do in the west.

I realise I am not eating much of it, and I don't miss it. So what? Do I need it? Is it a desirable consumer marketed product?

I feel healthy and good, vibrant and light! I enjoy this new simple way of eating, with clean hands, and no need for a knife, it feels right! I easily exchange my fork and knife etiquette for this culture.

Tony scores "Bang" for us.

The Sikhs are not allowed to smoke but can ingest whatever they want.

Bang is powder of Cannabis cooked with caramelised sugar and ghee, rolled into a soft candy. Sometimes it is covered in a diaphanous leaf of pure silver, or even gold according to budget.

Bang can be eaten as it is, or blended in a sweet and cold yogurt drink, called a lassi. Together it is then called a Bang lassi.

Bang can be eaten in pan leaves. Bang is a traditional product, sold in the pan shops.

What is pan? Pan is a heart shape, tender fresh green betel leaf, to stuff with betel nut and lime paste and other breath freshening flavours including Bang.

This is the favored digestive gobbled by the subcontinent, a stimulant widely consumed by labourers and all other workers of India.

The pan shops bless every corner and every middle of any street in all the cities. A small table with a stack of green betel leaves some edible flowers and twigs displayed on the tiny table with a drawer.

The dignified Pan Walla is sitting on a one footed stool. Dexterous and patient, he attends minutely to the precise orders of his customers.

He is very busy at times, but there will be some lull in the pace of his day, his opportunity to roll generic stuffed tasty leaves for the minimum price.

The pretty green and tender cones stuffed with their own stem, lay stacked orderly on the wiped clean table for which he uses all day, the same filthy looking rag.

All pan leaves must contain a piece of hard betel or areca nut to be slowly chewed and spit out.

Red abounding saliva and grits duly milled, expertly spat, land to blotch the road and sidewalks with long dark red orangey comet trails.

Many flavours can be ordered, the inventory of a good pan shop is a treasure of the earth perky savours.

Honey, cardamom and clove, silver, or gold, mint and asafoetida, a bit of bang, or a grain of coffee, opium, or a few crystals of cocaine.

You order and you pay, and the pan master deliver with flourish, the leafy parcel that your palate desires.

Most labourers carry a tied-up handkerchief full of a stash of betel leaves and a small box with areca nuts and white lime paste.

I enjoy a mitha occasionally.

Surindar and Tony takes us to the hotel Oberoi, an American five-star Hotel, with an Olympic swimming pool, steam room, sauna, gym, night club and a big fancy restaurant and bar.

Affluent Delhiites who want to be seen, are cruising in the bar lobby. Surindar and Tony enjoy imported American whiskey with their pouchy friends, paying top price for quality. They want to impress us, and each other.

The businessmen hands us business cards and show pictures of their wives and kids, waiting for them at home.

Men bring news linking their lucrative work to their family. That network comprises the world at large if not going abroad. Marriage is the only way to expand.

A proper wife is devoted to her husband and sons, father-in-law, mother-in-law. The Singh patriarch is a modern man whose only daughter is well educated and a working official justice lawyer.

Apart from her court job, she never goes out without her husband or the matriarch of the family.

We are invited to display and familiarise our hosts with our own customs. The men who do not smoke are curious about this forbidden sin. They encourage us to smoke our cigarettes and hashish joints inside their houses, observing us to find out if it really affects personality.

Tony scores some dope for us.

For most of our stay in that house I am charmed at home with the women. We laugh together at the absurd difference of wellbeing. I learn some cooking skills and some Punjabi. From the patriarch I learn to say "*Atcha*" a word repeated through so many times that, means: "well", "okay" and "everything acceptable or not?"

Sylvie is getting restless and starts exploring New Delhi on her own. Sylvie is having some guys calling her on the home phone. Tony voices the family malaise. We have intruded in this house for five timeless weeks free of charge.

I finally receive money from Bruno through the Singh's bank account with a parcel containing my unfinished book.

After clearing my debt to Sylvie, I still have fifty dollars. We can now move on, and part. Sylvie is going on a tour to Agra, I won't go with her.

I check my address book and decide to call Arvin Kumar, the Brahmin, and the quietest Indian friend we met in Teheran. I also need a change of scene.

Arvin invite me for diner at his family home, it is not far, in the vicinity of New Delhi railway station they live on top of their own shop, Vishnu statue palace.

The shop is full of luminous marble gods painted with vivid colours.

I climb the spiral metal stairs going up from the back of the shop, into a Hindu Brahmin family home.

I am invited to share the meal with strict vegetarian men who wear a cordon from their shoulder to their crotch, while the women serve us.

Arvin the elder and only son has a younger sister, a mother and a father.

I am welcomed in a sober devotional way by the whole synchronised family. They display for me another Indian tradition. I am soaking the different atmosphere.

No leisure time and more formality in this religious Brahmin culture.

Arvind is delighted with my visit; it will change his life for a while. He proposes to meet again and guide me in the part of Delhi I have yet to discover.

I take some distance from my Sardar adopted family. Showing chagrin and relief at my departure. I have savoured adapting to their ways, but I won't fit their mold any longer.

I have learned a lot from them, I know how to greet all Sardars, how to express basic needs politely in Hindi and the Punjabi way. How to be on my own peaceful with many and how to go on my way.

I have spent many hours with Biben, Tony's educated new bride and her mother-in-law, the mistress of the house Bidgi. Bidgi showed me many ways to drape and wear my new sari.

We went shopping together to purchase my one silk sari. Browsing every single sari shop on Connaught circus.

We were exhausted before I made my choice: a royal blue Benares silk with gold brocade bees all through the six meters of silk plus seventy-five centimeters with border but no bees for the blouse loosely separated by a few silk strands.

And afterwards, we sit for a rest in the middle of a green grass park at the Rambler Cafe with a refreshing lassi and samosa.

We go back shopping for a black cotton veil sari with a turquoise and gold border, and a dark blue petty coat. Bidgi and Biben order two blouses fitted for me, from their usual Punjabi lady's tailor.

At night we hang out with Surindar. Before unrolling the bedding and getting into our sleeping bags we smoke a joint.

Surindar wants to take a puff and dare the experience. We pass him the joint. Surindar seize it with some awe and turn the lights off.

In the ominous darkness, he experiences his first, then a second puff. Then he switches again the light on, and we finish our joint merrily laughing together and polishing off the box of burfi.

I am ready to enter India, more on my own. For Sylvie and me, no more clinging and depending on each other. We were never a team, but a crutch; we helped each other for the first steps. Now confident we are moving on.

With Arvind I explore ill-famed old Delhi and popular quarters.

We smoke chillums and pass hours with other Hindu devotees at home in ornate Hindu temples filled with fresh garlands of flowers. Smoldering agarbati sticks waft sweet smoke and oil lamps wicks burn softly. Doll sized statues of gods, brightly painted marble Murtis, get bathed by priests and dressed in brocade and silk and adorned with jewels, offered food and drinks and prepared to be worshipped for hourly rituals.

We sit on the cool marble floor, listening to the classic musicians plucking sarod, sitar, blowing the conch and flute and tapping their intricate rhythm on tabla, clay pots and mridangam.

While the singers tell the story and chant mantra, Ramayana Leela, their story unfold with sensuous ragas for each hour of the day or the night.

My favorite hangout and chillum smoking place is the spacious gardens of the Birla temple.

We walk between life size pink stone effigies of all heroes of the Bhagavat Gita standing with green bushes of roses and lemon trees. the temple is carved like a pink sugar confection.

Many hours, walking, sitting, smoking chillum and talking in the Buddha's Garden. We sleep a night in the Buddhist guest house garden at the Ashoka mission.

In the morning we climb all the stairs up the tower Koutoubminar. Arvind is just who I need now to show me sights on foot. He shows me an easily accessible India available for everyone's worship.

Arvind invites me to Jaipur to stay at his cousin's farm, it is not fancy, but we can stay there for free.

Arvind is related to artists in Jaipur and will introduce me. I abandon my Sardar refuge, and fade from the picture at Hailey Road.

I am shifting cultural interests from Sikh to Brahmin.

The ancient worship of the cow, the moon, the sun. Since or before Sumer. Ishtar, and Venus Astarte, coatlicue, Kali Mat, the cosmos above us mapped by so many observant priests dreaming of infinite religious reason.

This is a sober life, exalted through animist cult. It appeals to me with its precluding ritual and pomp I have a taste for this with my catholic upbringing.

Arvind's mother and his sister Sunita with their ceremonial sari on, flower wreath in their hairs, and a special shiny tikka dabbed on their third eye, perform Arti Puja. The butter lamp's tiny flame like a stretching light point. The shiny center reflects on the bhindi illuminated on their foreheads.

Sundown salutation in devoted trance. They cross the living room with offerings to the altar in the east corner of the house.

On their shiny brass tray, a charcoal and camphor fire burns bright, beside incense sticks, flowers and fruits.

Sunita blow a small conch, rings the bell between each blow, put flowers and fruits on the altar and light the agarbati when the camphor fire is extinct.

I feel the gentle peace of their house.

I am eager to explore more of that.

20

JAIPUR

I store, at the Singh, the cumbersome bulk of my possessions: my puchinka, fur hats and gloves, my hats and wools, my silver boots, and my manuscript.

It's getting hot in March; I take only saris and dupattas, for the trip to Jaipur. I will gather all my things when I return.

In almost five months traveling with Sylvie. I learned Boston English, she learned French. We learned something important to us, from each other. Now we expand in differences, going solo.

I sit beside Arvind on the window side, in second class reserved train seat.

We stop in the Rajasthan countryside in the outskirts of Jaipur. We climb aboard a cheap old bus, and squeeze between two passengers on the narrow four seats bench.

On threadbare wheels, the bus progress, scraping painstakingly and slowly.

Arvind is a thin scholarly boy, not particularly good looking but with intensity. Arvind is serious, appreciative and respectful. With him I got a good brother to lead me where I want to go. Arvind believes in Lakshmi power, he does not speculate with risky business as a friend and business liaison with Channi, Raja, Saxena and Prabu.

He keeps in touch on a regular base and knows exactly what they are up to.

The latest news is not very reassuring, he just got the message from Prabu announcing that Saxena got arrested, charged and put in jail for illegal car trafficking between Munich and Teheran.

He needs some serious money for bail, his parents have been contacted.

With Arvind I suspect with no certitude, Channi and Raja could be partners in that risky business, they should be warned to avoid a similar fate.

I telephone Surindar from Jaipur railway station's public telephone to make sure he warns his brother to take no risks with any car.

They buy prestige vehicles cheap from Saudi visitors. The car trade between northern Europe and Iran is a well-known way to make good money.

All which is required is initial capital for the second-hand car and a driving licence. All previous transactions for two years have been successful and following smoothly one after the other so far.

American deluxe cars are driven and sold, and Mercedes deluxe cars are purchased, driven and sold the other way.

Good business back and forth. This is a first glitch for our enterprising stylish friends.

Since everybody knows, everyone must be warned.

I just had a good taste of Indian family culture. I had to hide myself confined in the sisterhood. For me it was temporary. I am not trying to be Indian.

Too many hierarchic layers to respect, too much hypocrisy and patient conceding in the patriarchal family.

The mother of the priest, and the guru.

Females must sacrifice personal turmoil's, to raise the children, be satisfied with no privacy and to resign any personal ambition. And getting fat, eating too many sweets. The caste system, so called abolished, still dictates the entire subcontinent.

For my absolute quest I can't tolerate any of that. I must understand and teach my self how to lead my own life. I, still naive, have made too many signs of the cross seeing and respecting so many churches. I see through on my way.

With that Indian humour sharp and down to earth, I can easily denigrate religiosity and laugh at taboos.

I hear office workers babbling about the new politics, they dream about new equality American style.

They drink "Thumbs Up" a similar cola drink, because there is no Coca Cola import permitted.

They dream about our freedom and our pale look. I think that real freedom is not what happens in America, there is no decision in generic conformity.

But the modern Indians are dreaming of jeans and Lacoste tee shirts and sneakers, they will pay a good price for used Levis and western import.

I, politely endorse resilient tradition, betting it's enough to adapt deploying charm and still, progress safely towards my clue.

Since I left Sylvie, I speak only American English. The traveler lingo that everyone is relieved to speak and to understand.

I've improved a lot; I can now express myself fluently. I sincerely believe that I've cut the links binding me to my roots. I became free to scrutinise.

Jaipur, the pink capital of Rajasthan, is a thriving center for Indian artisan business. Precious and semi-precious stones, block printed cottons, garments, camel leather art are for sale.

Jaipur's pink palaces still inhabited by their impoverished Maharajas. Their family royal suite and rooms a tad decrepit are for rent at a competitive affordable price, while the Maharaja tells customers his fabulous history.

A deserted arid desert plateau with hard working crafty peoples.

Entering through majestic pink stone gates, we navigate through a wall of bicycles. At first, only bicycles, but also bullock cart and horse cart and rickshaw, and motor cars, and miniature painted trucks with the warning; "SOUND HORN PLEASE."

People on foot, between, bullocks, camels and elephants each animal harnessed of braided colours embroidered bells and jewels mounted by drivers goading them.

All creatures merging in the pink flow. No fear, and no agitation, everyone aware of the pace and their place.

With the old bus we progress slowly, we are getting through, then out of the big city.

We reach the farm of Arvind cousin, in the middle of a lush, tall cornfield. We stand in front of a ten-by-ten cement shelter with a corrugated asbestos roof. I see a door with a small lock on and Arvind Brahmin cousin greets us and give us the key.

Inside the room there's a small window with iron bars and no shutter, two Indian wooden bed frames with rope crisscrossing instead of a mattress called charpoys, one wooden chair, dangling bare electric bulb and one electric socket.

No tap and no running water, no fan. This is home!

I put my bag against the chair, and I plug in my record player. The cement room feels unbearably hot.

We walk to the middle of the field to check the irrigation where we will bathe before sunset. We are looking forward for that to happen.

We savour the welcoming chai cousin Soubash brings us. We smoke a pink marble chillum, present for me from the Jaipur Vishnu statue palace.

We are in the periphery of Jaipur in rural India.

Our first bath just before sunset is one exhilarating joyous moment under the strong jet flow of the irrigation. The bath shares the cascading water with the vivid emerald perky corn.

Refreshed and clean, we drink chai, eat roti with small bananas and fall asleep. I prefer a mat on the floor, Arvind takes the charpoy.

A first morning chillum at sunrise in the field, with another irrigation shower in the lively presence of the growing corn.

I am dressing up for my part, in my new sari. The three of us climb aboard the splendid, motorised carriage. Our vehicle is butter coloured, buffed to gleam. The dashboard ornate, every inch of the interior walls displays miniatures of Krishna's various avatars painted on ivory.

The venerable ambassador is garlanded with fresh flagrant flowers. Soubash ignite three agarbati sticks; one of rose, one of sandalwood and one of champa before he starts the car for our temple journey.

For Arvind and Soubash I am the extreme center of temporary revolution in their universe. Everything happens according to my foreign wishes. I love to be treated like this. My fascinating fair complexion and my happening eager presence is sufficient proof.

My music box can play for this new audience entrancing western dancing music, it works with battery anywhere.

From the horizon and all edges of the visible world, people appear farmers, labourers, and shepherds. They are running and gathering around us to watch me dance and listen to my music.

I entertain my spectators, improvising my role of a white Apsara.

I hide from the sun under the palou of my sari as a veil on my head. Rajasthani style like a renaissance Madonna.

I enjoy riding in the temple car. We park in a shady spot of interest. Arvind hurries to step down, open my door and help me appear. Wherever we land, we gather a crowd.

I play my music in a deserted temple, we smoke a chillum, make puja to the god of the shrine, make more offerings of sweets and flowers before igniting agarbati sticks.

Arvind brings with the first chai new garlands of white jasmine and tuberose and some yellow champa flowers for my finishing touch.

After my morning bath at the irrigation spout with the corn, I take the time necessary to focus. I dress up, bejeweling and adorning my brown pupils painted around in blue. I place a tikka on my third eye in the sacred point of my brows.

A tikka can be made of earth, ashes, red vermillion, yellow curcuma powder or white ceruse.

It can be a flat jewel glued on, sold ready-made as bhindi with self-adhesive glue to transfer from the plastic sheet to your forehead, decorative inexpensive or expensive, but always precious.

It indicates if you are married or a widow by its marking. With its dots, lines and colour combinations, it shows which Hindu faith you follow and which ceremony you just attended.

Devoted Hindu men who worship get it dabbed on at the temple or in private ceremony.

Arvind and Soubash, by now, are worshipping me; they wish and pray about my incarnation. I get exhibited around, and I acquire four new saris in Jaipur's market.

I am fed with milk sweets, fruits and lassis and I grow into Kali's avatar. I start to paint a snake on my third eye.

It just happens as I am dancing to Ray Charles "What I Say" in the ruin of the mother goddess.

My first worshippers, Arvind and Soubash, augmented by many labourers gathered here, all trailing like one ant colony on the move from the jungle.

They look, uncritical, at my spectacle, my amateur theater, my spontaneous show, my inspiration on display. I've got my captive audience in awe.

I do love feeling in that center, no longer anonymous or lost. I can believe in that bigger self!

Soubash rolls in the cream ambassador, early, before sunrise.

We are going to bathe at a Kali temple pool. A new location, another improvised ceremony attracts one ever swelling crowd of curious witnesses.

I get soaked under a strong jet in my navy blue under sari petty coat and blouse. A decent display performed by all women who enjoy a lavish freshwater bathing in sacred places.

I am in no rush, the fresh running water blessing so welcome after the night on the uncomfortable mat on the floor in the hot cement cube house.

No shame, no striptease, and a charming spectacle I don't mind providing.

The presence of the curious crowd does not bother me. It's my dance to my favorite song of the Creams "Tales of brave Ulysses", involving water.

The mystery evolves, merging and infused in this Hindu culture.

My father voice's, faint and far away, reminds me to be careful with trampling on details and challenging bigot's rules. Where men go and where women go, it's my game.

This is no longer teasing, when I choose the men's pool, to dive in and swim for my bath, but a deliberate iconoclast sacrilege.

This crowd never saw it before. I can hear murmurs rising, chanting "Kali! Kali!" when I get out of the water pool to dry off.

I like to perfect my number.

With Arvind and Soubash we finish the temple tour.

It's time to meet the artist guru. He is the one who has painted the miniatures on ivory in our worshipped car. That man is a renowned sculptor working on a bust order for a V.I.P.

Guru Banou Ji is chiseling at the white marble bust of a minister, admired by twelve apprentices and disciples. Guru Ji speaks and everyone listens. Revering his words.

His mother and wife bring chai for everyone and savoury seo and boiled chickpeas.

Guru Ji is curious about me. He shows me how to make a paint brush for miniatures. The bristles made from a few hairs brushed off his wife's mane. We will stay here for a few days.

I am to be his new student teacher; he wants to know all about my curious mind.

Guru Ji drills me to compare his with my notions of purpose: integrity, intensity, what is divine?

Guru Ji has got the wide-open eyes of a tiger.

Everyone calls his mother Mata Ji. She makes a mala for me with a hundred and eight tulsi beads including a big central rudraksha, the sacred seed stop for malas.

When Mata Ji offers me the completed necklace, a solemn Guru Ji places it around my neck.

After that his devotees ask many questions about themselves and me. What should they do?

Everyone is listening to my silencing advice. They line up and listen for days to my foreign teaching, I just don't have a system, but I am inspired.

One artist is drawing my miniature portrait. The disciples invite us to visit and bless their home.

Between my appearing here and there, Arvind and Soubash are having my saris dry-cleaned and keeps everything I own in perfect condition.

Like a shooting star I shine my light on while passing by. I am soaking in the nurturing divine essence of worship.

Banou Ji's reception room is a continuous firm mattress. Covered in white sheet. Everyone sits comfortably under the spinning fan drinking lemon water or chai.

It's hot in this desert state. And getting hotter now just before Holi spring festival.

This favorite festival starts now, today is the new summer moon. Celebration at all neighborhood locations will happen for twenty-eight days.

Everyone is allowed to go crazy for one full day in his area. They throw coloured waters and powders on everyone they meet, or request money not to do so.

Gentle people turn wild to play Holi.

Banou ji whole household prepares to play.

To help the fever climb to its glorious pitch, everyone drinks bang lassi. Including the women who stay at home with water buckets brimming full of coloured water.

Everyone fills their bottles. The kids have got hand size packets of colour powder they throw on me.

I down my glass of bang lassi with everyone else I am dressed in my white cotton sari. Instead of a blouse I put my white pleats and mini lace Mexican dress.

I step out into the courtyard as everyone's favoured target. The bottles and lotas, jugs of frosting coloured juice splash on me.

In a moment I am polychromed, entirely soaked and dripping colours before I run out onto the street.

I get from house to house welcomed by unleashed wild ladies and hysteric children. They tip the rest of the pink and the orange buckets all over me.

We take off by Tanga, an open horse carriage, pursuing each other with dry powders spraying and bombarding madly nonstop at the various family houses.

All ladies and children, poised at home, their buckets full, ready to dip or to strike any moving target.

I got for sure more buckets on me than everyone else, but every creature, dog, bull, camel, elephant, cow, cat and all humans of Jaipur, transform into a fast rampaging monster rainbow.

By the end of the seamless full-on day. I become a frightening-coloured monster. From the roots of my hairs to the soles of my feet, not a speck of white skin is left on me.

My eyes are red rimmed, my hair matted fluorescent pink and orange. My face is blotched with all the colours, and so are my clothes.

I absorbed the violent colour orgy, like a chameleon. I feel exploded and spewed. The party of exhausted players is all over at sun set.

No scrubbing and soap lathering, and no irrigation showers can wipe this. I will shampoo daily more than a month before the purple, pink and orange colours start to fade from my hairs.

After my Devi play for so long, I feel drained by all that attention. I crave anonymity. I just want to feel tired and ordinary again for a while.

I go back to Delhi on my own by train. Arvind and Soubash drive me to the train station. I get in the cream-coloured Ambassador with Banougi, his mother his wife and son. Twenty more disciples follow us cramming into two cars.

I climb aboard the train with all of them to find my seat number, secure my place and place my bag. They all rush off before the door slide shut. I wave at my group standing along the quay.

I feel some relief getting away.

I am seated in a second-class compartment. I need distancing from that absorbing experiment. I still wear a painted black cobra smiling on my third eye. I still dare to feel it, now it belongs to me.

I meditate and dream while the train whistle blows for my departure. I leave the devotees fading quickly with the dust and the smoke of the locomotive gathering speed.

This snake of Ma Kali, the renewing mother of India, now a lurking presence in my body temple.

21

RETURN TO NEW DELHI

As soon I reach New Delhi, I fetch my belongings at the Singh house.

Sylvie is visiting Madras.

I am planning to stay in a guest house before going further, I don't know exactly where on my way.

Sylvie and I both abused our welcome at the Singh house.

My latest warning about Channi has considerably cooled their cordial trust.

They told me he is selling dry pet food in Germany; this is not an illegal activity. Sat seriakal Ji, Choukria. Let's forget each other for now.

I deplore some embarrassment and a growing uneasy gap.

Thank you so much for your generous hospitality, sorry If I did not give enough in return. But I did my best to amuse you.

I take a room at the Goan guest house of missis Kolaco, near Connaught place.

When I register, I bump into Nicole. Nicole travels, like me, on her own. Sharon is gone to South America to be with her boyfriend; she never went further than Kabul.

Nicole shares a room with Susan, another American girl she travels with since Kabul.

This Susan is currently in Goa, shortly expected to join Nicole before they go north together, maybe to Cashmere, or maybe to Nepal.

As for me I don't know what I want to do yet, I now have three hundred rupees left to my name. With that I plan to live without care for a few weeks.

I take a long shower and shampoo my bright pink hairs. I paint a freaky blue cobra on my third eye. I lacquer my eight-centimeter-long nails with fluorescent pink polish, and my toenails to match. This colour is all the rage on the city posters for Bollywood movies. Shocking pink, like my brocade chole blouse embroidered with gold and silver, stopping under my bosom.

For a belt I wear a long necklace of cherry sized false pearls hugging my forty-eight-centimeter waist on bare white skin. I wear a low waisted Rajasthani pink billowing skirt covering my knees.

I've got silver bells anklets tinkling, and golden sandals on my feet. Multi-coloured glass bracelets clink on my wrists. Gold and silver rings with semi-precious and precious stones on each of my fingers.

Around my neck sits the mother of pearl mala from Teheran mullah, my blue glass bead mala from Erhat and my coral beads from Venice and my new rudraksha mala from Banou.

I wear a white and a rose cotton lined veil, a Dupatta. On my shoulders sits my black crocodile saddle bag, my papers and all my money inside.

My hair is already dry and flying around me, loose, shiny and still very pink. My amber eyes are set in blue kajol to match my snake.

Dressed like this, I am ready for anything to happen. I open my dormitory's door to the lobby.

Nicole comes to see me with two cute friends she met in Bombay. They were begging on the street of Colaba. She gave them some money and they are friends now.

These two guys have had no cash of their own for quite a while, and yet they seem to manage very well.

The two are looking suitably impressed by me. I notice that I've got their interest.

I set my music up in the lobby and we listen to the Creams. I play for them the part of Aphrodite who rides her crimson shell.

Rick at Musoorie in July 1968

Rick from Montréal and Harry from Berlin will come this evening again to take me and Nicole dancing at the Cellar.

This is a discotheque, bar and restaurant at the corner of Connaught place. Across the grassy park of the Rambler café, in my familiar walking turf.

I had lunch there before with Arvind when I ordered my steak rare, which felt rubbery and barbarian. I could not and didn't finish it.

I also realised the full extent of Arvind's discreet horrified shock. Arvind paid for that steak, and I still wonder what part of my barbarian D.N.A prompted me to challenge this generous, strict vegetarian, mammal brother.

I pay six rupees for a night at the dormitory. Waiting for the evening, I fall into a deep sleep in one of the eight beds.

It's only three rupees to sleep on the floor.

When I wake up, I am rested and ready for my next life.

I first see Mrs. Kolaco, a Goan catholic lady, she wants to talk to me. This shrewd opportunistic lady nags me for my record player. She wants it for her business, and she also wants to buy it for a very low price.

I refuse, she insists.

I get out of the guest lobby, all huffed up, I slam the door. I wander around Connaught circus and enter the Indian coffee house.

This giant aquarium for humans is bustling with Indian businessmen milling around.

A dozen waiters in white uniforms with orange and green turban caps take orders, clean the tables, and bring tall glasses full of drinking water. The busiest and favorite hangout in New Delhi.

With one or two hippie clusters noticeably attired on adjacent tables. They all stick out from the elegant Indian crowd.

In 1969, we are, memsahib first, and treated with respect.

Here we can get the novelty of American style food like hamburgers with ketchup. I sit at a hippie table. I dive in, with my brotherhood company.

I am merging again with my own kin after soaking in two months of Indian immersion with the welcoming super keen host country.

I feel saturated and need to wean myself from it. I got a good inkling of the divergences. I eagerly embrace my crossing back at the meeting point.

I know now to isolate myself. I belong to no one. I can merge with my kind, be together and aloof.

I decide to reach for the leftovers on the table. I drink a half-full glass of iced coffee and eat the rest of a hamburger somebody left.

I am now with the people who have discovered that money is nothing and surviving is what everyone must learn.

To introduce myself I ask about New York Nicole from Haiti, did anyone see her today?

There sits a rare Indian hippie, who speaks nicely to me and makes me feel comfortable in my chair.

This is Sami; a tall, seventeen-year-old, Bengali pretty boy from New Delhi. He has long dark curls, clear matte skin, eager light brown eyes under rounded brows and soft fine features, with a smiling mouth well defined.

He wears colourful brocade trousers with stripes and a cream white cotton lightly embroidered Kurta shirt. He carries with him his guitar in a case still loosely strapped on his shoulder

Sami is just breaking up with his English rock and roll band, and now going solo looking for a new group. One day soon he hopes to make a living by singing his songs and playing his guitar.

He studies design at art school but rock and roll music is the life he has chosen. Sami does not care about money, and he digs hippie life day by day.

We chat and I tell him I am staying, since yesterday, at Mrs. Kolaco's. It not so far, but I don't know my way back to the guest house.

Sami propose to accompany me there, he knows the way very well, and it's not so far.

He escorts me and wants to listen to my records. I got The Beatles, The Creams, Ray Charles, Jimmy Hendrix and the Doors.

First, he sings me a poetic song he wrote, his voice sweet and a tad fierce. He plucks his acoustic guitar.

In the lobby we chat and listen to the music for quite a while. Sami's father, retired from directing the railway stations lives no more. Sami likes to be free and unsupervised, his mother and brother let him be a hippie.

They live on Connaught place nearby, he still needs some time, to see his mother and his brother, for a helping hand out and proper food in the comfortable orderly Brahmin house.

At that exact moment Sami is getting bored. He puts on his gears and fiddle with his guitar case strap thinking to split. Nicole steps in with her two friends, Rick and Harry.

Sami decides to stay.

Harry, the smaller guy is faery-like, bleached and bronzed by the sun with even straight hairs whipping his collar bones like sun rays. He's got clear insolent forget-me-not blue eyes. He addresses me with a piercing trumpet voice barking English with a charming Berlin accent.

He wears blue and yellow striped trousers and a lapis-coloured shirt. He shows to be the aggressive leader of the two bare foot guys.

Rick appears standing tall and cool beside him. Definitely not the front man. He wears his longish wavy brown hair sun bleached half down his neck, he has a roman classic face and a roman nose. His two fleshy lips have a dimple at the meeting and he's got a rosy, evenly sunned complexion.

He vaguely reminds me of something, I guess he looks a lot like the roman centurion I made a copy of for my first modeling assignment.

He speaks little with a muffled voice a bit deep, and just for me he spells a few relevant French words, lazily steering me with a good accent.

He's got blue and slow eyes and they are exactly the colour of the blue glass bead mala I have around my neck.

He wears a Kurta with assorted pyjamas. Cream colour covered with pink roses on green stems with thorns and leaves and no shoes.

Rick seems to have seen me before I did.

I am still a grazing unicorn in my head, not sure to be ever able to get out of this interesting point of observation.

Do I need to step in the arena with the lions and shed a bit of skin to feed them?

I remove my mala of hundred and eight blue glass beads for Rick, and I put it around his neck as a gift.

Suddenly Sami decides to stay. The five of us smoke chillums, listen to the music, and communicate animatedly. We are a well assorted bunch in our colourful garb, all harmonious and disparate authentic hippies. We prance our mindless distinct flair on this sunny stage of the world none of us played before.

We dominate our stage; we are not conformist and ordinary. We are consulting with all new beauty, self-reflecting to be.

Since Matala, Nicole has transformed. She has discarded the well ironed tourist look I did not like.

Her afro hair, way longer, spike her halo, just like on Jimmy Hendrix's poster.

She wraps herself with a majestic negligence in her lavender fully embroidered cashmere shawl filled with milli flowers. Her emerald green eyes a beautiful surprise with her dark skin.

She wears Tibetan bracelets woven of three metals copper, silver and brass, studded with amber, turquoise and coral beads. They tinkle on her delicate wrists.

Nicole carries herself lightly and gracefully. She has no more traveler's checks from her savings of steno typist work.

All is spent now.

Rick studied for a year in general art and Russian at Sir Georges William University of Montreal. He had a summer job working the baggage ramp for Air Canada. A hired student, obviously chosen because his father was a senior flight instructor for twenty-two years in the company. He made enough money to travel for at least a year.

Rick's friend, Mahoui, disappeared on the road in Istanbul. Rick got a bit of financial assistance from Mahoui's worried parents to locate him. Rick was going anyway.

Rick's passport picture in New Delhi

He flew for free to Paris with his Air Canada family perks. He met with his elegant friend François to enjoy a great time at his posh pad in the Luxembourg gardens.

Rick and François met when Rick was learning French at summer school in Neuchâtel, Switzerland. They became good friends when Rick was sixteen and broke his leg skiing that first winter. It was a triple fracture, hard to mend, necessitating physiotherapy.

Rick had no patience for that. He walks a bit funny now since that leg grew crooked when he was still growing.

Rick went on the road and soon found Mahoui who was experimenting with junk at the Old Gulhani hotel, where Rick got his first experimental fix of morphine from Rasputin. Then Rick and Mahoui went on the together just like everyone here did.

We are all interested by our various synchronised story. Rick traveled with Mahoui up to Rishikesh. He got hepatitis and got cured at the mission hospital in Massurie hill station, where Mahoui's auntie was a missionary doctor.

Rick ate papayas and bland food, rested, got well and then went to Goa with Mahoui. Mahoui went back to Canada to his parents.

Rick went to Colva beach with a bunch of hippies all staying for free at Eight Finger Eddie's house, one hospitable groovy older guy.

Harry was at Eddie's Colva house. Rick and Harry went broke and were too hot in Goa. They got a car ride to Bombay and started begging on the street.

That is how they met Nicole and Nicole paid for their train to Delhi. They live in a guest room nearby, waiting for their money.

Everybody's plan is to go cool off in Kathmandu, where Eddie already is, for the next hot month and monsoon season.

Eddie does not go back to the west, he loves this lifestyle, all is cheap and great, the weather is perfect, he goes back and forth from India to Nepal since 1965.

Sami, my new friend, the budding Bengali rock and roll star, was inspired and knew all about Freddy Mercury, born like him, to Indian Brahmin parents in Calcutta.

Sami would prefer to be taken as a mysterious foreigner too. He does not feel too comfortable with his Indian identity. He is tall with fair skin, pretty, anxiously vain. Checking in the mirror and people eyes, if he can impersonate himself convincingly.

Sami is dropping out of art school, freedom seeking, getting incorporated with us beautiful hippies and the real rock and roll musicians.

At seventeen he is dodging the secure dwelling at his mother's and elder brother's, always accessible and not far, right here on Connaught circus.

Helpful so he gives me assistance, but needy, and he wants to share all I've got. He is a charmer, and we bond.

Berlin Harry was kicked out of his divorced mummy's protecting care, for objecting arrogantly to a good providing German stepfather he did not choose.

Since then, Harry has learned to hustle and survive from boys and girls on their own in Berlin. Just before he started his overland trip.

I observe so many experiences and commit to these chance heroes on my adopted hippie journey.

Together we are getting aware of being on our own. We are hopeful, the vibe is great. After a complete financial analysis, my stash of three hundred rupees is a considerable revelation.

We can celebrate our new friendship, and start spending it, at the Chinese restaurant, before going dancing at The Cellar this evening.

Rick waits for his money from Montreal at the American Express. He checks every day. Harry is waiting for his money from Berlin. They don't show any anxieties about having no cash, they convince me not to worry and not to cling to my pennies.

With my pitiful stash it so much more exciting to enjoy blowing it, while it lasts. All together we share a week of maximum pleasure, living it up.

I do feel that, and let's have fun. Anyway, it could not last long before I must learn to survive without it. The sooner the better.

So, we walk for dinner at the Chinese Buffet. I sit between Rick and Sami for this first celebration, with Nicole and Harry on the other side. We eat and I pay the bill and then we go dancing at The Cellar.

I dance again fluttering between Rick and Sami and after one hour at The Cellar Nicole and Harry are gone.

The three of us, all exalted in communion, smoke joints between the dances and drink lemon sodas with a pinch of salt and a pinch of sugar.

Spirits only up and rising, after midnight the music fizzles out and we walk together back to missis Kolaco's dormitory.

We spend the rest of this memorable night on the balcony, revealing to each other what's on our minds and smoking my marble chillum.

We don't fall asleep, but we groove on each other and finish the night the three of us lying on the floor, me in the middle of the two sighing smitten guys. Without a wink of sleep.

At nine o clock sharp, Mrs. Kolaco is doing her rounds, collecting the nightly fee from everyone. She demands twelve rupees from the boys who did not sleep but are still lying on the floor.

Both Rick and Sami are laughing, teasing her.

With despising air, I pay my six rupees for the bed I did not use. I decide to leave this place after my shower.

I refuse, again, to sell my music to Mrs. Kolaco. She insists to offer me a very low price. She begs me, she bugs and pesters me. I get out of her clutches.

Rick proposes me to move in the room he shares with Harry, on credit. Rick and Sami carry all my stuff in one suitcase and one bag.

We leave the guest house. I slam the door!

We walk, it's not far. I'm welcomed by Harry and Nicole joyous greetings.

We share a double order of breakfast, added to the mounting tab of three weeks. After a digestive walk to the Luna Park on Connaught circus we buy a ride on the Russian Mountain.

I pull the tassel and win a packet of Mary biscuits and a packet of Panamas cigarettes.

We get back to the private room. The landlord lives in one other room across us and beside his kitchen. He greets us to ask for his money.

He is owed three weeks of lodging plus food with room service and laundry, and we are four now instead of two. More work and expenses for him, he would like to see some cash, due now.

Rick and Harry must negotiate to gain a little time, the money is coming very soon, give us a little time.

Nicole first, then my arrival with luggage made him impatient. Only money can pacify him now.

We are not going to give away to this man whatever is left of my three hundred rupees, it is not enough to pay for the old bill, he must wait until the boy's money arrive like it was agreed.

The last of my money is for fun.

We climb into the five-seater old Harley Davidson three-wheeler bike taxi, a fast, noisy, exhilarating ride to Old Delhi Fatherpuri Channi chowk.

The hang out is the Crown hotel.

We climb all the way upstairs to the roof terrace where there is a couple of big rooms filled up with hippies and junkies. On the tarred roof there is a big empty terrace beside the cheap dormitory.

I see monkeys, pigeons, crows, cats, rats and chipmunks running. The colourful paper kites on all level of cascading flat roofs, and many people private gardens and courtyards, displayed to us; up above.

I see the city maze and the vultures circling around the Parsis towers, not far.

I can smell the smoky kerosene, the sooty city and the hot melty tar of the deck roof.

In the mid-afternoon, we hardly cool under the slow spinning fan inside our new friend's Mascot's room.

We hang out with Mascot and his pale mongrel dog that rowboat and jump on the bed when Mascot calls,

"Flash!"

Mascot looks a lot like his dog. He is a French junkie, our best friend hosting us at the Crown.

In that room Sami is inspired and he pulls his guitar from the case and tunes it for a long while then sings his melodious rock and roll compositions, plus, some hits.

We take place on Mascot bed to share a chillum with Angelo the pale Italian artist, facing us, all reclined on his bed under the creaking slow spinning fan.

Angelo draws beautiful pictures, Odilon Redon style.

He could make a good living doing portraits, but he is not really interested, and with Mascot, would rather play Russian roulette with his needle between life and death.

I think that is too bad they may prefer to die before they really grow up. Why is that a choice?

All of them here are at least occasional junkies, take a fix. It seems a good answer to every question they ever asked.

Rick, Harry and Sami take a fix, to be or not to be.

For all the love I received and hope to give, I drew the line. I want to be awake and avoid numbing.

It became clear to me now, the irresistible vibe calling for me. It's Rick, drawn to me.

In Rick and Harry's room, there is just two beds Harry and Nicole in one and Rick and in the other, two feet away.

In the intimate confine of our single shared bed, I am fighting a losing battle sharing the irresistible feeling.

I still maintain a weakening resistance, tempted, willing, but refusing to be conquered in a public show.

There are mental and physical fluids seeping between us. We are merging. There is no doubt, it is no cerebral convoluted fancy.

Each of the two of us, lost our footing on the world as we knew it just before. We are fusing in that magnetic field.

I resist, procrastinating firmly the special coming moment, the nights are exhausting us with battling and teasing exacerbated wanting.

Nothing left but that irrefutable intensity. I never knew how strong it pulls, that is love calling for me.

I am ready now...I know it's real, and I want it. I do not understand why it's so difficult.

We spend our afternoon at the Crown and with Mascot and Flash, I wait alone for Rick gone to score with Harry

Mascot managed to borrow five rupees. He really needs a fix. I am reluctant but give, no one can't afford this need.

We still enjoy dwindling fast rupees for a few days. The landlord turns aggressive on our trail pestering us, impatient for his due.

***

All the connecting dots the elements that make time count, to sort things exclusively Rick and me, in the life bubble rising and not bursting.

On such a high journey to that remote planet of love we hover above ground, riding that magnetic unrestricted burst of desire, split in two within us wherever we are.

We are disconnecting, seeing the rest of this unimportant distant world spinning away from us.

Any fancy call I had attempted to answer, just a trial fantasy which never happens. No one can even imagine, before falling in it, what love is. Nobody can sleep in our ardent state, and everyone is watching us jealously.

When we guess, Harry and Nicole are sleeping, we start making a little noise, getting closer, and that is enough for them to wake up complaining.

We must wait.

It happens in the morning when Nicole and Harry gone early out, leave us alone.

It is a discreet major change.

***

The landlord is fed up waiting for his due, he gave us the ultimatum to pay now or get out now, and he locks us out, with our belongings inside, as a guarantee.

That same night we climb into the room through the rear window and steal away with our luggage, abandoning the pair of my worn golden sandals.

I've got no more money. I am happy to walk bare foot.

We pile up in two rickshaws to Defence Colony with Sami and Scottish Edward to pay the fare, Nicole, Harry, Rick, and me.

Sami got the key to one small unfinished flat where we can stay until the end of April. A swift move in the night, Sami leads us to one unfinished modest building with only two floors.

On our upper floor there is no water and no electricity. There is a single bed and barely enough floor room for all of us, including Sami and Edward our new Scottish friend waiting for money, who had enough to pay for the rickshaw.

Rick and I are now the obvious couple. We share the creaky bed. Everyone else shares the cramped floor.

The Chokidar stays on the first floor. His flat has got water and a shower in it. He's got a second key for our lock, and if he is in the mood, will allow us to take a shower in his flat.

Beggars can't be choosy, for free, we take it.

We have a water closet with no water and one empty bucket and a lota. There is a water fountain with a hand pump down our street. We can manage.

I am now totally absorbed in my story with Rick, I try to keep it cool and together with the rest of life and every other member of this den.

We must relate like solo individuals, apart from our love-struck core. Every morning, Rick rekindles his bachelor quest for what is needed for the day, with Harry they hitch to New Delhi.

We will meet at the Indian coffee house early on, or later at the crown.

When Rick leaves, I stretch and enjoy the extra bit of room, then clean and tidy up.

Nicole and Edward go hitch their way. I linger with Sami. To take a bath, dress up, and listen to my music or Sami's songs.

We both take time not rushing enjoying the inspiration, getting ready.

Sami looks after me, he is sweet and considerate of practical needs. He won't let me get lost in this place unknown to me. He will find food, roti and dhal and chai.

He will talk sweetly to the Chokidar in Hindi, so we can take a shower.

In case the Chokidar is pissed off and won't open his door, Sami will go and get a bucket of water at the pump. If we are not in a rush, he will come with me to the pump, and I will take a bath in my petty coat like I see all the poor Indian woman do.

Nicole is not happy surviving this way, she rather goes back to Goa, and endure the heat with a breeze on

Calengute beach with a fan and the comfort of Susan guaranteed financial assistance.

She split the scene after three days. Edward got his money and split too.

I stay, I don't mind having no money.

I love the unexpected day by day, minute by minute, to dive in and survive.

I am here now the only girl, one woman, lover, sister.

Every one of my three guys company has a complaint with me, they left their mother, they had no sister before, they rebel at my female service, including Rick who feels depleted involved with me losing his precious cool personal energy.

That is the fundamental difference between the sexes, humbling me down to reality.

Rick says I should share myself equally since I am wanted by everyone here, he adds I should act like a hippie if I am one.

I don't care about this paradoxical bigotry. I'm still in my center, woman, hippie, but I am not equally involved with any of them.

I will not trust my body and soul to more than one other. Even Rick is bluffing, testing and confusing me. With him only, I know we can be a pair.

I do love Sami, as my brother, and I am wildly amused by Harry wicked outrageous arrogance, they will have to find their own sex mate.

If they feel lonely, my new brothers, so be it, I am not the one easy opening sister to screw them all.

Now all my money is gone. If money is nothing, I must try my own way

Harry is blaming me for disturbing his boys only happy survival team.

The two guys are putting me down. I must show them what I can do, now that all the money is spent. I must participate in procuring what we need as a group.

Rick and Harry suggest I try begging like they do in the street.

This is a giant step, a blow to my obvious high and mighty and so far, lucky self. I experience a moment of panic.

Begging, like prostitution, is not an option for liberating me. But, for my love I must try anything to be on his level. It's a challenge. I try my luck.

I walk alone down the corner of Channi chowk in my red sari, all made up with my snake and jewelry, jiggling my silver bells anklets I plant my bare foot at the angle of the street's narrow sidewalk.

I put my hand out and ask the first passer by some help. Like I have seen so many Romani doing at the church front where I come from.

I don't feel right about this. I am embarrassed and ashamed. I don't fit the part. I can't really be doing this, it's a farce. I tell my short story to a sarcastic charitable investigator.

The first guy throws me twenty-five paisas, and the next one fifty paisas. Ten minutes later, I go hide in Rick's arms. I hand him the seventy-five paisas proving I tried.

He soothingly tells me, "Just do what you can do!"

I go back to the roof three floors upstairs and look down at Rick and Harry's silhouettes standing at the corner of Channi Chowk. I can see them from the window, sitting on the bed between Mascot and Flash.

Ten minutes later Rick and Harry enter the room, cheerful, each with ten rupees bill they just hustled.

You know!

And we run down stair again to eat a plate of dhal fry, with chapatti and curd and a pile of white rice, and achar pickle. All nutritious and pungent, the Indian staples are cheap and best. And a sweet and spiced chai.

With twenty rupees we have enough for food, cigarettes, bidis and dope. We pay for a Harley ride to New Delhi for kulfi ice cream at the Rambler café, plus samosas and bananas and tangerines at the street stall.

We go home, hitch hiking to Defence Colony. We are bare foot in the inflexible mounting heat.

We want to go north soon to cool off in the Himalaya Mountains of Kathmandu. Every day we speak of what we will do in Nepal.

I want Rick to stop fixing opium or morphine. Rick says it's helping how he feels with the heat now, he says he will stop in Nepal, and it will be easy and cool.

Sami prefers Methadrine or Coke.

Harry takes everything and fuck everybody he can put his hands on.

The boys fix mostly in the hottest hour, in the afternoon, at the Crown, everyone in turn on display.

It is a casual affair, step by step, not hiding from me or anyone. A ceremony for their body experience.

I always look at Rick. I watch him. I watch his hands. He puts the stuff in the spoon to cook on the flame of the candle.

He knocks off the glass bubble at the top of the vial of distilled water. He adds the water in the spoon, let it bubble then cool.

He fills the syringe through a cotton wool filter.

He takes his belt, tie his arm just before the elbow and squeeze the belt to make the vein pop a little, and then carefully aim the ready syringe and shoot the mixture until it's all empty. A tiny drop of blood shows when he pulls it out.

He smooths the mark by rubbing it gently. I can see his pupils clearing when the flash hits!

Depending on the injected matter, it could be warming, speeding, or canceling any feelings. Here is the comfort zone of addiction. This, I don't emulate but I mind, it feels unclear and sordid to want out.

I am just looking at what they do for a kick. I could do worst to understand, I am in love, and I feel lucky with what we've got. Friendly support, a flat to stay, music to listen to, we eat and drink and sleep.

Due to the surge of our romantic life, Sami and Harry are feeling neglected on the back burner. We are trying to get more intimacy in the middle of the sparse common space.

We need to steal our time. We use any closed door to hide the luxury no one else can have with us. Like Juliette and Romeo, we must avoid proximity with each other.

We count on divine destiny. We are compatible and opposite. Rick blindly perceives and I see him expanding me.

Together we fill the world at play.

We step into the Indian coffee house. Rick asks me who is here. I can be his eyes and him my focus. Something is perfect between us. He looks at me, I look at him, we are a wonderful pair, and it is reality.

Long before we met, I dreamed of flying in a cathedral with him, creating outer space.

It is taking us time to relate, acknowledging imperfections, compensating mutual handicaps, developing patience and tolerance.

When Sami and Harry finally fall asleep, we approach each other quietly and to be sure no one sees us we close our eyes.

Rick goes away with Harry, from the flat, in that boy's club I do not fit in.

I stay behind with Sami.

I recreate, lightening up the trace of my lover. All concentred in the mirror. I paint a vivid cobra on my brows, my nails, my eyes. I do my hair, dress up and renew flair with inspiration.

Sami do his own fastidious grooming.

Sami takes a long time to get ready. He is obsessed with all details of his appearance, he put kohl in his eyes, and may want polish on his nails if we have time. He is impersonating a foreign artist from South America. Sami dreams to get out of New Delhi.

We are not ready to go out the door until we both shine. Then he goes with pride to gets us a good breakfast on credit. And we close the flat and hitch together to New Delhi. Sometimes he does not take his guitar.

I am comfortable with Sami he is considerate and attentive to all the details, unconditionally loving and not in a competition with Rick, my lover man, and his friend.

He may feel some melancholy at not being the one chosen, but he gets some satisfaction from my sisterly appreciation.

Sami is a whiz at getting credit and gets us all welcomed for a feast in many restaurants where he knows the food is all right. We can only go once without paying. I harness mixed scruples I can't afford.

Most mornings Rick lingers around with me, until Harry whisks him away.

Rick and I we have left the creaking bed to Harry alone, now threatening on top. I am in the middle cuddled with Rick on my right. On my left, lays Sami at the respectable distance of ten centimeters.

It could be all cool, but Machiavellian Harry menace coldly to rape me while I sleep. That scenario cannot last any longer. I know now how easy it is for me to survive alone.

Four of us is too much responsibility. There is no power and no fan, and no water. To keep our brains cool, we can only speak about the mountain and dream cool dreams in the stagnant increasing heat.

We are going away from here to the next Shangri-La, it will require a boost of fortune to leave Delhi.

First Rick needs three hundred rupees to recuperate his passport and visa at the Nepal embassy before we can go.

What strategy will yield the cash?

Rick and Harry can put a bit more time at lucrative panhandling.

I do my part around the emporiums on Connaught circus. I demand ten rupees in advance then I tell the short version of my fascinating story to any Indian who like to have a drink with me.

If a cruising car stop for me, it is twenty rupees for all people I met previously.

I establish my strict tariff, for an appearance, a coffee, ice cream or lemon soda with me at the Rambler establishment where my Indian customer can be seen as a good friend of mine.

That is what I devise for earning, and so, I do my share for the common pot.

Sometimes a couple of the Singh's friend insist to take me to dinner at a club in a five-star hotel. After two hours in that lobby, eating, dancing and talking about nothing, I get bored and anxious to go back with my hippy crew in our squalid personal space.

I get drained by the respectable drinking businessmen showing off with me. They are not overly generous with the little cash they relinquish.

Only Sami can extract some real money from the rich Californian hippies. They find him groovy, and they love to pay for our group dinner.

Sami's unassuming charm and persistent generous humility has produced hundreds of rupees from the Californians.

In the late morning, Sami and I, all dolled up to our maximum, hitch a ride to Connaught place then start walking barefoot through old Delhi.

We savour our time grazing our gifts from the fruit vendors gaping at us on our way to the afternoon rendezvous at the Crown.

We appeal to each fruit and fresh vegetable stand on the way, eyeing our wanted backsheesh from the distracted curious merchants. They give us apples from Kulu, some mango from Goa, grapes and tangerines from Bangalore, sweet gooseberries, white daikon radishes, refreshing cucumber, and red, purple and orange carrots, all the way to the Crown.

I get from shampoo, soap, laundry soap and toothpaste from generous Helen. She has a private room beside Mascot's. She is a friend and a survivor, she gets loads of extra toiletries in the five-star hotel rooms where she entertains an Indian businessman, glad to pay her fee.

***

The barber is an affordable beauty parlour for men. For one rupee the boys get a shave, and up to three for the deluxe treatment, which includes a head massage, shampoo, and perfumed lotion. It's a relax pampering for each man's day.

Of course, I prefer imported cigarettes. I get a packet from any host inviting me for meals and refreshments, and a ten-rupee bill.

We are the junior embassy on a drifting raft, we represent the valuable foreign exchange.

It's already the end of April a time to clean up our act and gear up for the next move. I get the urge to do all our laundry since the two weeks we are without water in defense colony.

Laundry is a big project in the heat with only one bucket. With Sami's help we bring it all to the fountain in the street.

In the inferno under the blasting sun, we get through the whole pile. Wash, rinse and dry everything draping it bit by bit on the fountain. Many locals halt to contemplate our feverish activity.

Three hours of hard labour, then we carry it all clean and dried back to the flat, furious and exhausted. But we did it.

We speed up to get ready and hitch to town, it is getting late.

Without any shoes we all have multiples cuts and sores on our feet. We constantly hit our toes, scrape our heels and bump the sides of our feet. We get used to all that and develop leathery skin and our feet are not burned by the hot asphalt.

I get beautiful sandals offered to me, but now I enjoy walking bare foot.

On the day that we washed the laundry, when we reach the Crown, I write an aerogram to my parents.

I have no shoes, that's like a joke, but I am sure they will think it's a serious matter.

I tell them I have no money. I don't want to come back. I met someone. I need to go to Kathmandu, to the roof of the world. I could use some financial assistance. I put the aerogram in the post box near the Crown.

We hitch home to Defence Colony. It's later than usual when we reach the flat. With the light of a torch, we open the lock. I notice the sorted laundry has been moved.

On further inspection, my electrophone, the records, and Sami's guitar are missing.

The one and only suspect is the Chokidar who's got the double of the key.

Sami and I yell at him. We demand he give us back our things. Suddenly, he understands no English and no Hindi. I get mad and drag him to the police station

This is one outrageous theft. I must follow the matter by a formal accusation. I have no delusion about recovering our valuable music, it is already sold for sure.

I know it's the Chokidar, but he may not even admit it if he gets a good beating from the police, now already waving their big lathis with glee and menacing him.

It's entirely up to me, and for sure he could use that good beating. He deserves it.

My compassion prevails and the fact that a tiny doubt lingers about his crime. We have no proof. He let us take many showers in his own bathroom, we never had any money for him. I am not letting the cops beat him.

He won't go to jail on suspicion with no formal complaint. We let him go, and all of the party goes home separately.

We swallow the blow, we come down, and we go to sleep.

Sami, Rick and Harry are all agitated about me calling the cops, we have illegal dope on display, no money for backsheesh, and we squat this place.

Next blow, when we come home that evening there's an extra lock on top of the one we've got a key for. Apparently rent on the flat is due now. It's the first of May.

We have to beg the uppity Chokidar to let us sleep the night and take our stuff away and clear out next morning.

That's it, our last night in Defence Colony.

Rick has chosen my company; he gives me all the money he made that day. Time is up, time to separate from Harry. I am now Rick's girlfriend in function.

We are the last ones to leave the flat, Sami went to his mother's home feeling smaller without his guitar.

Rick and I rent a private room with private bathroom, for ten rupees a day at the Crown.

For the first time in my whole life, I am moving in with a guy who is my lover.

Both of us are timid and uneasy about this, we are sure we want to be together, but we are not at ease with this intimacy.

We have a room, we have the key, we have a bed, and we want to make love in it. We can be private and a couple.

It's too obvious, and too easy, we want it, but we are embarrassed and mixed up. Still like complete strangers, paralysed at the bottom of our story, not yet able to be ourselves with each other.

For Rick's passport and visa, he needs three hundred rupees. He wants to sell my things including my suitcase, I allow that and choose with him what I can live without.

I wait impatiently for him in our room. He comes back with forty rupees for the lot, it is not enough. He gave my worn-out silver boots to Shorti, his opium dealer at the red fort. Later, I see Shorti strutting proudly in my boots, way too big for him.

We spend all he made in two days. Then we have to hustle. We will need to pay each day. Again, and again.

We need a change; I get impatient with our clumsy couple. We make many friends at the Crown, the ones I like are not the ones he like.

We are quite different, but we do understand each other. And we laugh together.

I definitely favor the rosy side of life. Rick listens with interest to gossip and any prediction of imminent doom, can occupy his mind. I can't believe he is considering believing any of that crap.

We get more of Helen's extra shampoo, tooth paste and soap, she is making a good living selling her body to Indians who can afford a foreign girl. Receiving soap from her taught me not to judge hastily and it expanded my scale of tolerance.

My friend Helen gets ashamed about her way of making a living, it was easy for her. But she suddenly lost her self-respect comparing herself to me.

We talk about it and decide she must retire and try another profession.

Since she loves brass jewelry and collects it, I suggest she start her new business with that. She will probably earn less, but it will be a start.

All can change. She has a good head for trading.

Helen bursts into tears. She will go for a retreat in Shivananda ashram in Rishikesh, she offers to pay for us if we go with her since she still has lots of cash.

I only want to go to Kathmandu with Rick.

So, Helen put a brass swastika mala around my neck, and I give her my mini Mexican pleated dress splashed rainbow colour since Jaipur Holi.

We hug and she leaves.

Rick succeeds to get the three hundred rupees for his passport and visa, but he still must wait for his money, and he won't make a move before he gets it.

I am restless. I am fed up. It's too hot for hustling in New Delhi.

We sleep for free in the loft of Subash, an artist from Paharganj that we met with Sami. Anyone can stay in his workshop, somewhere in the maze of old Delhi.

Subash welcome us and shows us where to clear a minuscule space in the tiny, crowded refuge hosting a dozen of hippies, half of them moaning junkies in need of a fix.

We clear our place to lie between a cardboard folder and a bag of clothes. We spend a long night, not sleeping in the turpentine fumes.

Next night, we try the Sikh temple on the marble floor with no blanket under a mighty spinning fan.

I catch a cold.

We go back to the Crown. Rick must stay until he gets his cash. It's not easy being in love for us.

He told me he loves me. He was sincere and matter of fact about that, I accept to love him too.

But love did not make me patient in the heat, it's not easy, and I feel paralysed depending on his inflexible reason.

I have to get my expectations happening on my own before I learn to compromise. I need to leave Delhi now.

In Helen's old room, we have a new neighbour, his name is David, he is a rugged looking guy who just got out of the Vietnam War.

With his severance money he is on a personal mission to discover India for three months, before he returns to his prairies in Minnesota.

I decide I will hitch with David to Kathmandu, very soon. It is easier to get a ride with a girl; he will pay for my food.

Nicole came back by train from Bombay. She visits us at the Crown and stays at Missis Kolaco's. She joins me to hustle some cash in Connaught circus. We quickly earn enough for the day.

I am taking the opportunity to go away with that guy David, I will be helping him, and he can help me.

I am fed up, dragging my sore feet in the heat of May to just hustle enough to survive in the endless loops between the Crown, American Express, the post office, and the Indian coffee house.

Rick is also impatient, depressed, moody, and snappy and we are not even married.

I need time on my own.

I am going down the stairs with David and my luggage

I bump into Rick, my love, going back to our room upstairs. I so much want him to be with me, but he is waiting for his money. We kiss so lightly on the lips. He goes up, I go down, and we are torn.

Early in the morning David and I lift my big bundle of things in a rickshaw out of town. To lighten my load, David stores the single draft of my book in progress and my painting kit, in the suburban part of Delhi. I don't have a clue where it is, who is the guy, his name, address or telephone number.

I don't even bother to write the address and the name of the people we leave my stuff with.

I am thinking only of Rick alone without me, so blue, like I am without him.

We keep the rickshaw going until Connaught place and I sit for coffee at the Indian coffee house. I wait for David gone at the tourist office to get a map of the road to Kathmandu.

I slowly sip my coffee and then I ask politely the waiter for a glass of water. He stares at me and ignores me.

When I toss my empty coffee glass, it shatters on the tiled floor. A surprised murmur, followed by silence greets my exploit.

White glass brings luck!

22

AGRA & BENARES

We step in a rickshaw Vespa, all brilliantly painted with Hindu gods and stylised flowers. After the Delhi Bridge the driver drops on side of the road at a suitable spot for hitch-hiking.
In five seconds, we are surrounded by one fast thickening Indian mob, which hides us from all possible rides.
Eventually a bullock cart penetrates the wall of people yammering at us and extracts us from the crowd.
Slowly, effortfully the driver coaxes the two white humped bullocks with painted red horns and the cart takes us about two miles further on our way.
We are suffocating at the noon hour, powdered by that dust coating every object.
I've got my light cotton sari on as a filtering veil enveloping me from head to toe.
We are relieved and grateful when a truck stops. We climb aboard the empty trailer bouncing behind. The truck just emptied its cargo in Delhi, will get a new load in Agra.

David installs his quickly inflated air mattress, and we sit on it like on a raft in the turmoil of a moving storm. David has tied the mattress up with nylon cords to the metal railing we hold on for dear life.

Thank God for David's guerrilla war survival skills. We sit on the mattress while the trailer rolls and bounces on the horrendous pot-holed road.

We get tossed up in the air fifteen inch up, by each chaotic jolt. One endless ride we luckily survive in one piece.

We reach Agra, the first stop. Relieved, we praise the air mattress.

In the pitch-dark night, we rest our pounded bones in the cheap trucker hotel among clouds of buzzing flies and mosquitoes. We fall sound asleep after that first part of the journey.

After two years of mandatory war service David was discharged from Vietnam. He still looks straight and hardened in his hippie disguise on his well-deserved peace tour of India.

He will go back home to the family farm in Minnesota. This army war service is his only travel opportunity.

David kept clutching his grandfather's guitar the whole way. In the hotel snack bar corner, he shows me, and anybody interested, the family pictures he has in his wallet.

That is where I write my first letter to Rick, before going to bed, glad to reach the first city on my way to Nepal. I had to leave him, but I can't wait to be reunited in Kathmandu.

We get up early, well rested after a bucket shower with a tap in the lavatory, Turkish style. We go directly to the Taj Mahal; the only reason Agra is the number one honeymoon destination in India. The city we cross is small, dirty with nothing impressive until we reach the Taj Mahal.

Better than its picture, in the middle of stylised geometrical water basins and gardens, doubly reflected in the pond. This empty tomb of eternal love illuminates the sky with its white translucent delicately carved marble lace.

Each white marble stone was imported from Carrare, Italy, where the precious white marble is the best in the world.

Shah Jehan had this most celebrated monument realised by his genial architect. Who was later blinded for his reward by this jealous master.

This abusive tyrant, eventually died a prisoner in his own palace, eating nothing but chickpeas for the rest of his life. Captive of his own son, the new Shah.

Every minute detail of the cenotaph is magnificent. The great white marble work has enchanting proportions and inlaid patterns of precious flowers of lapis Cornelia, turquoises, agate and jade and malachite, aventurine and tiger eye.

The visitors whisper quietly about the romantic landmark of the Moghul Empire.

That is all we need to see in Agra.

We skim through the ugly crowded town. Of course, there are many honeymooners first class hotels, but that does not matter to us.

Our luggage is waiting in front of the café close by the Taj Mahal where we had a copious breakfast of dhal, roti, curd, and chai.

From here we take another painted rickshaw scooter out of the city. Right away, we get a ride.

This time a truck fully loaded with hemp bags full of dhal.

The obvious place to sit is on the roof above the driver. We sit on David's air mattress in the box hemmed with iron rods to tie nylon ropes to and hold on.

We hold at the railing with a firm experienced grip. Defiling under trees canopies we can touch with our heads as we tumble on the road.

This time fearless and exhilarated, riding like on a mad elephant stampede.

The driver brakes for frequent stop discharge the allotted bags to shops all along the road.

We come down from our perch to refresh and relax our cramped, stiff limbs walk a few steps and drink a chai.

At the last stop, we stretch at the roadside chai shop. A Renault car with an open roof zoom speedily by us, come to a halt, back up and stop at our level. The girl driver asks us if we'd like a ride.

It is a French girl, her name is Christiane, she is going to Kathmandu with an stopover in Benares. We are delighted to accept the ride.

Immediately, we thank our truck driver and shift our gear and bags from the top of the truck. David deflates the mattress and rolls his ropes, we pack everything tight in the small car's trunk, and we shift ourselves gladly to this deluxe personal transport.

I am of course sitting in front and chatting in French with my new friend Christiane.

What good luck and good suspension in that new car. A four-seater, two door sporty road warrior.

Christiane is happy to take us as passengers. We are a welcome shield plus company against unwanted curiosity.

She is fed up getting assaulted at each stop by a crowd of idle curious.

She is traveling from Paris as an assistant on the film crew of *Les Chemins de Kathmandu*, a film realised by Cayatte on the scenario of Barjavel.

Christiane is an intrepid fast driver. In the new unstoppable car we zoom across villages, past cows and crowds.

We travel all night when it's fresher, and less dust falls from the open sky upon us. There's less traffic, apart from the speedy monster trucks spraying dust clouds and trying vainly to stall our speed.

At about six in the morning the sun starts to rise when we roll more slowly into Benares, now called Varanasi, but Kashi is still its holy ancient name.

David and I have already discussed to stay in the house boats, the cheapest hippie hang out on the Ganga river.

For the entering night with Christiane, we stay at the tourist bungalow. It's a hot and hazy welcome.

Benares swallow us in a spectacular blushing glow with the sun rising. We are too tired to move and gladly stay around in a comfort we have missed. A shower and a bed are rewarding luxuries quite forgotten.

There is nothing special about that place except its full of regular tourists and priced above David budget.

We sleep away the whole day's heat. We wake up just before sunset ready to discover the sacred city at its most glorious time.

In a rickshaw to the Ganga River, David and I get down at the burial gath.

Hyper grandiose, the sunset dive among fuming and flaming pyres. After glowing and lingering saffron and pink, every colour merges promptly with advancing shadow. The sunset engulfs Mendicants and pilgrims who mill about in the fainting glow, alighted with incense smouldering sticks and marigold orange flower garlands.

Lepers extend a maimed hand exhibiting what is missing of their nose. They show healthy babies, they care for them.

Proving to me, this is a lifestyle profession and a community of their own, not only a frightening and compassionate obligation for our charity.

Some hippies wander the street looking around, opening their eyes. It's all ablaze with dusty dark reddish smoke. I am impressed, in awe of that vision. A new experience of perception. About the edge I prefer to walk on. I see it here, hiding with all ending circumstances the smells of hot air saturated with smoky dust.

Dusk fades. I see white shrouds wrapped around floating corpses gliding precariously on narrow rafts. They sway in the slow current and soon sink. Tipping over Meandres to oblivion in the river teaming with many hungry creatures.

It cost fifteen rupees for the wood, to get burned on the funeral pyre.

Launched into the river by their living family members who can't afford the wood, incense, and the ghee for the fire. They sink into the river which disposes of the departed.

I see the vultures fighting on top, digging fast and deep with their crooked beaks, for viscera through the anus, and for brain through the eyes.

Is that why these birds have no feathers on the neck?

Kashi's multiplying human infestation endures and nourish this earth rich mud made of ashes and water for thousands of years.

Ganga absorbs ended desires.

Earth is celebrated in so many temples along the wide river.

All the buildings askew, confronting gravity. Inclined, leaning at extravagant angles. Shift their masses like tripping dancers on a quaking ground trampled on by the endless pilgrims reaching for their end.

That dominant saffron hue gives Varanasi its renunciate colour.

All devote India pilgrims wait for this auspicious moment, at least once, to walk and bathe into this spot in The Ganga. We step through a mass of beggars waiting for alms on one side, on the other, prostrated dying waiting for their end.

Each bather goes down, step by step, with offerings to the river, then submerge performing the ritual ablution.

They throw flower garlands and launch leaf boats with tiny clay clarified butter lamps, grains, camphor and vermillion powder.

As many rats as people scurry to retrieve edibles from the offerings. As many crows as people gather twigs and shreds of clothing and some food for their big cawing young waiting with gaping beaks. Dogs and cats etch and retrieve all edible substances.

At the bottom of The Ganga, buried in the muck, the peaceful scavenger crocodile, called a gavial, is waiting for all the rest with sweet algae.

From the fierce heat there is no respite except for the grey fresh river. We go across it swimming to the other deserted bank.

We found two high wooden carved Daws, gently rocking. Our hippie shelters. It cost two rupees per one night to make your own bed with your own bedding. On the upper, or lower deck.

From the upper deck we dive again and again. Dry after one minute and too hot, we jump again.

We swim back to the shore; we get back to the tourist bungalow and get our stuff. Mikel the Australian backpacker is coming with us onto the boat.

Christiane is already gone, zooming to Kathmandu. She did not have the inclination to pass any more time in Varanasi.

David and I want to explore more of the mysterious holy city. David, buzzing with enthusiasm, decides to rent the entire second boat for ten rupees per night.

Mikel the Australian moves in with us, still on the first leg of his slow way to China. He has no money for any luxury, and start immediately to work for his keep, Mikel lugs the luggage.

David splurges on a marble chillum and a water clay pot. I fill it up at a fountain and carry proudly on my head on the cushion of my rolled-up dupatta, just like I see all women do and the *coolies*.

We get installed with blankets and sleeping bags on the air mattress in relative comfort.

I do notice how generous David has become. He now wants his reward and expects me to be nice. It would have been nicely convenient if I did not fuss and opened my heart and my legs to him. But I won't and I will have to pay the consequences.

No more solicitous mister nice guy and I can go and sleep on the wooden bench on my own like I prefer to do.

I am one ingrate bitch, and I can keep my cold distance. David is not going to support me in style, with no extra. So that is that.

It's hot and getting hotter all the time. All I can do is dive from our deck and climb aboard the other Daw.

I am welcomed on the deck by two feverish thin French guys I met in Kabul during winter, two months before.

Such long time ago for them like for me.

Jean and Louis are on their way slowly back home to France from Kathmandu.

They had a difficult time. Getting sick from everything they choose to eat, the spicy food, the fruits, all they consumed or drank specially the Kathmandu water.

Everything gave them the shits. Everything for them has been dirty and polluted. They are barely recovering from their case of hepatitis coupled with amoebic dysentery.

Of course, they cannot stand the heat of Benares after the cool weather of Nepal.

Jean and Louis share their safe food with me. The rest of the hot afternoon we dive in and out of the Ganga holding our breath out of the sweltering heat, into the cool vital river.

At night I go back to sleep in David's boat, and I sleep on my puchinka fur with my Norwegian sweater as a pillow. I don't need David to feed me.

David, who does not hold a grudge, has forgiven me for rejecting him and reverts to a welcome neutral friendly attitude. He promises to help me when I decide to go on my way.

I go around walking with Mikel and David and we sit under the Bamian tree.

With sadhus we met in the street, we smoke a chillum with their Ganja and share our hashish. Mixed with tobacco, we all enjoy that.

The sadhus tell us where to go for Prashad. We will get free feasts in all the best temples. So many temples provide survival necessities for the pilgrims to exist here.

Everywhere I look, I merge intimately with these multiple gods and its death parading in so many disguises. No one ordinary, everyone implicated, ego-less and wanted.

Worship and death in a moment.

I am part of that flow of humans, beast and spirits, all looking for sustenance and shelter in the biggest temple calling everyone home.

That was a complete day program.

I come back home to the boat to dive in the Ganja and smoke chillums.

The boat owner invites us in his deluxe vessel at sundown around prayer time and just before Arti.

All the bells are ringing. Calling at each other, ringing shrill all around the temples beside Ganga, filling all the air. Resonating, echoing, urgent.

This is the momentous hours when the day call the night. This, a terrifying intensity I can't dismiss. I salute, I respect.

Our boat owner and our host is a priest.

At that exact moment, he applies something sticky on my brow on my wiggly snake, on my third eye.

A dab of death. Made of ashes and grease gathered by the agori after the corpses are burned, and the mourners came to clear all what remains of the departed from the pyre.

This is my hypothesis about the matter I am anointed with, something intelligent explaining my fright. I could be wrong.

Jasmin, musk, amber and sandalwood, the prevalent agarbati wafting in Benares.

To wash my clothes, I emulate the Banarasi. They do their laundry in a row around the river, before the main leaning temple. They plant their feet in the water, they dip the clothes and use the mud of the Ganja, instead of soap.

We beat the clothes on boulders right here, then lather with the mud, then twist, until all the pile is done, beat, then rinse and put to dry on the bank draped on the boulders

I start whistling the happy tune of The Bridge over the River Kwai, a little boy whistles back, and then all the dhobi launderers, start whistling.

I see a barge with a few foreigners quite naked and pale sticking out of the blue. I recognise New Orleans Fat Sammy, a lucky dope dealer I met in Delhi, a mentor of rock and roll Sami my favorite elected brother. Fat Sammy handed Sami a new guitar and enough money to go to Kathmandu. He is a generous affluent part of our family scene. We are friends. He invited all of us to great feasts with Sami, Rick, Harry, Edward, Nicole and me.

With him we went dining and dancing at the Princess and the Cellar, the only two foreign discothèques in New Delhi.

Fat Sammy has paid urgent bills for us. While he passes on his barge, I swim toward it. I climb on the barge dripping in my Tahitian bikini and emerge to greet him.

Fat Sammy ties his barge to our Daw pontoon at once. I dry up and dress and we go to the best sweet and lassi shop, to celebrate this divine chance meeting.

We gorge on sweet burfee, ladoos and refreshing lassis, gulab jamun with warm rose syrup and special masala chai. That feast with many chillums induces a comatose siesta before sunset.

With fat Sammy, we're still digesting our feast of sweets, all reclined on the roof of our hippie carved houseboat, everyone is falling asleep. I look at Kashi's stars and I think about Rick before dozing off.

***

With Jean and Louis, we are adventuring in the mysterious maze of little streets. We are a target for curiosity and this time we have to run away from aggressive beggars.

We risk into a narrow lane and get attacked with stone volleys. The beggars fear us invading their turf. They don't know what we represent.

With all my jewelry, my festive brilliant clothing and the snake clearly vivid on my alabaster forehead. Many Chant "Kali, Kali" when I pass.

I could be one momentous incarnation of the goddess queen.

Since Jaipur, I welcome her playing, feeling her place in the temple of my body. I accept willingly, honoured to host her.

I am now in the mood to walk solemn. I am the center of all streets. I won't budge for anyone, I am following my straight line, imposing my own will, churning some waves.

Around me everybody makes waves. Cows and bulls, car drivers and all the passersby. In my India. I just got the clear inspiration of divine importance.

I am unique, isolated, a treasure full of bursting love to discover and worship.

I am the incarnate illustration of destiny meeting ancient culture. A magnet for beliefs and hopes and fears.

All the dreams of knowledge and spirit of wisdom free me into this fresh chaos.

I am love, who knows love seeking love.

All is worthy. Gathering and hunting on my way, with my bare feet firmly on earth, I get it all.

Still, I must protect my choice and my desire, personally tiding up my fragile life puzzle.

This is Rick, a love so hard to get, who blew my way. Is that my link to destiny, my place in order?

How difficult it is to go alone on that liberating quest and still hold that secret choice and merge the dreams with reality.

I am the wandering sister of many brothers, but my love is hidden from them. Its remote for me to hold and cling to and carry and nurture. I must reach the next refuge with my tranquil humble and divine leader.

I must respect inspiration in its coming order.

I lost all my freedom to stay indifferent. This is when I prepare to lose all previous taboos. My work must be done, and we have time.

So far, I'm still irresponsible and childish, I want to smile and shine. I want to discard and pulverise what is in the way of my clear reflection. Rise above material bondage and despair, just like a butterfly.

Was I ever a rampant caterpillar? I am sure I enjoyed that state too.

***

I have been here and nowhere else for a while, when I meet Joe, a rugged Jewish young man from the Bronx, traveling alone for ten years.

He just arrived from an ashram in Bihar, on a charitable relief mission for the poor.

He got persuaded by the master he still follows. That the end of the world is coming on the nineteenth of September, counting on my fingers I tell laughing at him, "that's in less than three months!"

Joe is on his way to Kathmandu. On top of the roof of the world he must prepare. He has no time to waste.

I decide to go with him.

23

VASSARENA

David is generous with me as he promised.

He lays on me fifteen rupees to help me out on my way. I take it gratefully, we had one interesting time traveling along.

Joe is leaving the boat and I follow him with my big bundle of clothing on my head. I hold it together with a tensor cord and ribbons. The zippers all exploded and busted at the seams with some parts of my dresses escaping like so many colourful snakes.

It is what remains of the soft leather bag I got in Istanbul bazaar. We march away the way I came, we leave the Ganga sacred ground, and we get a Vespa rickshaw at the road to the next town to the north.

And from a curious crowd we get extirpated again by a gentle bullock slow cart. A perfectly decorated Hindu truck takes us on board for the interminable, dusty hot and tedious journey. We are let down on a road in the middle of nowhere at a railway station, this is Vassarena town.

We are exhausted. I see a village formed around the railway station. The earth is dusty, dry, and deserted with no green foliage.

There is no hint of public motorised transport. Only two travelers on bicycles speeding away from all the pedestrians.

This railway is the main city axis with all shops and houses along the rails.

When we get off the truck, a crowd encircles us. From so many humans diving into my eyes I feel assaulted by this entire inquisition I can't escape.

No one has seen anyone like us before. I feel sucked dry and weakened in one abysmal pit. I hallucinate in my unnaturally taxed mind and taxed spirit, forced to look inside all the eyes and connect.

I am too tired to hold my boundaries it is scary. I faint.

I revive a little checking out the scene with half closed eyes.

One properly suited gentleman lawyer greets us and introduces us to his credentials. He invites us to refresh, have chai and food, and rest in his town house.

We walk there and enter one of a few adjacent narrow houses. The entire curious crowd follow us, and they pile up tightly filling the lawyer's house.

I am just able to catalyse this vibration I perceive I answer questions with monosyllabic grunts. Everyone speaks to us in flowery English.

Joe too, emits monosyllabic grunts only. I am lying on a mattress, and I concentrate on the fan. This fan irritates me; it creaks noisily and spins too slow churning hot air. I concentrate and will it to stop, and start, and spins faster and it does.

I comment, "now I command electricity!"

That is funny, that is a miracle, I became a capacitor.

The lawyer with folded hands invites us for dinner at his lawyer friend's house, two doors away.

We are eating spicy mush with roti and rice, drinking warm Limca that makes me thirstier for the water in the stainless-steel cups. We get bombarded by incessant banal inquisitive questions.

We do not bother answering. We are in a trance, indifferent to too many hosts presenting us their credentials. Like a contest for us to judge how educated and hospitable they are. Their eyes looming on me like microscopes.

We are so welcome to sleep here!

But this is one accidental landing, a mistake. We are cornered in exile on this other planet.

Our host for the night keeps touching my feet. I've got white and plump feet with lacquered fluorescent pink toenails, and silver ankle bracelets with little bells tinkling each time I kick the guy daring to touch my divine feet.

He persists the whole endless, restless, annoying night.

We're served a morning chai. And we get moving at dawn, it is still almost dark, and it's hot.

I got eaten by mosquitoes at night. My skin feels itchy and hot, my feet are tired of kicking the insistent lawyer.

We go stand on the road where we came the day before. A policeman stops to help us.

He explains "There is no traffic here, and you should take the train it is the only way to get out of here."

We don't believe he's telling us the truth.

Not one single truck or car passes during the five hours of fruitless patience in the increasing heat with no shade. The concrete houses radiate more heat and dust.

Then we capitulate to the policeman's obvious advice, and we enter the train station. Joe purchases two third class tickets for the next unknown town.

We waited in vain for too long. We feel crushed, dissolving in a daze and find some relative comfort sitting in the waiting room with no fan.

On the tiled floor in the station a woman agonises, surrounded by her family. I come closer. It concerns me. I decide to help. Everyone gets out of my way, and I approach her.

The burning creature has turned purple, she is rasping for air. It is a desperate last fight.

I pull out, from my pharmacopeia, a powder against fever I mix it with water in a clay cup. She manages to swallow it.

Everyone watches expectantly.

I am galvanised, In this dangerous situation.

At this point, any compassionate intervention can help a destiny in extremis.

I retire with Joe to rest and consult the map David gave me with the fifteen rupees.

We wait for the train in a smaller more private waiting room with a lock on the door reserved for first class passengers. Five minutes later I hear piercing scream shouting,

"Kali! Kali!"

The crowd of the station is chanting it!

I say calmly to Joe, "I am sure the woman is dead! Go and find out."

Joe gets out of our remote waiting room. He comes back one minute later, bewildered, and shuts the latch on the door.

"Yes, the woman is dead."

The crowd is moving and swelling like a storm at the station chanting.

"Kali! Kali!"

They witnessed Kali give her death. Me, the white Kali!

It was coming and I did not fear it and gave ultimate energy to my departing sister

Vociferation mounts louder. Joe does panic and attempts to escape through the back window facing the country wasteland.

I severely scold Joe, and say:

"Don't be stupid".

I feel so calm and collected he listens to me. He can see I can handle it. He comes down. I know I can repel all that violent fear and the mounting frenzy.

I tell him to unlock the door while I am sitting in the Lotus Asana of perfect equipoise. I meditate on nothingness.

I am ready to face the crowd banging at the door.

Joe still is super nervous, but he obeys me when I order him to open the door.

I am ready, exuding serenity, peace and poise.

Looking at me through the open door the crowd subside. A few people enter the room silently. They are contemplating me now!

The station master announces a delay, the train will come here four hours later than expected.

During that waiting time, the Indians who come in the small waiting room are asking the usual questions.

"Where are you from?"

"What is the purpose of your visit?"

"What is your program?"

Nobody alludes to the already fading incident, they leave us alone and we rest, until the station master himself warns us of the coming train arriving now, four hours later.

I thank the station master and we leave this refuge.

I lead and Joe carries my bag. I feel my inner Shakti rising powerful. That is a trial run on containing the spirit rising.

The crowd murmurs at our passing. We climb aboard and find a seat in the third-class compartment.

With a whistle blow we travel away on our journey

I hear "Kali! Kali!" Bouncing calls all the way from one station to the next from the train getting more crowded from station to station.

We don't buy a ticket for the three days of this entire journey.

I clearly hear more voices calling the name of Kali. I can no longer distinguish my delusion from that reality.

Joe also hears it, from the churning wheels calling "Kali" all the way.

The dead woman of Vassarena is calling me that name, and more curious people are pouring in our compartment asking some more questions about me.

I do not open my mouth.

Joe does answer their questions. They feed us and buy us drinks of chai and soda water. After three days we arrive at the Nepal frontier of Rexhaul.

Before that the ticket control master asks for our tickets, we tell him we have no tickets, we are sadhus.

This response is acceptable.

We have no problem getting out of the station through a short cut. We pass many rails; someone helps us find our way to the road.

We spend our night sleeping on the ground at the border.

We cross on foot to Nepal with minimum formalities, surprised about the fact that no one bothered to check on our visas.

Here we are!

We pay in advance fifteen rupees, all I got from David for the ride to Kathmandu, all the way in a colourful painted temple truck.

We climb on the roof of the driver's cabin, holding the metal railing for dear life, like I know how to do by now.

We put all my warmest clothing on. The glacial mountain air hit us with the howling wind.

The terrain is hard to negotiate for our braving old truck, dangerously overloaded. We're squeezed up against the railing with twelve Nepalese. All of our bodies cushioning the bumps and shakes at every turn of the wheels.

Beside the maximum cargo on top, there are more passengers, five are seated inside beside the driver.

The open remork is filled up with heavy burlap sacks full of wheat plus another dozen people holding on to them.

We proceed at a snail pace with frequent stops at shacks beside the mountain mud road. The driver refills the water of the parched radiator, and we all drink hot chai with biscuits. We all pee in the filth like the other stinky humans, smelling like wood smoke and fried mustard oil in their old clothes, never washed.

We progress imperceptibly, this is time traveling through the never-ending journey of one hundred kilometers. We are frozen in time.

I am wrapped in my karakul fur puchinka with my embroidered hat, socks and gloves under my woolen shawl. Joe beside me wears my Norwegian black and white sweater.

We sit imbricated intricately with the other passengers, all sharing the remaining body heat on top. We are all a part of the brilliant ancient glorious truck which bring us higher and higher still. We sail all through the moon lit night.

24

KATHMANDU

It's dawn when we reach a timeless, feudal, magic town.

Stepping down from our truck like snails unfurling horns, we breathe the air, and leave our broken shell behind. We admire everything around us, we are in a valley on our way to inspect lodging option.

To the first hippie we see, we say we have no money. He directs us to the Quo Vadis hotel. There we be welcomed and can sleep in a bed, even if we have no money, the dormitory is free for people like us!

The perfect name of that hotel fits with us.

It's simply marvelous to pose our belongings beside a bed with a mattress stuffed with coarse bran and to refresh with a first cold invigorating shower.

Joe finds his bed in another room.

I go down to the bathing and laundry area in a roofed courtyard with low brick walls. From the courtyard I can see the empty alley leading to the street.

The hotel has eighteen rooms, including a dormitory with eight beds on the three floors. The number is written on each door. A wide wooden staircase leads to the upper floor behind the lobby.

This bare minimum place is adequate with ideal location right in the center of the old town behind Durba Square.

Everyone lodged here calls the patron Uncle. This kind, generous, attentive man lives somewhere in the hotel with his small and strong hunchback helper Ganesh, the Chokidar and room service attendant.

I enter through all unlocked doors behind Uncle. Some of my friends are here.

English Philip, who's fancied me since Delhi, stays in room number fourteen on the third floor.

He is delighted to see me without Rick and propose to guide me and buy my dinner. We can walk. Nothing is too far in Kathmandu old town.

First, we walk to Yeti Travel, the American Express center on the other side of the square. It's just across from a well-groomed park with shading trees and tall *jacarandas* in full purple bloom.

This is the King's Palace of Mahendra. A yellow and white handsome mansion, but not very imposing. I cross the road to admire it, and even pinch one of the wafting blooms of creamy gardenia with shiny dark green leaves.

I reach across the wrought iron black grate around the royal palace. The mansion is just a good-sized opulent villa. It is possible to get invited here through the embassy.

It's possible to meet the approachable Hindu king Mahendra. Vishnu's divine protector incarnate, the ninth emperor and Shah of the unconquered Nepali kingdom.

King Mahendra is happy to welcome the visit of well-behaved foreign hippies introduced through all embassy in residence. King Mahendra is an integral tolerant part in that Kathmandu scene.

A letter from Nicole is waiting for me at the general delivery post office. She stays at the Jet Sing hotel and tells me to come and see her as soon as I arrive.

Philip tells me Sami is also here. And Harry was here too, but just left for Pokhara with his new French girlfriend Valerie.

The Jet Sing is a few streets away from the Quo Vadis.

In Nicole's room, we smoke a first celebrating chillum of Nepali charas mixed with 5-5-5, American imported cigarettes free of tax here.

We are happily reunited, we made it. With Nicole, Sami, Philippe and me, we go to eat at the Blue Tibetan *thupkas*. Tibetan style unspicy noodles cooked with some boiled cabbage, onions and pumpkin broth.

I walk back to the Quo Vadis with Phillip. I meet Jimmy another guy I met in Delhi at the Crown.

Jimmy takes me to the Himalaya cold drink, just across the square and he buys me a cold lassi.

We catch up.

Half a dozen of specialized hippie hotels host most of us.

With the Quo Vadis, the Jet Sing, the Garden Hotel, the Coltrane, The Oriental lodge and the Match Box, spread around, within walking distance.

We visit each other in lobbies and dormitories and private rooms with en suite bath. Expanding our circuit to half a dozen restaurants and popular tea houses.

We also meet to listen to music, groove on and share our meals, our drinks, smokes, and pills at The Linkesar, the Cabin, the Tashi, the Ravi Spot, and The Blue Tibetan.

Plus, a couple of new age enterprising hippie health-conscious eateries. The German bakery just opened by German Woody, who makes whole wheat bread, and earthy soup with the help of very beautiful friendly Nepali boys.

The Swiss mission sponsors a dairy shop, where we can buy Nepali thick yellow curd in clay bowls, pasteurised fresh milk in glass bottles, and gouda cheese and white cheddar.

The cheese and whole wheat bread comfort food, reminds all of us of our faraway homes.

Kathmandu has a distinct perfume. With the slow burning Kush, vetiver grass, braided twist of doop, the sweet smell of hashish smoke, beedis, and kerosene stoves.

Like a herd without a shepherd, we are roaming capriciously within the perimeter, meeting at refueling stations up to Yeti Travel, including the slightly intimidating immigration office.

After a two-month initial visa, everyone needs to apply and pay a fee for a two-week extension, or a trekking permit to climb up the Himalayas.

It's just a walk away and a short climb from Kathmandu, the capital, to the oldest crowning temple of Swayambunat, the famous satellite village.

I go with Nicole and François on my first walk to Swayambunat. Nicole travels with François the short guy from Paris. Nicole has flown direct from Delhi to Kathmandu, she got paid by Missis Kolaco herself for professionally typing important paperwork.

Nicole and François are paying six rupees per night for a private room at the Jet Sing. Nicole and François decide to join me and start to save their money at the free dormitory of the Quo Vadis.

Nicole spoke to Rick in Delhi. Soon he will join us here. When she pronounces his name, my heart skips a beat.

The foot of the sacred steep hill is only half an hour promenade away across the bridge of the Baghmati River. The crowded river now low, slowly slushes between exposed boulders through Kathmandu.

The river is busy with various groups of citizens. Some washing laundry, taking bath, filling buckets, refreshing vegetables for the market or relieving themselves, in this running wet road. All of them pollute the water's muddy flow.

We cross that bridge over the sacred river of this Hindu kingdom never conquered.

Every five years, the Gurkhas kingdom hosts the massacre of a multitude of water buffaloes, and so many pigs, goats, chickens and pigeons. This carnage runs blood on the earth and into the river.

The sacrifice to the power goddess Gudimai will happen again next year to the left of the bridge I cross.

The brave Gurkhas warriors are not afraid to kill or to die. They make the greatest brutal bloody show cutting bewildered buffaloes heads with their Kukri, dull curved scimitars. For four hundred years, a multitude of Hindu pilgrims come to assist at the spectacle, held once every five years.

The ritual is due again next year. The biggest animal carnage on earth, according to the Guinness book of world records.

I first saw the Gudimai sacrifice in the Italian film Mondo Cane. A chocking documentary about the entertainment industry of human cruelty and traditional crime. A very commercial market happening in popular venues as we speak.

We march on the dirt road to Swayambunat. Soon, we see a field with an isolated museum. We enter.

It displays silver griffin, and gorudas, and minor Hindu god's effigies, of brass and stone and wood, piled on the floor behind the carved entrance door.

All is dusty in the spacious neglected room.

One guard receives us. He is not grumpy but disturbed from his nap.

We are the only visitors, free to hold and touch all brass wood and stones carving brought here from abandoned crumbled temples.

Old relics, forlorn here, without worshippers.

We progress across the empty field to a few houses in a row, the beginning of Swayambu village.

Nobody greets us but a few wandering chickens, dogs, crows and curious kids.

Through a path in a square garden with fragrant roses, gardenias bushes, and Datura with yellow trumpet. We enter on the first footstep of the monkey temple.

Many hippies prefer to live in this village. They rent a room or share a house with a Nepali family.

To get in through a minuscule carved wooden door, where everyone must pass through and bow deep to the threshold, or bang hard his forgetful head.

In and around Kathmandu, we are encircled by the gods of Nepal. Their effigies carved in stone or wood, painted and worshipped in altar, anointed with ghee, saffron and vermillion powder.

Doop is lit and wafting. Prayers are chanted at every corner of any alley. The eyes painted on all the temples are watching and challenging me.

This place may be answering me.

The Tibetan Buddhas greet us surrounded by smiling monks in saffron and maroon robes. Playful on the dharma to illumination.

One open Bazaar for Tibetan refugees to sell off relics and replicas. Hindu Buddhism products for sale with the Dalai Lama's teachings. The refugee industry is alive and doing well. They sell:

- Prayer malas made of turquoise, coral, and amber beads
- Packs of three metal bracelets
- Brass, copper and silver statues of their protectors
- Silver skull pendants and human bone trumpets
- Tibetan sweet grass incenses of Potala, Kailash, and green Tara, hand rolled, waft a sweet aroma of smoldering hay.

- Tibetan wool carpets, colourful with rainbow dragons, phoenix, flowers, wheel of life, griffins, and snow lions, thick enough to sleep on.
- Hand woven yak wool shawls, knitted with beautiful designs and wool socks.
- Tibetan Thankas, prayer flags in rolls on strong string, of course, Tibetan flags, all sizes with a rising sun and a snow leopard.

The ladies in their dark uniform dresses, over white cotton blouse, have a lined multi-colour apron with a pocket.

Around their neck, they wear their wealth in heavy ancient turquoise beads, fossilised coral and amber.

Heavy earrings distend their long ear lobes.

The refugees request donations for the good cause and call to free the exiled nation.

All the high lamas, the *Karmapa*, and the *Rimpoche*, all are smiling, convivial, and humourful.

All astute and pleasant people, able to get their maximum price.

There are hardly any motor vehicles disturbing the tranquil pace of the capital, apart from the taxis. They are yellow with black stripes all painted like tigers with black rimmed green eyes. They honk imperiously forcing their way, spewing exhaust fumes of leaded oil like the few foreign vans and cars.

Vespa rickshaws and cycle rickshaws, wooden wheelbarrows, and some trucks miraculously squeezing through narrow streets

All city traffic mainly on foot and hoofs. They all follow the bully rules, according to size.

I walk in the middle of the street, like the big bull, nobody bars my way.

City police in blue uniforms and army Gurkhas in pale khaki attend to the traffic.

A Gurkha is trained for war since early childhood.

The mercenary tribe of Nepal produce fearless fighters recruited to fight other people's wars.

They all learn from this same mountain village to fight for the Nepal kingdom, or outside of Nepal to serve the colonial armies.

They wear khaki shorts skirting wide over the knee with one assorted short sleeved shirt and a topi hat.

Uncle is a retired officer from that Gurkha tribe.

The Eden Hashish center, government shop, has got a catchy poster on the door.

The daily menu on the black board, with the price for ganja, hashish and opium.

The doctor's office is next door. This accommodating physician will inject you hygienically with your choice of drug.

Plus, in his pharmacy he supplies vials of sterile water, cotton fluff, new syringes, and what anybody wants to inject on their own.

On the way through the cloth bazaar. The black-market best rate is right here. With twenty-five per cent more exchange on Indian for Nepali rupees, and no queue or paperwork at the bank. One American dollar brings twelve Nepali rupees at the black market and eight at the bank.

We follow our hippie circuit. Everyone is guaranteed to meet everyone.

At the bottom of the Hindu Buddhist temple, we are greeted by three giant guardian Buddha's painted yellow with maroon-coloured robes.

We climb each deep step, edged by stone gods, all the way up to the stupa. We rest on top. I gape at the sacred, display under the sky. A giant silver and gold giant bell, and a huge drum.

Gods, Buddhas and their accompanying animal guardians enthroned in their carved niches between sets of silver and brass prayer wheels for everyone to spin, with a flick of the right hand, in passing.

Priest, monks, Lamas, and devote pilgrims, circumambulate, mumble mantras, and perform pujas. They offer garlands of fresh flowers, vermillion powder and saffron, incense and clarified butter, dried coconut pieces and bananas to the effigies they honor.

The eyes of the temple follow everyone on the ambulatory circuit, we spin the prayer wheels and bow, shy about stooping so low like real humble and sincere devote believers.

I observe them flexibly progressing like inch worms, diving flat on the ground in the deep prostration of supplicants, all kissing this sacred ground.

We beat on the gong at the start of the circle display beside the temple school for children monks.

Some very young and small, all dressed up in saffron and maroon robes. Their skulls all shaved like their adult master. They follow each other run and jump to their class of dharma teaching

I notice a white kid, shaved and wearing the same monk dress. His name is Ossian, the son of Angus and Hetty, Scottish scholars. He is a Lama avatar.

Circumambulating, we turn all prayer wheels, ring all bells and sound again a final gong.

We go down. Followed by many mischievous red monkeys.

We leave reverently the temple, slowing down the deep stone steps, turning up to the sky, digesting the new spiritual practice.

My first time of many more.

Now. I look!

I feel the many eyes from above, cascading down from the snowy highest peaks, crowned with ice. Glaciers lay sparkling, mellowing in the sun.

Eyes search bare rocks where the ice melts and the spring forms the icy river.

Their gaze sneaking down and looking at the greens and lichens from the shrine. They shine on me.

I feel the grace and stand joyous, blessed in pride. Crowned by cascading stupas with blinding painted eyes looking down on little me.

I am honoured and humbled, aware to be a part of this.

Nicole, François, and I are discussing our encounter with eastern rules versus those in the west. We shake our shoulders and conclude its all bullshit.

We feel safe at the Quo Vadis, and its free. We sleep on a burlap straw dusty mattress; it is what I expected at the end of the world.

We share a room in the dormitory with Jean-Pierre and Jacques, we met them at the Crown in Delhi. We are old friends by now and comfortable with each other.

Jacques is French, a gay artist of brute art. With Jacques I get into a passionate discussion about the mystic quest we are living now. We share that same hopeful spirit. We trust in divine destiny, our common ground.

After sunset, the only place to hang out is the Cabin.

There, we wait for the night, share many chillums, get stoned, and listen to the latest music on the barely audible voice of America radio.

For the new music revolution, we perk our ears, tune in to the latest hits of rock and roll, the music we identify with, lyrics we can barely hear reflecting our basic feelings.

We want, we believe, we trust all that gushing about love. That is all we can hope to gain, just aligning with our life and wanting it.

The Cabin is hidden behind a courtyard at the end of many meanders. I could never find it on my own; I need to be guided by my friends.

This smoker den is also a restaurant.

The Nepali patron, Rana, is a dynamic ruler and minister of the royal family. Rana can afford this experiment with meeting us and observing us. He provides this hidden gloomy space where so many chillums and joints are smoked in a confidential dark, hushed space.

Everybody whispers in a cloud of hashish smoke. We sip tea or drink real imported Coca-Cola. I find this atmosphere rather sinister, and the vibe is heavy for girls who like fresh air and to have fun.

With Nicole's support, I want to modify that scene in the room with the music. I plan to start to dance.

Here comes the dancing queens!

On our second evening before going out to the Cabin, we dress up at the Quo Vadis. I lend Nicole my red gypsy skirt and put my mini silver satin dress with pink piping and my fur puchinka on top.

We are prepared to start a revolution as we march through the darkening evening streets.

Bouncing through the courtyard we make a swinging entrance, irresistibly starting the dance. Willing the dim sound to be cranked to the max.

We dance and transform the Cabin right away in the first dancing of Kathmandu.

That does not go too late at night, but it is a fun change.

The previous afternoon I met eight fingers Eddie, the older guy everyone says is cool.

At the Linkesar, on the second floor on top of the restaurant, Eddie smokes beedis in the tearoom, sips chai and nibbles dry cookies. He sits cross legged, lingering in comfort on flat cushions and straw mats, surrounded with younger Hippies passing time.

Nobody speaks too loud here. Eddie is receptive, obviously interested in newcomers, he is glad to meet me.

He is about forty-five years old, long brown curly hair carefully combed, skinny with dark smiley eyes, and wrinkled matte skin, wide shouldered and tall, vivacious and present.

Not beautiful but noticeable and ready to joke with doubt about anything anybody wants to believe.

Eddie has a big, crooked nose and a pale olive grey complexion. He has a nasally but clear speaking voice and very long skinny legs and arms. He wears a kurta with a Nehru collar white with blue lines, and grey pyjama pants.

To greet me, he advances his three-finger palm like a punchy blessing,

He obviously does not take himself seriously. This man enjoys a chosen frugal experience.

With practical wisdom easily generous he jokes with this hippie entourage of fully grown, boys and girls, still confused.

Rick told me about Eddie, he stayed in his house in Colva beach in Goa with:

- Berlin Harry
- English Tobias
- Big Eddy
- Australian Peter
- English Scott
- English Peter
- German Wolf
- American Simon
- T.H.C Jack from the U.S.A
- Italian Giuliano
- English Jerry
- English Broderick
- Caribbean Felicity
- French Remy
- French Philippe
- American Mary

Eddie likes to tell jokes, and to narrate his life story.

The eldest of nine brothers and sisters, his Armenian American family with all the kids born and grown in the states.

His short career as a bass player with three strong fingers, his wife a glamourous call girl, who kept him as her house husband. A cook, writer, and entertainer, Eddie was the father who raised the baby son she had with someone else.

Eddie left America when he realised he could become free from any responsibility.

His wife paid him for all his services for twelve years, he saved the money she gave him and put all of it in a separate account, like she did with her black money, tax free in Switzerland.

Eddie does not like the word "work", and he does not think too much about people who work for a living.

Eddie is glad he avoided work and did avoid service in the Army. Thanks to his three fingered right hand, which would not pull a trigger.

Eddie lives on the interest from his bank account in Switzerland. It is not much, but enough in India and Nepal for his frugal lifestyle.

With no concern for money, politics, morality, drugs, religion, sex, or any rules of spirituality.

Eddie does not waste his time playing other people's mind games.

Eddie likes good simple food, a bit of rum, easy friendship, joking at the center of attention, listening to good music on his radio, sitting cross legged, and dancing with his arms and hands to ragas.

He renounced recently all drugs and sex, he only smokes beedis, the poor Indian cigarillo. A few strands of coarse potent tobacco inside a dried rolled betel leaf secured by a tiny, knotted tread, all handmade. The bunch of twenty sold wrapped in paper cones.

Several brands to choose from: Ganesh beedis in pink papers, 20-30 in tan papers and many others...

In the streets of Pakistan, India and Nepal the strong aroma of smoking beedis permeates all the other distinct perfumes. Amongst kerosene smoke from the cooking fire, the dried dung fire smoke, pungent spices, stench of stale urine and shit, flagrant flowers, sweet smoldering sticks of agarbati incense or doop, the smell of beedis rules.

Eddie is surrounded by his court of young followers. They all wear the same type of seer sucker cotton, pyjamas pants and kurta shirts. Their cheap rubber tongs, all waiting for their bared feet owners in front of the doorless entrance of the tearoom.

Eddie's got a dry warm funny heart like his laugh. He likes us who like him, and everyone claims he is very high.

So that evening we lead Eddie and his disciples to the Cabin. They are all dressed like him, all with the same haircut a bit long on the neck. American Jack, English Jerry and Italian Guiliano and a few others, everyone who followed Eddie from Goa to Kathmandu, follows Nicole and me to the new dancing floor.

This is 1969 in May, the first time Eddie dance with me at the Cabin.

We are taking off flying like birds. Eddie and I we like to dance extending our arms like wings in the wind on the music of The Doors, and the White Album of the Beatles.

The faint music volume, suffice for us to prance and groove. Eddie and I are the most ecstatic's dancers. Eddie with long skinny arms and legs is a great contortionist reaching for the sky. Nicole and the others are trooping along, more subdued but dancing steadily this special first time.

But soon they take a seat on the wooden bench and look at the show, of Eddie and me, dancing forever.

Anyway, we started it, the party spirit is on.

Dance is the essential ritual worship. It can be frenetic or contemplative. I am here, we are here, exuberant, oblivious to our indifferent spectators, the sedated smokers.

Dancing beats all stagnant torpor. It dissipates the clouds, it does not cost anything, and you don't need to be a specialist to enjoy it, bare foot or in flip-flops.

***

With trekking shoes, you can climb the mountain just above us, to the tallest peaks of the Himalayas. Here is the world ultimate destination for mountain climbing.

The goal for the planet's mountain fanatics, the most ambitious earth conquest with good equipment, good legs, good eyes. Up to, Everest, Annapurna, Kailash, so many mountain treks.

Available permit and Sherpa's coolies can be obtained for a fee. You will be guided and cooked for; they will carry your load and make your camp.

Not for me, you need so much money and heavy equipment, I like it spontaneous and not so difficult.

Others will succeed to make a perfect enduring hardship tool of their body, but that's not for me.

Joe is determined to go all the way to the top of the world, before the nineteenth of September.

With no training, no money, no shoes, no trekking permit and no guide, he just starts up bare foot. I don't believe he can do it, but he can try!

After three days in Kathmandu, time stands still.

I feel remote, getting no further on the road. It begins.

Sami pop up at the Quo Vadis with his new guitar. We are at the end of the road, it all makes sense, everyone who matters is here.

Sami moves in, immediately, onto the vacant third straw burlap mattress in our dormitory.

All of us are riddled with lice. Nicole and I diligently try our best to get rid of the tenacious pest.

Powdering D.T.T special hair remedy. We oil our manes with Licel, combing each other oiled hairs with tight teeth combs and crushing the tiny critters and tinier eggs between our nails.

Extermination of the hitching guest takes persistent dedication.

The invader spreads again, one single pregnant escapee multiply in the semitropical humid optimum medium in the long-haired jungle of all of us.

All this diligent poisoning and grooming and pitiless crushing should destroy a weaker species, but the mighty Nepali lice proliferate and spread again, if only one of us still hosts it.

A curly friend, scratch surreptitiously and we know the battle is not won yet.

Survival in Kathmandu is way gentler and cooler than in Delhi. The Nepali loves us like children love their new toys. They open their heart to us and since they have no money themselves, we share with them the survivor knowledge that money is nothing.

American hippies, Peace corps volunteers, world class remittance travelers, exploring baby boomer trustees, all have extra money to share.

We came overland, but they flew. We all believe the world is entering the Age of Aquarius with us as pioneers opening everyone's eyes.

Uncle, the patron of the Quo Vadis, provides for us credit, food, shelter and respect.

Kathmandu is another word for Shangri-La, a magic land with no rule totally exalting and divine.

I think I found the place to realise my dreams right now. In the street, many ceremonies, holy rituals and devote believers.

We walk again, at night, to the village and climb to Swayambunat.

Glowing in the full moon, the round top of the world celebrates in light. It flows down, touches the earth's core and showers all of us with free L.S.D for the celebration.

A wild cool fire engulfs all of us. It eventually abates with the morning light.

Back at the Quo Vadis dormitory I must push away Sami who got his straw mattress beside mine. Something to do with the full moon makes him creep into my territory and overstep his boundaries.

I stop him with sarcasm and remind him of Rick, our friend, I am exclusively committed with to be faithful to. I won't permit Sami to forget that.

Rick has written to me, he is answering my letters and coming to Kathmandu. I keep desire burning for him.

But of course, I don't mind teasing Sami a bit and keep him inspired to write a song about love. By my side he is, my selected platonic brother.

No damage done, with teasing the hormonal flow. It is so inspiring, when dominated.

We play, we talk, we dream, and we share a small and intimate respectable distance.

Fun with suspense in the dormitory, with six of us on straw mattresses in close proximity, jeering and laughing about all that noise for nothing.

No risk of confusion, I pray to keep everything simple and hopeful. I got already involved and mixed up, but not yet familiar with Rick. I wait for his presence to progress.

I will not weaken and cross the line, I hide my light in his shadow, there is nobody else for me.

Still Sami is my brother and play mate, but we are not a pair, he will find someone someday. I keep him close with Nicole watching. She criticizes me and does not approve.

For Sami, Nicole is not beautiful even with her green eyes. She is dark, too curly, and too skinny for him. An English educated Brahmin boy who prefers fair skinned girls.

Sami is fair for an Indian, he would like to pass for a foreigner, from Argentina or Cuba because of the music. Sami worries about his looks.

He says "Am I looking all right! What about my eyes?"

In this overpopulated chaos, the proven remedy, the abolished caste system, has no substitute in this democracy.

The landless and restless Europeans went to America and Australia to colonise a better place for themselves.

We come here to understand what we should do and what we refuse to do to have a life. I broke the mold like anyone of these various people, on my way to try free life.

I hope we are changing the world with peace and love. I hope the world accepts us, we share it, we are it.

Sami plays his guitar every day, gradually improving. He sings convincingly, like an inspired Bob Dylan and so many other singers I heard before.

"I want you, I want you soooo bad"

Sami write his own songs. He's got nice Moghul eyes and a clear appealing voice. He's getting taller, asserting his talent.

We all rely on each other in the close proximity of the dormitory.

We smoke hash, beedis and cigarettes. We communicate, drink chai and eat boiled peanuts and cookies and the local triangular bananas

We listen to music. We are totally occupied.

We keep happy cooped inside the hotel room before we venture out and meet others to play music with, eat and share exciting new ideas.

French Therese lives with Larry and Dany on the way to Swayambunat. Therese sings. Dany play electric guitar and sings. Larry blows the horn, the trumpet, or strums the harp. There is always a gifted amateur percussionist passing by for their jam session.

Sami plays acoustic guitar and joins the singing in their house. I dance and sing along to their music, and we smoke chillums and drink chai.

Each idle day, flows lazily, nearly empty, like the Bagmati river.

Jacques and Jean-Pierre leave the Quo Vadis to rent a floor in a Newari house they found hidden in Swayambu village behind a hedge of orange and yellow verbena bushes.

Jacques invites me to move in with them, but he does not want Sami to camp with us, Nicole and Susan are allowed.

Nicole speaks French and Susan is bothering no one, just fixing morphine and sleeping it off. She wakes up to eat, that's it. She has money to pay our share for the food, so she is cool. She pays for three burlap mattresses stuffed with straw for eighteen rupees each, like the one we sleep on at the Quo Vadis.

With all our stuff in the tiger taxi we arrive ten minutes later, it's not far.

Jean-Pierre waits for us on the balcony of a small wooden house, our new home.

We cram the three mattresses in the tiny space with no door. No extra room remains to walk, we must dive into our beds.

Jacques and Jean Pierre are in the bigger sized room with the balcony and a window.

The owner lives on the upper floor and passes through the shared living room. Five Tibetans occupy the street floor with three black goats. Everyone has to pass through our living room to come in or out of the house.

By the steep common staircase springing from the tiny carved entrance, everyone must bend their neck carefully looking where to stand to get in or out, it's like a rabbit hole with lots of traffic.

No electricity, no water, no latrine, no glass on the windows, no kitchen. All Swayambunat houses are basic shelters like this.

Walls and floors of beaten earth host flies, horsefly, mosquitoes and tiny scorpions. All tiny ferocious creatures hungry for blood.

Kathmandu in Tibetan lingo means diarrhea. Hygiene here is yet another undiscovered American mystery.

We sleep through our first night with a lit candle and a twist of smoldering fragrant doop.

We take turn to fetch water at the distant hand pump fountain, the sole supply for all villager's cooking and drinking. Never mind bathing!

Sami sneaks in at night, lonely in Kathmandu, he invades a part of my straw mattress. It annoys me in such a confined space.

I kick him out and he is forced to move with French Marie Therese, our neighbour junkie who likes him and shares her dope.

She looks unhealthy, but I am not interfering. This is not my choice.

I believe money is nothing, but I search for what energy is needed instead. I can ignore Susan right under my nose in our shared space.

We follow Sami to Kathmandu's finest new restaurant. Sami is beaming in a white embroidered kurta, with all of us spiffy, ready to feast.

Sami orders from the menu.

He checks the quality of the food, he chats with the owner, he promised to come again with his friends to his restaurant.

I take my place beside Sami, he takes care of ordering, we occupy the center table.

I'm still slightly uneasy, cringing about knowing we have no money to pay for this meal.

But I am one experienced part time International Situationist, of the Estro Harmonico, and I can handle uncalled for scruples. Individual reprise is a must, and we do enjoy this feast.

We take our time eating slowly, drinking fresh squeezed *mosambi* pale orange juice, savouring every pungent bite. I indulge in a banana pancake with chai for dessert, steering further guilt into my catholic crusader heart.

Sami takes care of the bill, reassuring the restaurant owner about the accidental lack of funds we are experiencing this moment.

The hopeful patron shall be for sure paid later tomorrow, or the day after. We will come back and eat again here, maybe as soon as tomorrow, when we get the money, already sent, at Yeti travel. Thanks for the outstanding meal!

We depart easily from the table through the door, to the street, all together seven of us.

I jeer, casual and easily guiltless about our day-by-day survival. By now I should be liberated, but it takes some more time to flex the honesty rules.

Each day brings hoped for fulfillment.

I get food, shelter and even deluxe American import 5-5-5, and Marlborough cigarettes to fit in my sophisticated cigarette holder.

I am satisfied and grateful, and boastful. Every day, all I need comes to me, even money pass by my hands, it gets easy.

Having no money is no longer a concern. I feel good about getting used to it. I refuse to sell any of my desirable belonging. I have been so lucky.

I need everything I got to play my leading part in this mysterious play at the roof of the world. How could I renounce now, the special attributes of my identity? I explore unknown territory, banking on further divine protection.

Jacques adopts Krishna, the wandering Newari little boy of maybe seven or eight. Krishna wears a tan *topi* and Nepali pyjama courta and no shoes, he follows us everywhere.

It is Krishna who guides us to the spring where we bathe in fresh running water and wash our clothes.

Krishna chose to follow me into a beautiful world for free.

Krishna carries my soap, shampoo and dirty laundry to the spring. We walk through the field, down the gurgling water hole deep enough to float in.

I wonder about Krishna's parents maybe they work at the soja and amaranth field near the spring

Krishna's English is very succinct, like him. At night he disappears and goes home, to be back in the early morning to tag along with me.

At the creek we gobble ripe yellow raspberries. Krishna and I pick them carefully through the prickly bush

With Krishna, I feel closer to my innocence and protected by ancestors. We wander looking for food, like the red monkeys.

I float mindless and free, in the secret shelter of the remote spring, I detach, so far removed from anyone I can think of.

Nobody I know can imagine I am here

25

A HIPPIE WEDDING

Austrian Barbara and English Charlie will get married at the monkey temple.

They approached the Buddhist priests, who agreed to perform the ceremony in Swayambu temple.

Jacques announced to Barbara, "Brigitte can cook for a big party!"

I am the only choice to prepare the feast. We meet the future bride and groom. Barbara is excited to get married. She met English Charlie, only a month ago, but it's love at first sight to be announced and celebrated to the world without delay.

Barbara and Charlie have converted to the Buddhist faith and no longer belong to the world they left behind. Barbara announces to me, "It is a slap to traditional society, with my Christian background, and my Austrian family!"

A real wedding complete with a Buddhist priest and flowers. All the hippies from around Kathmandu are invited to witness and enjoy a party they'll never forget.

An official ceremony, abundant food and chai for everyone. I am honoured to be chosen for this great, anti-conventional, occasion!

Renegading her proper religious background for another exciting one is Barbara's winning ticket. I don't think it will make any difference, but I keep my mouth shut and encourage her enthusiasm.

Any religious ceremony, with ritual pompe seems to be the best way to sanctify committed true love.

Charlie's budget is a thousand rupees, exactly my estimate to feed all the hippies invited to attend. It's enough to satisfy all the ravenous freaks hungry for sweets. I propose we serve a nutritious and tasty menu for everyone.

With Charlie's thousand Nepalese rupee in my hand, Jacques and I go shopping the same morning in Kathmandu market.

The wedding ceremony will start tomorrow before midday and the afterparty will go on to sunset, we have just enough time to get the food ready.

With Barbara I composed a simple menu: a huge Suji, a huge custard and a curd, savoury finger snacks, fresh fruit salad and chai.

We buy a five-liter jerrycan of kerosene. We borrow two pump stoves from Dany and Therese to add to our slow cooking wicker stove.

At the market we buy:

- The three biggest clay pots and one aluminium pot with a lid we find at the market.
- Three kilos of white crystallised sugar, and three kilos of golden raw jaggery.

- A half kilo of the best quality chai powder.
- Five kilos of semolina,
- two packets of corn starch.
- Half kilo of raisin best quality,
- half kilo of sun-dried pitted apricots.
- One kilo of pure ghee,
- one liter can of pineapple chunk,
- two cans of pitted cherries
- one kilo of imported swiss cacao,
- five pods of black vanilla.
- One *thola* or ten-grams fresh cardamom,
- two tholas cinnamon,
- one thola cloves,
- one thola black pepper.
- Two-Hundred-gram fresh ginger root "one Pau",
- one kilo shelled almond,
- five liter of fresh milk and two kilos of full fat milk powder.
- Three kilos of apple,
- three dozen of triangular local bananas,
- two kilos' tangerines,
- two big papayas,
- the biggest watermelon,
- ten woven leaf baskets of yellow raspberries from the hills
- and a one kilo pack of pressed pitted dates
- A burlap bag full of puffed rice,
- two kilos of roasted peanuts.
- Half kilo of shredded coconut
- Five one-liter clay pots of yellow firm curd.

- Two hundred plates of dried leaf woven with their stems and two hundred paper cups.,
- fresh garlands of orange and yellow marigold.
- Doop and agarbati.

I haven't had so much money in my hands for a long time, and it's all spent so fast in an extravagant quantity order, paid in a flash and delivered to the taxi.

I spend most of Charlie's money, I kept enough for the taxi to carry everything to and fro, all our goods piled in the tiger taxi.

We get home and start to labour right away. I delegate pounding the spices to the landlady, in her stone mortar.

I am synchronising the tasks with my friends, to deliver the promised feast in time

We cut the fruits in the plastic bucket, pour in the tin of pineapple and the tin of cherries let it macerate overnight with the dry apricots and dates, the fruit salad is almost ready.

In the middle room on the slow wick stove, we toast the finely pounded fragrant spices, add water and let the elixir simmer with ginger. We add more water, little by little, until the giant aluminium pot is two thirds full.

In a clay pot, we add water with turmeric powder on the fast pump stove and when it starts to boil, I whisk the in powdered milk, and then Jacques starts steering, like a conductor until the milk rises. We lift the pot away from the hissing stove and let the perfumed milk cool off.

Nicole puts the other empty clay pot on the hissing pump stove and slowly roasting the semolina, stirring evenly until the nutty aroma develops. We add a third of the sugar, stir it into a blond caramel and incorporate the ghee. Then the blanched almonds, made by Jean-Pierre who patiently popped each almond out of its brown skin. Finally, we add the shredded coconut and a deep spoon of Himalayan salt.

I transfer the pot of semolina pudding, called Suji Halva, onto the slow wick stove and incorporate the cooling golden milk little by little. I finish stirring in all the raisins until all the liquid is absorbed in a final homogenous, sticky, sweet, nutritious main course, easy to scoop onto a leaf plate.

Next, on the hissing pump stove, a kilo of crystallised sugar is dumped into the second clay pot and stirred vigorously until a sputtering volcano erupt, then we add all the cocoa powder. The Dutch import quickly turning into lava and immediately doused with milk. Jacques turns the bubbling chocolate lava slush into a smooth quagmire.

Next, I slowly introduce three liters of powdered milk well whisked with water and vanilla pods. I whisk in the corn starch smoothly diluted by two liters of fresh cold milk. Mix evenly until it bubbles into smooth chocolate custard with no lumps.

The very large pot of perfect chocolate pudding soon forms a smooth dark shiny skin on top of the slowly cooling clay pot.

In the last clay pot, we stir the last of the milk powder with enough water and remaining fresh milk into the ready spice elixir, still simmering slowly in the aluminum chai pot. I add the chai powder and let it steep while simmering for two more hours then finally I add the jaggery to sweeten the chai, and cover to simmer with the lid on.

The fruit salad, macerated in the bucket since morning, is ready to transfer into the third clay pot.

The middle room is a flagrant hive, where we sweat hard at work performing each phase of the feast. Until we deliver on time, in the late morning.

Two by two, we carry the heavy clay pots of sweet *deva* food. The main course of suji halvah, the chocolate custard, the fruit salad garnished with yellow raspberries. The aluminum pot filled with chai is still simmering on the wicker stove. Along with the bag of puffed rice, the peanuts and the curd.

At the riverbank all the food is displayed on the square table carved, some thousand years ago, in a massive boulder.

Two monks guard the feast while we climb to the temple for the wedding ceremony,

Charlie and Barbara, resplendent in white robes and fully garlanded, descend from the temple summit, walking on air. They are announced with pomp by repeating joyous melodic calls. The bells ring. The conch blows and the long call of the *dzung che* trumpet call us to attention.

Charlie and Barbara exchange gauzy white scarves assisted by a monk and three acolytes, he puts another scarf on them and more garlands around their necks.

It is all sealed by a kiss, loudly cheered by everyone present. That's it, it is done. The wedding ceremony is performed, not a long one, and not boring.

All guests hurry down to the riverbank for the feast.

All hippies from Kathmandu, Bodenath, Swayambunat and Pachupatinath gathered and brought offering for the party of the newlywed. More garlands of fresh flowers, more incense sticks, biscuits, fruits and peanuts, and more dope.

We follow the example of Barbara, seizes a leafy plate to scoops and sample all there is. Barbara offers it to Charlie who load a plate for her. The newlyweds start to eat, and everyone is happy with copious delectable suji halvah, the chocolate pudding the fruit salad and curd, and the hot chai.

The musicians play their first set for many of us, over a hundred freaks plus Nepalese and Tibetan and monks.

Dany on lead guitar and voice, Therese sings, and sitar Steve plays his sitar.

The band dropped Sunshine L.S.D. for the circumstance.

The food all gets consumed and the chai drank. The leaf plates, the, paper cups and the empty baskets fuel the bonfire. All is eaten and the fire is over quickly, everyone rushes to the top of the hill where the band is moving to play.

There are no flat spots on top of the hill. We all find places around the newlyweds, throning in the center, on top of a heap of garlands. Both wear white turbans and flowing white robes with superposed white gauzy scarves.

The entire assembly all dressed for the party displays in splendor. I've got on my favorite crimson purple Afghan dress. fully embroidered, a purple snake, alive on my third eye with tiny purple dot all along my brows.

I am really stoned after cooking all night, I smoked chillum only but got the contact high with the general acid vibe.

I feel the air pulsing around me, lightly directing me on one unknown ride, only Jacques and I are dancing.

I am twirling round and round, bending my neck resting on my shoulders perceiving my spine axis center holding me steady. My crimson purple skirt flares like a top.

I keep spinning, like the *dervish* I discover I am.

Barbara and Charlie look content and magnanimous on their throne. Our queen and king gazes at us celebrating them. Each of us is grateful and satisfied.

Everyone hangs out in the moment. The cameraman for the French film, Les Chemins de Kathmandu, is filming the party, he follows me with his black lens eye when I spin around. I am aspired by the sky and lose my ground hovering for a flight. I am dizzy when the music stops. I wonder what I can do to get higher

I look up. I notice German Kurt sitting on the treetop of the one lone small tree. I climb impulsively to the treetop; I seize Kurt foot expecting his help

Kurt's foot slips away from my grip, and I fall straight down like one heavy fruit, right beside a big boulder on the hard rocky ground.

I am all bashed and sore, I wonder what I broke. After a little time registering my pain, I try to stand only to faint a moment.

My friends want to bring me to the hospital. but I don't want to go. Kurt is fast down the tree to my rescue, he is strong enough to transport me on his back, all the way up to my bed in our house.

I have a very sore ankle, I can't walk. I cry in pain; I can't sleep at night. In the morning, slowly I pose my foot on the ground again.

Two days later, I am still suffering laying on my mattress. Rick sails into the room tagging behind Nicole.

Here I lay miserably crippled on my straw mattress. This is not a good look. I feel bad and deflated and ridiculed.

Rick wants to move here with us, but I don't think it's all right. There is no room for our private reunion, with Jacques and Jean–Pierre, Nicole, Susan and Sami always here.

I wish Rick would get a room just for the two of us. I can't even tell him that, he should know. Rick goes away without a word. I am shattered in my discomfort. How can we reconnect?

I desperately want to mend. I start to apply my foot on the ground, I can walk carefully limping on my feet. I was invulnerable, but I am sorry for it now, wounded in my leg I lost my pride.

Now, it is everyone for themselves, here and now. At this edge of the world, there is no room to expand, and no failure allowed.

I am lucky, my love still looks for me. I must learn where my humble limit is and protect us so we can share our span of life together.

I lean on Nicole to walk carefully from the Swayambu house, all the way down to Kathmandu. We meet by chance with Rick and Sami having a jolly good time together.

They barely say a word to us. Therefore, we ignore them as well and we walk carefully back,

Two days later, Rick visits me again. He comes forth a bit hesitant and says, "Why don't you come and see my house?"

He hands me fifteen rupees at the same time.

Rick scored a nice big empty room in Swayambu, with a mud floor, not too far from our Newari house.

Rick and I, flushing in a pink glow, laugh nervously. An intense vibration blasts between us. Our friend's keep silent, but no one can doubt we connect.

We are still love struck in silence. I make a pleasantry, "Why don't we all move in right now with you?!"

Rick replies "You better go away. Now!"

That evening, I escape from our house and secretly pass the night with Rick. All seems uneasy, complicated and weird between us.

It started since we fell in love. Already in Delhi getting close has been difficult. We separated to regain an identity. We are still love struck, that is clear. We yearn for each other.

I prayed for this paralysing attraction. We are fully magnetic, and disturbing, but we are not quite ready. I must find a way.

Between Kathmandu and Swayambu, Rick and I are wandering, lost and seeking each other. We trust the divine fate to help us. Love's fire must take its flight and engage with us.

I prepare to tackle all the piling up obstacles one by one. I must reach a simple normal life with him. But our friends want to own that intense feeling. They interfere to distract us.

We are caught, pinned by the same arrow. We fell at the bottom of our story

I must climb and level up with my attracted stranger, remove all pretentions to connect again. He feels that too.

I walk alone, away from Kathmandu to Swayambu after sunset.

In the moonlight all the barking dogs call each other. I greet them with my gentle child voice, they greet me with a gentle bark, they follow me.

I remember why, I wear a striking snake on my third eye. I lead the pack of dogs. I improvise a song, addressing loud and clear my challenging goal.

I sing to the night I trust.

I follow my direct way, to trust, to adore, to revere. All shadows merge in the moon light.

That sky, that Earth with all the eyes alive on the temples. I remember to address each entity.

Love with fear, forgets no one. Worship, appease, praise. One day it will be time for my turn.

I can trust my friend Jacques. He does not need more than the hopeful friendship I can spare.

With all the other I bluff to pass with no damage. At the end when they get tired of distraction and silent, I must find my way out.

With so many chillums and joints. I bloom psychedelic. I swell to a new connecting capacity. There is no normal future in this edgeless fleeting world.

I can dance liberated in perilous equilibrium. I just embrace this with all I got.

Since Matala I meet only those who fit in that freedom.

Apart from Rick who is a sort of cherry on top, I am evolving in my role, rather positively, with loving human and sentient creatures on my way.

I shy away from boring safety routines, for the next far out discovery.

Rick tells me I should be a hippie leader, and why not? Since I have nothing to lose, like all of us, I can be a hippie leader, for a while. Jacques and Jean-Pierre take L.S.D., and Jacques says I should try it.

I observe everyone who's done it. Jacques did not change with this experience, but I am not so sure I want to be an acid head. I get drug overdose paranoia with one puff too many.

Should I risk that short cut to enlightenment? It has not transformed Jacques. We celebrate his L.S.D. come down by taking a ride all around the temple to Bodenath in a bicycle rickshaw, 10-kilometer roundtrip from Kathmandu.

We know we don't have enough to pay for the fair price, but we install ourselves anyways, joking about that fact while the little rickshaw guy pulls our weight.

At the end of the long ride, I give the guy the only two rupees we've got, with extra laughter. Well, it is still better than nothing!

High hopes deceived, our driver runs behind us to complain, but we have no more and no shame running away to lose him.

At the immigration office I am denied a trekking permit for the second time. I neglect to renew my Nepalese visa for two months. Every two weeks they require more money for an extension.

No money, no stamp. I don't care anymore about all these silly rules.

Jacques and Jean-Pierre got no extra for the next month's rent.

Nicole, Susan, and I move into Rick's room in Swayambu.

We bring our three mattresses, the wicker stove, the three clay pots, ladles and spoons, the green bucket with a tap and a lid for our drinking water.

We install a sari partition in our new house for Rick and me. All is well until Rick's friends arrive from Goa.

I meet a blond bespectacled pale gay guy, that's Peter from Brighton, and a dark hair bespectacled ardent looking genial artist, that's Simon from New York a bi sexually active deviant looking for action.

They move in with us, invited by Rick. Rick has spent and shared most of his money. The rent is paid for another two weeks.

I cook and we playhouse all together in the big room. I have delimited our private corner with my saris. We rest barely secluded in that reserve; our shy love inhibited by so many observing friends in that communal room.

Nicole helps me to cook and clean. My parents sent me forty dollars at Yeti travel. When that money arrives, I plan to settle comfortably alone with Rick as long as possible.

Rick decided to clean up, to quit fixing. Rick wants us to go to Kakani. I got the cash for a week excursion. We will be secluded and view clearly Annapurna high up in the mountain.

Peter and Simon stay behind, but we have Nicole and Susan coming with us to share expenses. Susan is joining us to decrease her morphine habit. This is her first sobering phase before she quit entirely to meet with her parents in a couple of weeks in Portugal.

I buy a thola of hashish for Rick and me.

Climbing to Kakani takes more than three hours in the weekly bus, which stops for every voyageur along the thirty kilometers of winding road.

Just above us, the sky is clearer and bluer. The serrated white summit of Annapurna shines its many peaks.

We halt at the only cottage on top of the hamlet. We rent the biggest of two guest rooms, with two single beds for us four.

We pay for the full week in advance, the exorbitant tourist season price.

This includes morning tea and meals, always dhal bath, and white rice, with a very spicy cabbage sobji, chapattis, and chai with some very sour curd, if we are lucky.

All we can eat of this harsh monotonous diet with guaranteed hiccup and burning guts.

Rick stops fixing right away the first day with no problem. He feels good about doing that so easily.

Now he makes fun of Susan in her half narco-torpor, she stays glued to her half of the bed where Nicole is, Susan only sits to eat and play card games with us or fix at night.

When Susan sits to eat or to take her half fix, she raves about how clean and fresh she feels in the crisp mountain air.

It feels good to be remote. We play card games on our beds and get going early to walk around the winding mountain path.

It's high up here. I am surprised to recognise every blade of grass and life form, so very similar to what I've seen before.

We come back to the room to take a cold bucket shower, eat our burning guts food, smoke chillums, play cards. Our life drastically simplified, with only us and the owner stepping in with his loaded food tray. The crows croak, a tabby cat jumps in from our open window and miaw for a taste of the sour curd and petting.

That full week of leisure and spicy food passes slowly. Far away from the freaky scene of swinging Kathmandu, the valley below, waiting for us down the winding road.

Left over from my forty dollars I've got just enough to pay the tailor in Durba square, for my golden Nepalese suit with assorted pyjama trousers.

Decked in my new cheap shiny brocade with a pink flush, I parade like the sun for Rick and the proud tailor.

Rick approves, admiring me, he does not criticize my extravagant spending. He does not mind and does not think about the future. We had nothing before.

I already know he can be morose and gossipy, tactless and so blunt it makes me laugh. If I feel insulted by him, he knows how to be forgiven.

I appear in my gold suit at the Linkesar, arriving at the same time as a new batch of pink strawberry L.S.D.

T.H.C. Jack offers me two tabs and suggests I drop one, but I decline to accept his gift now on my own.

With Rick eventually, I may try, but not yet.

I meet German Peter. He just drove from Munich in a Volkswagen minibus with his Japanese wife Miyeko from Tokyo. They are a handsome couple in the cultured pearls import/export business.

Peter always dresses in a black elegant business suit, with a white shirt and a black tie. He speaks English with me, he knows Italian, Spanish and French of course German, besides fluent Japanese.

Peter speaks a lot about what's continuously happening. Peter emerges from his office, the Volkswagen bus, for a walk. Hidden in his jacket pockets are his speed and syringe. I follow him listening to his fascinating commentary about every detail of his world.

He shut up for a silent moment, to shoot up casually on the street standing in front of Durba square temples. Just a brief respite of his discourse.

I listen, attentive to the flow of words pouring tirelessly from his mouth.

Peter informs me about anything he is about to accomplish, like opening the door of his Volkswagen, and why, and about the absence of windshield.

Any banal gesture deserves minutious obsessive comments.

I am just, for now, the sentient witness of the unraveling cartoon of his speed freak life.

A sorting wonderfully precise, proving mechanic and electronic evident life form.

Like the angel in Orpheus, the Jean-Cocteau movie, he runs to some urgent seriously delicate affair.

My head is about to burst when I can't endure one split second more. I run away on foot.

In a blink...

Peter and Miyeko reside in a spacious clean room at the Matchbox Hotel on the bank of the Bagmati River. Miyeko is beautiful with a porcelain complexion, dark straight long hairs, perfect in her clean room.

Sami presents us and asks her if she could spare some sandals for my sore feet.

Miyeko hands me a pair of golden sandals, very comfortable, a gift I am very pleased to receive.

It is her pleasure to give to me, and she cracks open her smile revealing to me a full denture of protruding beastly teeth between her perfect lips. I am surprised by this hidden rhinoceros smiling at me.

From the Matchbox Hotel, at the edge of the river right behind the path to the temple of Pashupatina.

I walk five kilometres to get to the Shiva temple near the ghats where they burn the corpses on a pyre.

To enter the temple, I take measured steps on the ominous suspension bridge, full of holes, and dangerous looking, it swings exactly to my hesitant rhythm.

I am exploring my fear. I pursue my curiosity step by step. I explore, I express myself to the receptive land at night, and all is alive.

I screech like a sea gull, my highest pitched sound. I call loud and clear. I chant to the sky. I sing to the stars, and constellations.

Every cloud responds. Moonlight, earth, rocks. All is aware and engaging me.

Rick waits and wonders what I am up to, never minding what I'm looking for.

I dialog with the open book of the night. Only Rick could stop my lonely quest. It's all a bit weird but I must inspect what is always above me.

I have to be lucky.

***

This morning Joe came back, after a week on his trek without a guide, without shoes and without money.

Joe is emaciated and haggard, his feet a bloody open tumefied sore. He came back starved, dehydrated, lucky to be alive to tell the story.

The poor mountain people he passed on his way up had nothing to give him, they were running away frightened by his pale ghost.

This intruder had nothing to exchange and no gifts to prove he was a foreign stranger.

He could climb no further, or even walk at all. He rolled his painful starving frame sliding all the way down.

We dress his feet with clean rags, feed him and water him tenderly. When he feels better, he can hurry back to Bihar with his guru, to prepare for the end of the world on the nineteenth of September. This date is approaching soon.

I see Joe limp away leaning on the helping shoulder of Philippe and Jimmy. Joe disappears and I meet Christiane who left us in Varanasi in her fast Renault car.

She rushed to Kathmandu and she's still here, her movie work is over, she lingers and plays her part of our hippie scene.

Christiane has met her soul brother, François the Parisian, the guy I met with Nicole before.

Christiane's type is Cro-Magnon. François is short and stocky with bushy, long dark hair, and a ten-day beard. He has a lot to say. He looks nicely wild and sure footed.

Christiane is no longer so *straight*. They are together, Christiane changed into a cool chick, with enough to share, no more bourgeois.

We are grateful to be at the receiving end of her metamorphosis. François got a stash of S.T.P, some ultimate new psychedelic experience like L.S.D. for sale and some to distribute to personal friends.

The rent for Rick room won't be renewed. There is no more money, we spent all of it for the week in Kakani, we have only one more week paid for our room.

Rick and Nicole are going to the Quo Vadis, in number one room, to help Susan through her three days of cold turkey. She needs to get totally sober before she flies to Dubrovnik and meet with her parents.

I will stay in Swayambunat, I cannot take care of us, and Susan's urgent request is too taxing for me.

I have to realise myself, to clear a direct path allowing human love. I am wanting union, it will happen, but everyone I know here tears us apart.

Nicole managed to lodge Rick away from me, I am allowed visits, but I am not welcomed to stay the night and disturb her sleep.

I am losing my grip. I am perturbed, unleashing, like a brewing storm, becoming wild. I am getting lost between worlds.

My friend Sylvie from Matala is here, but her interest in me is long gone. I have become strange and possessed. I frighten her with my wiggly snake.

I haven't got the least interest for the rest of her hopeless predictable journey, back to Boston, at her parent's windmill shop. She is a normal adventurous girl.

I am madly unraveling. Rick calls me a space cadet. I am obstinately assuming my space cadet mission at this moment.

***

The monsoon rain has started. Two or three hours a day the rain pours, and the rest of the time it is cool. I watch the greenery growing fast and the flowers blooming.

I must stay on the roof of the world. I am convinced it is my place to become wise.

The only one I want to link with is Rick. Each time I recognise someone else, I want to know, where Rick is, if they saw him, if he knows where I am.

At night I walk back to Swayambu. I sleep in a dormitory with a dozen familiar hairy freaks, not far from Jacques and Jean-Pierre's old house.

I am on a drill to get into my own world with Rick. I take the short cut across the hill where the Gurkhas are practicing with their guns. They don't shoot at me when I dare pass. I feel am a dangerous target they could shoot.

Every morning I walk down to the spring to take my bath. I pass through a lush meadow, constellated with pink iris, ten o'clock fluorescent small flowers, yellow dandelion and wild roses.

The creek fills up the bedrock basin with clean water. I need to purify my growing confusion.

With my housemates, we lay in the water to wash ourselves, our clothing, and our hair. We pick yellow berries, and we smoke chillums. We are grounded in that pristine nature.

Time passes like this.

Every afternoon I walk down to Kathmandu. I spend the evening with Rick and with Nicole; it is always Nicole who says I should leave the room so they can get some sleep.

When Rick starts to fidget and yawn, I walk back to Swayambu by myself through the short cut with the howling dog pack, who follow me.

Harry is back from Pokara. He lost his love groove with the Parisian Valerie. She came back with him, but she's trying to shake him off her while he clings to her like a creep. Harry is not a man, but a whimpering boy. Harry protests her unfair rejection to Eddie at the Linkesar. Eddie laughs it off with a joke. Valerie comes closer to Eddie and Harry sits beside T.H.C. Jack on Eddie's other side, dejected.

Room number one is on the ground floor, two floors up is Staff's room, number eighteen.

Staff has a blond crewcut and officiates in his black lama dress. He splashes fine brushes soaked in watercolours onto translucent, handmade, daphne paper.

From the ceiling hangs myriads of colourful mobiles depicting galaxies and forthcoming space, all dangling and floating by single tread.

Staff the artist spends his nights splashing many new galaxies on virgin paper. His gaze intense and blue, his pupils dilated, he expects my visit.

In the dormitory on the first floor, room number nine, I've got my bag of dresses and things, and a straw mattress if I want to rest.

Uncle is looking after me with Ganesh his hunch back servant. I can ask for food and chai, they will give me whatever I need. I am one of the protected long-time guests.

I get myself ready. I paint my fresh snake in Staff's room using one of his paint-soaked brushes.

I twirl around between the new galaxies dangling from the ceiling, floating at me. I tear some down. Staff is waiting for someone to decide which ones to keep, and that's me.

In the open shelter of the Quo Vadis, we are cared for by Uncle, he knows what's going on and he looks after us.

We are Uncle's migrating fledglings, protected here before flying our way. Uncle and Ganesh enjoy seeing us dance and party, he wants us to remember a good time at the Quo Vadis.

Uncle hires musicians, offers food and drink, no alcohol, we drink chai, lemon soda, we smoke hash, grass, beedis, Indian Charminar, Gold flakes, and Imported 5-5-5.

We dance in the lobby space. I warm up the dance floor all by myself. I hook with invisible lines the dance to pull in more swinging dancers.

Sami and Neil play guitar, Drummer Jimmy beats on the drums, Gino blows his silver flute, and Steve pluck his sitar. We rock and roll with all voices. Everybody sings and dances.

Dancers move, vortex spins, everybody jumps and rides to the beat with Eddie Eight Fingers, who grins. He spreads his long arms like a giant skinny spider making a big engulfing shadow that everyone jumps in.

Everyone dropped the pink strawberry field L.S.D I got in my purse, except for Rick, me and Eddie.

Every new day some friend proposes me to take a hit of this short cut to revelation. The L.S.D. can wait for me until I am ready, no rush, I doubt a pill will change me! Peer pressure may force me.

What do I fear exactly?

So, on the following beautiful afternoon, I climb upstairs at the Linkesar. I feel fully shiny like the sunny day, in my cotton veil tie dyed multicolour sari from Jaipur. I look like a tropical fish with a rainbow snake on my third eye. I feel splendid, I smile lovingly at everyone here.

I sit beside Eddie and entourage. On his right, sit his number one follower T.H.C Jack and number two English Jerry, both seriously subjugated by what Eddie has to say about L.S.D.

Jack and Jerry are not a laughing type, nor good looking, but, like me, they are still naïvely building the dream of their future. Jack is researching scientifically how to purify the toxicity from the therapeutic psychedelics.

Jack hands me a couple of fresh pink pills, two hundred and fifty microdots each, called Strawberry Fields, like the beloved Beatles song about that same pill.

Eddie tells me, "Take it!"

I won't swallow it right now, I take it with me and go back to room number one to consult with Rick, and Nicole is there.

Rick will take the trip with me. Nicole will look after us.

I take the precaution to cross myself in catholic fashion, and I swallow that pill.

I have my doubts and I want to believe, I close my eyes, just like I used to swallow the host.

Rick is cool, he does not need to make a show. He swallows his pill, we drink chai and smoke a chillum, waiting for the trip in room number one.

I take a bath and put on my golden suit; we get closer. Love is all I care about.

It takes a bit of time before I feel any different, after an hour I almost forget we took the pill.

I feel a shift of perception. My body feel lighter, and I feel smaller. A tinge of anxious fear sinks in me. I watch out!

Rick and I leave the room with Nicole and walk to the Joint, the opening club at the Garden hotel. We are hoping for a real party to groove with the swelling hippie tribe.

So far, every party in a commercial establishment has been halted by local police.

It's still before sunset when we arrive at the Joint. The party is starting in the courtyard, decorated with banners of glittering saris.

They made a stage with planks for the band, and Larry is playing a track on a record player of the latest album of Jimmy Hendrix, "Are You Experienced".

Through a loudspeaker, the sound floods our ears, and we feel the beat. It's pretty loud and a real groovy start. The rejoicing party enters dancing and fills the courtyard with more and more hippies. Everyone I know has arrived.

I am babbling, feeling like a bubble, so light. not so experienced or grounded.

The crowd is oppressing, the sound too loud, and the air stifling. I perceive the dancers as surrounding vampires waiting to suck my life.

The sun is setting. I lean on Rick and grab Nicole's hand. I am ready to flee.

Simon and Peter Scott are sharing a plate of banana pancake with Rick. I won't touch the food. I am too busy transcending. Putting weight and fire and darkening my transparent body.

The sound surges to galvanise everyone in the crowd. Eight Fingers Eddie was the first to dance, leading in his shadow T.H.C Jack and English Jerry. Harry and Valerie follow.

I watch Eddie, a giant grey spider, projecting his colourless menacing shadow on all the colourful sparkling dancers.

We escape the party.

I am holding hands on both sides of my middle. The night is here on the street. I see lemurs and griffins and ancient mythic beasts emerging from the ground and creeping from the walls. I see banshees charge at us from the temple faces.

We flee the menacing hostility.

We are safer now and we slow down our pace. We stop in front of a lit shelter where firemen and police are doing exercise. They fire their guns but not on us.

We get back to room number one. Nicole climbs on her bed and lay there. I land on the bed with Rick. My own blood is coursing between us, through the veins of Rick and Nicole.

I cannot get away from Rick, he needs me, and he needs my blood. It feels so dangerous to be in love. We are paralyzed clinging to each other.

We don't care about life or death, it's all the same.

I get a grip and will myself to get back to the middle. I leap like a deer from the bed and out the room. I find Ganesh and order milk and bread. I urge Uncle to snap out and help me out, I got to stop the blood between us.

We are growing strong. Bring us the food to change the peoples of the world.

Everyone still looks like a restless vampire to me, but no one resist me. The hotel is full of people running, upstairs, downstairs, slamming doors, getting in and out.

I go to the lobby and Ganesh gives me the loaf of bread and a bottle of milk.

Back in room number one, I watch Nicole put on a blood red shirt and scratch her head, then metamorphize into a werewolf with human limbs.

I am horrified by her change. Rick looks dangerously infected, blood swollen, darkening purple and blotched.

I slap him, and I slap him, and I slap him again and he comes back paling slowly to the life form I can accept but still blotching between slaps.

The three of us cling to the bed like to a raft escaping from a sinking ship.

I start to chew the bread with some milk. I watch Rick and Nicole, wildly agitated. Terrified and terrifying.

I throw the chewed balls of milk and bread into their open mouths. They eat it and are tamed again, slowly chewing and swallowing, they become normal humans again.

I watch myself in the mirror, I am all deformed and horrible. I slap my face, again and again to suppress that monster, to replace it with my previous image.

I will remember not to trust our form again and forget who we turned into.

Rick does not want to stay close to me. If we lay together a single artery pumps blood between us, more and more flooding from one to the other, hooking and drowning us in too much blood. We sink to extinction.

Rick manages to tear from the bed and leap through the door. I can rest now. I am fully relieved with him gone. Nicole is sound asleep; all is back to normal.

I fear for Rick, going back to the Garden hotel, what will endanger him there. I am afraid to go and find him out in the night. I forgot the way.

I force myself through the door, two dogs are waiting for me. I hope they will show me the way. I follow the dogs inside a courtyard, where a group of Gurkhas are doing a drill. I watch them for a while.

I step back on the road and march with two Nepalese soldiers. I want them to take me to the Garden hotel, and the two dogs keep up with me.

I stop at every fountain to wash my bare feet and my hands. Two fountains later I lose the soldiers. In their place two drunks' approach and hassle me with some restraint.

They are pulling stacks of rupee notes from their pockets and waving them at me, flapping their stack under my eyes.

I spit at them and the dogs growl and bare menacing fangs.

When they touch my arm to indicate my way to go, I kick them with my fists and feet, while the dogs bark loudly. More and more dogs follow us, in cortegio behind. The drunks still follow us at a respectable distance.

All night, I search for my way back to Rick. The night is lit by the cool waning moon and bright lamp posts, it is never dark. I find my way back with the dogs in front of the Quo Vadis.

I marvel at the light display. One explosion of thunder and a phantasmagoria of frozen fireworks hang on a cloud. They shift, here again, jump to a statue, here again on the stupa it lights up the eyes of the temple seeking me.

The drunks are coming closer to me. With the dogs we look up at the light and lightening dance with the sunrise.

A blue blinding spark lights a plume on top of the lamp post. The two drunks' freeze, the dogs run off, and I run to climb the Quo Vadis stairs up to the dormitory.

I grab Nicole's hand mirror to watch the world in it until Ganesh brings me my morning tea.

Down in the courtyard I take a cold shower, I watch the rain drumming hard and filling the holding tank.

I dress and climb the stairs to Staff's room. I pick the smallest brush and paint a blood red snake on my third eye. I run down into room number one. Rick is back. We leave the room arm in arm to eat porridge at the Cabin.

I lose Rick again when Nicole shows up. I am alone again. I borrow a bicycle from a cop who stays for hours chatting with Uncle. They are both intrigued by me.

I pedal speedily with all my power to Swayambu.

The monkeys call my name, "hou hou, haha!"

Monkeys are all over the hill looking at me, jumping around to show me the way.

I go for a bath at the spring. I pick wild roses and grass and weave myself a crown.

My Nepalese gold brocade suit start to frays at the seams, but it still catches all the light.

On my bicycle I speed up through the village, dispersing the scared chickens and pedestrians.

I concentrate on speeding in my straight line, I avoid accidents faster in the middle.

In my friend Nacoul's chai shop I order the usual, egg nog, on credit. Christiane is here, I sit beside her. She is so worried about François. He personally sampled a dose of his latest batch of his latest superior psychedelic, called S.T.P. (Serenity, Tranquility, Peace) guaranteed to enlighten all of us.

François is claiming to be God. The almighty one, nobody can bring him down, it is hopeless now. I try to calm

Christiane, I say "Everyone here believes to be the only god, one day or the other, don't worry, it will pass".

I pedal back to Kathmandu with Christiane on the carry-on seat. I keep in the middle having wild fun terrifying Christiane, the cows and the passerby. I speed fast to the Quo Vadis, and I hand back the bike to the friendly cop still chatting amicably with Uncle.

Uncle tells him about me, "She is very happy, she never thinks about tomorrow!"

I relax and I fall asleep in room number one. Early in the morning, Jacques wakes me up with a bunch of roses, gardenias, and the gift of a silver ring with a beautiful turquoise, my birth stone.

Jacques is leaving Kathmandu returning to Paris, via airplane, we shall keep in touch.

26

FULL MOON AGAIN AND MORE FOOLS

Tonight, a full moon gathering is happening in Swayambunat at the temple.

The Swayambu hippies made a plan. All of us focusing to make a wheel of life, our revolution will change the world for the better.

Before sunset we meet on the lower side of the hill at the three giant yellow Buddhas.

I am the priestess to lead, here and now, swollen big with faith by all seekers inflating my self-creed. I am squirming in my own skin. My inner child revolts, feeling threatened, obliterated, innocent, and shy and hiding well.

I am still learning. What is this overwhelming insane masquerade? Our pretentious laughable Babel tower of folly? It was picked up on the road hitch hiking, just passing through, building a me, me, me.

Since morning I hear the roosters calling, "Kathmandu! Kathmandu!" Not "cokeldoado!"

The mighty town request me to perform that role at the monkey temple. I've been groomed since birth for it.

Do I take myself seriously?

My ancestors with their ancient arms push me with their shadow life. I will harness the occult pressure I always listen to.

They passed their glove to the dying woman in Vassarena, I am still listening and responding to all the mixed voices.

Nothing can be ordinary. I give up on the ordinary, on rules and regulations, on Visa stamps and identity papers.

Since more than two months, I've got no mail and no news from my parents. I disconnect from my illusion of continuity.

Rick is real, my concrete link going on with time. Without him I am lost and no longer human, a powerless prisoner, trailing behind this giant self, unleashed by the mythic snake of Kali painted on my brow.

Rick warns me, "you walk like a nut, you dance like a nut, and you get lost like a nut!"

I know. I watch myself, trying to keep my own life beneath the heroic picture. I am mixed up, unraveling with insanity.

In my memory I can recollect honest efficient peoples, clear facts, the spirited magical things.

So many L.S.D. freaks exchange lukewarm moral belief for Buddhism, yoga, Islam, Sufism or Hinduism. They can't wait to renounce the hard to keep freedom, to let go of the shiny regal hippie costume, and to adopt and propagate their newfound religious dogma.

I am a daughter of the wind funneling that great power, an open channel of the wind, I hold my grip on the mad horse I am riding on. I am letting this take my charge to the end.

When I enter the room at the Quo Vadis, Nicole leaves it in a huff. Rick spends a lot of his time being patient with me. Together we get away from the friends following our tracks.

We walk together in the night, tumbling on each other between the temples watching us.

This cosmic ending world, our ending space fuses us as it disintegrates. For the wheel of life, I bathe in the spring.

The mighty high priestess self takes over. I dress in white with a crown of wild shrubs.

The old druids are pushing; I climb the hill through prickly brush and gnarled trees, snakes slither beside me, red monkeys call, the owl screech, I hear a tiger roar.

I reach behind the temple for the sound of guitars and sitars, accords, drums and tablas softly beaten, horns blown, bowl sing, gong resonates, and the long ornate Tibetan trumpet, the *dzung che*, calls my silent voice with its forlorn mighty sound.

With hidden faces behind wood painted mask of Swayambu's peaceful and wrathful gods all the musicians play together for the ceremony.

Baskets full of tangerines and bananas, puffed rice and peanuts roasted in their shell, spiced roasted soya beans, and milky chai for everyone.

I sit on the back of the big stone lion and start to howl with the music.

Then we drink and eat, and we dance under the moon with many obscuring clouds pulsing to the beat.

I am in the middle of a circle of fire, burning twigs, paper cups, dry leaf empty plates, dried dung cakes.

My voice the wind channel, the Mantra of transformation. I am only an instrument. I swirl, I chant, surrounded with fire dancers. All of us dressed in the pale colours of moonlight under the moving sky often eclipsed by clouds.

We dance and chant and play until the fire extinguish, until the musicians remove their masks, and the thunder strikes lightening showing everyone faces, and the rains starts pouring.

The clouds glide fast in the wind, hiding the moon, the lightning tears the haven. Everyone finds a place under the roof covering the school hall of the open temple, we watch the end of the storm and the moon sets.

We walk down the temple to the village; most of us sit in Nacoul's chai shop and order chai.

Afterwards, Peter in the black suit drives me back to Kathmandu in his van.

I am all spent, and I need to find Rick. I was hoping for us to meet at the gathering in the temple. I thought he was on the other side with Simon, who came to deceive me, in my mother's cachemiri blouse, pretending to be Rick.

Simon tried to push me from the cliff of the temple, but I stood strong, and he left. I never saw Rick at the temple.

Peter drives his manic way a menacing bullet on four wheels, drilling through the circulation.

He halts in front of the Quo Vadis; he comes out to open my door and we sit for a joint in the hall.

The hall is unusually silent and empty, that is weird! Ganesh is hiding from me, and Uncle is not here, room number one is locked.

I don't understand why all is unraveling.

The people I meet scurry around like rats in a sinking ship, no one reacts as they are supposed to...nothing is granted, I should understand the unrest. Not expect habitual logic to rule this circumstance.

The merchant does not sell us food, the police control no one. It's a panic! Rick and I finally meet in Staff's room. There we sleep together

I conclude it must be the 19th of September, this world is ending, and that is why no one assumes responsibility. I am forgotten and lost anyway. I went too far.

What I took for granted, like everyone, moves as fast as possible away from this end of my story.

I find my way to the Cabin and dance with Eddie smiling and engaging as usual.

When I see Nicole, she flips and she won't talk to me, she is on her way back to New York, she has her return airplane ticket in her bag.

I would also like to leave this confusing mess I am in, but I have no return ticket, and I want to go with Rick.

I have no idea how to do that, what's in my power, what's home? Aren't we home here anyway?

I meet with Sylvie for a heart-to-heart talk. She scolds me about losing it, about going the wrong way, about embracing madness, about acting as if I was not vulnerable, about clinging to the wrong boyfriend.

I understand all she says and agree. Except for my boyfriend, no one can interfere with us. I'm engaged in the cyclone of my uncontrolled discovery mission. I must clear my own way to happiness.

27

S.T.P. THREE WEEKS AWAKENING AND HOW TO NEVER SLEEP

It's been a full week since I came down from my first L.S.D. dose. Christiane and François are hanging out at Nacoul's chai shop. François is cool again.

Not so loud about being God. He's still magnanimous; he hands me out one orange pill of that same S.T.P. that sent him rocketing to the ultimate self. François, sobered up, offers it to me now.

I figure it is just another brand of acid which I should experience fearlessly now.

We enjoy our snack together and I gobble that orange pill with my eggnog, just before I peddle back on the cop's bicycle to the Quo Vadis.

Rick and I simultaneously step into the open door of room number one. Rick takes me in his arms and locks the door from inside. We hardly ever make love.

This is a dream unfolding one hour later when the added orange pill pushes me into the enchanted expanding universe of Shiva and Kali.

When we rest, I become intensely unhinged and Rick splits from the room letting me rave. I blew it again, I scared him off.

I clamoured for our true love to rule this whole world, nothing can be put in our way.

I am now alone, tripping in the room. I want to put everything in order, and I see all dimensions covered by a monstrous layer of dust.

I won't be able to remove all that dust with my hands alone. I search for a broom to get rid of the dust. I open the door and Larry hands me a jar full of beautiful shimmering peacock feathers...

With the feathers I send clouds of dust through the open window. The dust flies outside, swirls back inside again change space covering everything again. It lands in billowing dust layers.

I am desperately flaying that dust.

Nicole comes in, she looks at me with compassion, I am trying so hard to get rid of the dust, but it is not possible, and I cry still feathering it.

Nicole consoles me, she says not to worry, it looks much better now, it's all right, I did my best.

We leave the room. Just across the square we sit at the Himalaya cold drink. I don't want to stay a minute, the hostile vibe makes me feel terrible, and the waiter refuses to serve us.

We get out fast and walk to the dairy to get a bottle of cold milk. But there is no more milk for us. Other hippies still drink their milk bottle, I snatch a bottle from someone's hand.

Everyone transforms in front of my eyes into ferocious beasts, even the nice Julie changes into a feasting monster. I tear the bottle from her hand and pore the rest of her milk over her head.

Nicole grabs my hands and pulls me back inside room number one.

In the room Nicole cook mango jam on the slow wick kerosene stove and feeds me some. Rick is here now.

I pass out. When I open my eyes, Nicole and Rick have left the room, and I am alone.

I remove all my rings of gold and silver with precious stones, and I toss them through the open window. I remove all my bead necklaces, all bracelets, and my anklets. I toss them all through the open window. I remove all my clothes and toss them through the open window.

I look at my image in Nicole's rectangular mirror then shatter it over my head. On the biggest broken piece of mirror, I smear toothpaste, peroxide, powder soap and fresh mango jam.

I smear that muck all over my naked body. I jump through the open window and climb on the Pomelo orange tree, then slide down the tree into the courtyard.

I climb back up on the brick wall and back into the room. I get into the rooms with music.

I speak to no one. I watch myself, aggressively determined to achieve the capital task to severe the very solid cable holding me in some bondage.

I penetrate forcing my way into everyone's world, nobody seems to mind, including Uncle and Ganesh. I want to reintegrate into room number one, but that door is shut and locked.

I dance wildly in front of the door. I sing to the door. I supplicate the door.

Nicole and Rick are inside, they have barred the door to me. I renounce the door; I climb upstairs and enter Staff's room.

Lots of hippies hang out there, some of them offer me my rings and bracelets I tossed through the window.

I want nothing back. I put on my naked smeared body some very old patchwork trouser and a blouse.

I am searching for Rick around in the hotel, but I do not find him. I crash on a straw bed in the dormitory with a few hippies beside me, I pass out.

In a blink I surface again.

I can't stand the clothes on my body; I get naked, wandering through the hotel again.

Uncle has called the police and two officers are asking me if my visa is up to date. I find my voice and I tell them, "I don't care! I don't need my passport anymore; if someone wants it, they can have it!"

Uncle takes my passport and my crocodile shoulder bag with all my papers. My bag with all my clothes and my belongings is here in the dormitory.

I decide to shower and walk downstairs in the courtyard. I take a long cold shower. The rainfall is pounding hard on the asbestos roof over my head.

I put on my blue brocade Benares silk sari. I get out in the street, this time through the door.

Six armed soldiers in camouflage fatigues with rifles on their shoulders appear and take me away in a Jeep painted like a tiger with green eyes.

They leave me at the police station in the hands of plain-clothes Nepali police who address me in English.

I do not understand their questions. I do not understand what they want from me.

What does all that have to do with me?

I push them away and fight them when they come close enough to touch me. I see men but I know they are hidden tigers.

They grab me and carry me to the tiger Jeep. Six of them hold me down. I laugh wildly through all that. I am the body Kali chose, a furious female god that no man can tame.

I am dragged into a feudal fortress with high grey walls. I am taken and carried over by women.

On entering that garden space, I dive in a muddy crocodile pond, I know no crocodile will harm me.

I roll around in that pond. Four women pull me out of the mud, remove my muddy sari, and douse me with a clay pot full of water. They dress me in a tattered colourless robe.

They put some chains around my ankles, shackle my wrists on my back and let me lay on my belly, in the grass of this garden for quite a while. It feels uncomfortable in limbo like this.

I soon get used to it.

I lose all track of time I am dragged and chained to one enormous brass wheel by one ankle. My hands are still shackled on my back.

I am trying to assess my situation,

"Where am I?"

"Why like this?"

"What's the story?"

I heard Jimmy Hendrix is dead; he drowned in his vomit from a life overdose.

"What's happening?"

I am speaking at the sky, still waiting for its answer.

Nobody speaks a word of English, and the sky is not answering any of my questions.

I speculate I may be here in the center of earth, a hostage captured by Tibetans rebels.

I am chained into the labyrinth to the wheel of life I must turn. I have to turn that wheel to free a captive world. I am very thirsty on that metal wheel heated by the sun.

Part of my corner is covered by a long narrow roof running along a wrap-around deck covered in cow dung. It's a step down to the large grassy garden courtyard.

I am stranded, chained at the wheel at the corner of this antechamber. I see many closed narrow doors, all behind me. I hear other muffled female voices babbling behind the doors.

That garden has got green grass and small bushes, some chickens and ducks roam with the women.

Two of them in a cotton khaki colour sari, and three covered like me in a tattered colourless robe, only one is nude and agitated and mumbles loudly.

I am in the center of the earth, restrained by my chained right foot. My hands are still shackled behind my back, but I am able to stand up and I can walk just around the wheel. My vision is partially obscured by the columns holding the roof over my head.

I am wondering if I am dreaming or if it is real?

Soon a woman in a khaki sari comes with a key and unshackles my wrists. She hands me a plate of rice with some cut pieces of vegetable and a lot of little black stones.

I eat it. It may be maggots white and plump, grown fat on dead bodies, kept here for feeding us in the earth's center.

Another woman brings me water and more of that food, and one smouldering incense stick and a brick very humid which smells like sandal wood.

I eat everything on the plate. I swallow the little black stones and bite and gnaw at the humid brick. I drink all the sulphuric water but feel thirstier.

The two women in the khaki saris with all the others swirl silently around me.

I scream. Loudly I demand other clothes and to be freed from my painful tightening chains. I won't be able to attempt to turn that wheel in my abject condition.

Night falls and now nobody is paying attention to me.

It is my time to turn that enormous wheel, I must try. I've got to channel and push with that ominous superhuman force which possess me.

Three times I use my pain with hopeful despair. I climb push and force and seizes, and I believe it has moved.

I understand the whole perilous equilibrium of my new world. It is pushed, now, the limit snapped, the cable is severed. I turned the wheel.

I come from the bottom to the center in the middle of earth. I am here now, the humbled one, I accept that.

I wail, releasing from the open gap of my mouth I hear my own clamour filling the night

"Kali! Kali! Where am I, is Brigitte gone?"

"Shiva! Shiva! Shiva! Is Rick gone?"

Rick must be captured, like me. He has to do big work, and he must not know I am here.

I scrutinize all I can see. I can't see him. I don't know what's happening. What has been done with me? Where will I go, and when?

If...?

Did I properly turn that wheel? Well yes, I do know that force is all gone now.

Rick will come and get me, we will remember, and we will be allowed a couple's life.

I protest about the disturbing duality possessing me.

I don't want to be Kali, only simple-minded Brigitte. Same goes for Rick, but now that we're still possessed by that terrible force, there is no way to refuse it.

All the restless night I still push further on the wheel exerting all my strength between pushes.

I cry, I scream, I plead, to the sky and to Jimmy Hendrix floating where he kissed, to the clouds taking the forms I am searching for, to the stars guarding all space.

I am sure Rick is around, close by, maybe behind one of the closed rooms around the antechamber. I suspect all the hippies are hiding close by, restraining Rick impeaching him to rescue me.

The woman are slaves of the earth's center. They follow orders here from authorities, Tibetan lamas, enlightened spirits, and freed hippies. The unforgotten dead are helping, and the unforgotten gods are helping, it is a fight for peace and love, with us spilling across the universe.

I see myself floating high in a passing cloud, I yell "Do not believe it, I am not up in that cloud. I am down here tied to the time wheel, forcing to move it, still chained!"

I claim my love deliverance and peace. I pray, I supplicate, no one should obstruct love and peace, and no one should distract Rick away from me.

I chant clearly my story all night long, laughing at hope, crying at obstacles. In the semi obscurity from the garden grasses, I see a blue dragon and a black dragon, they have many heads, and I watch several centaurs emerge from the earth from hidden holes to stand in the garden.

It's pouring rain in the flooding grasses, some feeding maggots shimmer on muddy corpses.

Still, the rough women at the corner under the roof, sit like stones. Could they be real?

One of them pulls on my hair and starts unraveling my hair like silk. They pass that silk tread growing continuously from my head to other crouched women carved around the walls in front of their narrow, shut door.

They all spin and weave my hairs round and round. I want to stop that. I fight to repel them, but I am tied up and shackled, my head is endlessly letting silk thread and the women are weaving like the busy limbs of a spider.

I understand this is the new cable woven from my new self. I need it after I turned that wheel.

I can only climb on the wheel or sit on the dung floor. I am more and more thirsty, the rain is pouring just outside my reach, and I hurt from pulling on my chain trying to drink the rain.

I cry at the dawn's misty light, exhausted and empty. I hear Rick voice crying too.

I answer him "It's better like that, you know! I prefer to cry, but it's idiotic!" Then I burst to laughter, then again start crying profusely.

Two real women in khaki saris detach me from my chain; they remove my shackles with a key. I feel tired and fragile like the mother of an infant just born.

I look around leaning on them, I see the multitude of design and scenery in any little thing.

The walls are made of sculptural minute details, layered upon each other, so is the ground, so is the sky. Everything I see is meaningful and tells me too many personal stories.

I am so tired of observing and following vainly the clear tracks.

The mist dissipates, I see acidulate colours with a plastic shiny varnish on the running chickens and ducks and every blade of grass.

The women become flowers, grow vibrant, bloom colourful in this humid saturated garden. They are holding me, linking existing gods and the unforgotten dead.

I am so happy to be freed, I lean on the flower women. I trust them, and they help me tenderly to walk in the soft grass. I just shed my training wings.

The flower women are my friends. They are happy I did turn the wheel and produced all that silk for a new strong cable.

I will surely get out now, I passed that test. I am flooded with emotion; I cry with joy and relief.

The flower women help me walk. We approach the fountain in the warm rising sun, we walk slowly to the growing corn rows entwined by dark green climbing squash.

We walk under the shade of a sumac tree with velvety crimson blossoms, over a blue stone bench, beside a tiny shrine. We reach the fountain of blue shale.

I am so close now to the country cottage of my paternal grandparents, they meet me here, they show their spirit to me now.

Now, I hear their voices whispering about me, they loom from my memory to the rescue of their curious troubled little girl. It's all logic, I am not completely lost.

The tender flower women are washing me gently at the fountain, from my head to my toes. I can see my own feet plumping white and clean with the cool water. My limbs shed dirty old scales, my skin getting glossy.

They pull grasses and wild mint growing at the fountain to rub me with.

I see and feel my sores, bruises, and blotches.

In the middle of the dark flower women, a small blond child with green eyes is gawking at me.

I don't want them to wash me when he looks. I feel so vulnerable, I can't bare his penetrating gaze; they take him away from me.

I feel perfectly scrubbed and cool. They dress me, in my own, clean, blue Benares silk sari with the brocade gold bees.

I do recognize it, but no texture feels right, not the grass I sit on, not my own hairs, not my own skin.

It's difficult to take a breath of air, inhale I am growing, exhale I am shrinking, almost disappearing and sinking into the grass.

I feel so tenuous. They lift me with precaution and sit me on the blue stone bench to comb my tangled hairs.

I am a new queen doll in the attentive hands of my rugged captors, a delicate import rescued from a lost kingdom. I am in between worlds, lost, humiliated, looking for the kingdom where I belong.

I am seeking guidance, attentive to the voices of many ancestors. I trust I am getting out of this place, soon back to a world I can live in.

In this limbo place I wish to be granted some boon. I wish my hairs to grow silky and strong, to my ankles and every one of them to be split in four.

I wish every one of my long nails transparent, showing the pulsating iridescent colours of the course of my life. The nail of my index on my left hand shall be longest with the design and colour of a brilliant peacock feather.

And I wish for my youth and loving compassionate beauty to be vibrant and spread prodigious eternal love.

The flower women sit me in the soft grass. They fuel my secret hopes. With my wishes granted I shall get back my newborn responsibility.

I am appeased and I stand up to dance with my own shadow. I carry in me the earth goddess riding a wild horse. That is my own death experience.

When I get out of here, I will meet Rick eventually, and all will be familiar again. All evil is blowing away from me. I close my eyes ready for harmony.

I feel my silky hairs tumbling on my shoulders. Then I open my eyes to realize the flower woman cut my hair.

I am a bit surprised, but I accept that.

It's a question of time, it will take time, but my hair is growing now, and it will take time for them to be suddenly very long.

Maybe it is the normal way, better to start like this.

Two men in white blouses get into the courtyard. They speak English. They are taking me away from here.

It is all happening as it should, I feel good about everything. But suddenly everyone turns ugly and cruel.

Before that, one of the two men holds me and the other holds a very big syringe with a big needle and plunge it in my arm.

It hurts and I stumble and fall on the ground in pain and surprise. I lay there, inert feeling that pain, trying to understand.

The flower women pick me up and carry me out the medieval door; they transport me and sit me in a car.

The white blouse English doctor says he injected me with B-complex stamina booster.

I find myself laying on a bed, in a room in Bodenath. I vaguely recognize Joe my traveling companion from Benares to Kathmandu sitting beside the American doctor.

I realize I am in their hands, and they want to play doctor with me. They insist on giving me a shot of mescaline.

I don't want any more shots and I try to resist both of them. Joe clamps me down and the doctor injects my ankle. I lay mute after this abusive treatment. I am indignant, on watch mode; soon the doctor leaves the room.

Joe comes fast and jumps on the bed; he attempts to fuck me. I fight him. I manage to stand up and run away from him, I jump through the open window.

I land on the road panting, all fuzzy, and stunned.

Some people carry me gently upstairs, it's just one floor. Again, in that same room.

My head is all bloody and my thigh hurts.

Joe is here again with the American doctor. They, drown me with deceiving questions. Their treacherous hypocritical help upsets me, they try to confuse me.

I don't want to stay in their perturbing hands. Apparently, Joe tried to get me into a monastery for women, where I am not welcomed.

I am only waiting for Rick's help, I prefer to be left alone and wait, I don't want to be hidden out of reach.

Joe feels sorry he failed me. He helps me in a tiger taxi and brings me back to the Quo Vadis.

I say nothing, he still horrifies me, I spit in his direction. To avoid him I could only jump through the window injuring myself, now I can hardly walk.

Many hands settle me in Staff's room. Too many people are crowding me on the straw mattress. I want my own mattress! I want Rick, he must hurry now!

I crawl on all four and search. I don't sleep for three days and three nights. I can stand and walk crab like, on the side, my ankle and hip still hurt a lot and my head still on fire.

I see Rick, distinct, in a mass of others.

He comes to me, he asks, "where did you come from just now?"

I tell him, "I just come from Jupiter's thigh!"

He asks me what happen to my leg. I just tell him, "It hurts!"

He does not seem to know what happened, but I felt him connected to me that whole time.

Maybe his body was not with me, but he was.

I am puzzled, now sitting beside him in room number one. Rick is almost naked in a loin cloth and both of us pick our nose side by side, with a crowd of silent hippies around.

I want so bad to be alone with him so he can explain to me what happened and appease me.

The whole universe infiltrates us, I must keep cool.

Nicole announces me she is off to Delhi... I say "Ah! Good! I can forget her."

Rick looks at my new haircut and he tells me it looks very nice.

Around us many hippies dedicated at my service. They feed me, they get dressed in my clothes, they help me to dance. If I hear music, I start to dance. It doesn't hurt when I dance.

Eight Fingers Eddie come to visit me every day. Beside my bag of clothes, I use the broken pieces of Nicole mirror.

I pick a fragment and look through; I dispatch one hippie of my team at a time. Everyone is dressed in my clothes, executing a task on the mission for peace, love and order.

I can dance but I hardly can walk. I want to go for a bath at Swayambunat's spring, but I am stuck mending at the hotel.

Day after day, I drag myself painfully upstairs and downstairs. I enter all the rooms. I cannot sleep and there is no place for me to be at peace.

Rick is gone. He told me he was going home the last time we spoke. But I could not believe he left me by myself after the old world ended.

In Staff's room I inspect fresh blooming galaxies hanging on a thread and floating from ceiling fans, walls nails and the window frame.

I chose one to destroy, one to displace, and one to hide.

Staff is counting on me storming through to recreate his daily world.

It is what is expected...

My world is in two parts separated by a liquid drape. It's the flood; I am the captain of the Quo Vadis, like Noah in the Ark.

The Magician's Garden, a painting by my friend Marianna Rydwall

28

WATCHING PEOPLE IN MIRROR FRAGMENTS

In the mirror fragments, my helpers come and go. I emit direct telepathic orders if they get lost.

They search their way back on the other side of the water, each helping lonely seekers across the abyss.

With each rescue, peace, love and order can come closer. Rick and I are to be the last, then we can be together again...

Everyone must get free to love, but no one reaching across can be like before.

Rick must save the drowning one. I get help from the unforgotten, resurrecting for that revolution.

Joe brought me back to the Quo Vadis, to be forgiven he helps me. I am severe and suspicious, but I tolerate him.

I command confusion. Rick does not want me wild. I focus on him the only raft I cling to. The turmoil made him drift away.

Where is he? I glimpse at him, through the windows in many places, high in a plane flying, I see him on top of the temple. He is a temple, and he takes so many aspects. I pray he take his human form for me.

I can walk again. I refuse the food, the chillum and the chai. I look in the last mirror piece; I see the world is calling me out for my mission.

I must get out of the ark of the Quo Vadis and search very far for Rick. I revolt, I disrobe, I am naked, I feel power unexplored in my body.

Staff hands me the black Tibetan lama dress hanging from his door. I put it on and step on a cycle rickshaw. Waiting for me at the Quo Vadis door.

I don't sit; I stand erect in my lama dress, beside a fat placid young mother in red, who nurse her baby.

The driver goes fast speeding through the crowd, while I stand and remove my black robe and swing it over my head, over my white naked body. The clamouring crowd runs up in a gallop to surround us. They reach in to touch us in our carriage.

The rickshaw driver stops abruptly in front of the Match box. I enter inside the hotel, helped by Eddie with T.H.C. Jack and English Jerry, they live here.

They whisk me in a room, Eddie tells me to try to rest; I will be left alone in peace.

I am suspicious of them, I take a shower and put on the lama dress. When evening approaches, I run away from the hotel through the door.

No one is after me, I am free. I am only searching for Rick, by myself in the night.

In the bustling city I climb into a tiger taxi. When the taxi slows down, I open the door and run away through the dense crowd. If the crowd comes closer to me, I remove my dress, swing it over my head and screech high pitched sounds like a sea gull.

If someone dare to touch me, I fall to the ground and roll in the mud.

I climb on the statue of Goruda, the vehicle of Vishnu. incarnate in king emperor shah Mahendra.

Goruda's effigies are all around in Kathmandu, with his vulture head, this winged man, hold the head of two cobra snakes wrapped around his shoulders and arms.

I am searching in the sanctuary city. I climb on Goruda and spit on everyone coming too close, until they go away.

I hide quickly entering the night in the growing protective shadow of Goruda. The crowd forgets I am here.

I limp slowly toward Swayambunat, there I will go down for a bath in the spring, and everything will be normal again.

Nobody is around but the waning moon watching over me.

I am tired and sore; I rest on a low wall holding on a fountain shrine.

Here is the couple of married first cousins, Swayambu Billy and Susy. They study the marvellous ancient mystery of Swayambu, the oldest temple. They come to me and offer to put me up in their house for the night. I laugh at their charity.

This proper woman will never go naked like me, she signifies conformity, she wants me to hide.

Still, I follow them. They take me back to the Quo Vadis. I sit on a pile of sand, two drunks and a drunken hooker insist on helping me, they hand me a vodka bottle full of gasoline and we share it.

I wave them all away.

Ganesh opens the doors a tiny bit to let me in. I am lying prostrate, lifeless, and dull.

Two French hippie girls dress me up and bring me for a meal at the Ravi spot.

When I hear the music, I start to dance and cry.

I want to escape, but the girls hold me firmly by the hand and keep soothing me. I stay quiet and still, fearful of every move. The air I breathe oppress my lungs; I doubt this life.

I see only oozing disease, ketchup is red blood, meat is decaying flesh, all the peoples at the Ravi spot are dying or dead.

I eat porridge with milk and banana, the girls bring me back to the hotel, there everyone is taking care of me.

I am restless, I want to get out.

The morning comes with a hard rain.

I find a crowbar and swing it over my head to get out of the Quo Vadis, in my golden suit with my painted vivid snake. I spin the crowbar, clockwise, and then counterclockwise.

I march to the Oriental lodge into an open room. I install myself on a bed with the ominous crowbar beside me.

I stay put here. The manager of the hotel wants me out. I am not cooperating nor reasonable.

Six Gurkhas cops throw a big net over me, like over a tiger. So, I am restrained.

They put me handcuffs and a chain and carry me out at the police station, they lay me tied up on a bench pinch my tits and tickle me with their bamboo sticks. I spit at them furiously.

They make me stand and march me away in shackles through the city. Everyone can see and follow me going, tethered like a reticent beast, finally through the medieval door between high grey walls.

I am again near the big brass wheel of time I turned before. I am relieved to be back in this familiar place. I smile; glad and loving towards the flower women I know here.

I know I won't stay here for very long.

This place is different now, the shiny plastic wrap is gone, and the crocodile pit is now a rice paddy where little green shoots are thriving.

I am dumped for a while on my belly in the wet grass, I smell the earth and in that uncomfortable place, I rest.

They remove the shackles behind my back and chain me at the wheel, I am docile and grateful. I won't eat, I won't touch this food. I am in training with ascetics.

Now I think this must be an ashram where each of us is subjected to a pitiless discipline and I must, like everyone here, assume my share of the burden.

I only stay that night chained at the wheel. Early morning, they unchain me and take me to a cell through one of the narrow doors on the wraparound covered deck.

I am in a cell, alone, with no window; they bring a plate of rice and vegetables. I don't want to eat but a day later I feel weak and wonder "what I am doing here?"

Nobody can speak my language. I must pass through earth and through shit, I am ready. I will get strong, eat, and survive. I don't have a clue where I am. The flower women are nice to me, they let me out of that dark cell in the morning and I wander in the garden.

They comb my hair and follow me around; they share their food and cigarettes with me. I see the other women beat a woman chained at the wheel, and I cry.

Nobody understands or care about my feelings. I lost contact with ordinary life. I rejected the ordinary rules. I threw my passport and everything precious I had.

I am lost and now abandoned, I can be used for experiment, sent to other space in a rocket like they did to the Russian dog Leika in the Sputnik.

No one need my consent I can be used like a zombie with no will. I want to keep my will, I don't mind going into space in a rocket, but only if I go with Rick. And I want to see my parents before I go somewhere I am not sure I'll comeback.

I want to find out if I still have a chance to live my ordinary life.

I now realise Rick may be gone back to Canada, he talked about it the last time, he had no other solution, his parents had sent him a ticket back to Montreal.

I did not want to hear it, it's up to me to find my own life again, and this is not only about S.T.P.

I got lost into my experience beyond control; I want to return in the middle of life.

That trip is more or less over, but I am still lost. I count nine days and nine nights, and I am learning to be here now and to keep my space, my hope, my plate of food and to eat it.

The flower women call me at the door, somebody I know is visiting. It is Susy, she brings me cigarettes, a ballpoint pen, two aerogrammes and a letter from my parents. Susy tells me I am in jail, the prison of Nepal, called Jail Khanna, where I am kept with criminals and nuts, one of them.

My parents sent eighty dollars for me to get back to Brussels overland as soon as possible.

I feel relieved to know I am in a public establishment. I worry about the passport I remember I threw away. But everyone will cooperate, I just must be patient a bit longer.

In her letter Maman tells, my sister Martine is now installed in Paris with my friend Bruno.

I am perturbed by this announcement, my sister left her husband, and her two kids are taken care by the paternal grandparents. My sister goes to visit her kids every two weeks for a few days.

Well, I left Bruno. It's none of my business. She wants a life with a nice convenient admirer. Maman does not object to this change. Her stability is not up to me.

The jail's doctor come and talk English with me. He sees I am back to normal now; I should not stay long here there is no objection for me to leave Nepal and go back to my parents' home.

I feel free to tell the doctor, when I leave Nepal, I prefer to go back to India

I am planning to go live in Goa; I can stay with Eddie and wait for Rick.

How naively stupid on my part, I should only agree with this official observing doctor.

I am agitated, emotional, and unstable.

I am protesting all decision taken on my behalf; I don't want to be told what to do. Insanity still lurks dangerously close.

I still listen to all the voices. I don't speak to the doctor about that exciting, distracting, lifeforce threatening to surface again.

I cannot trust others and I can't trust myself either.

With the help of the orange pill, I took three weeks ago, I am awake. More and more in a violent restless confusing world.

I speak with this intelligent doctor about the violence here. The violence of uneducated confined peoples is their only manifestation.

Since I regain my foreign sanity, I am no longer everyone favourite. The garden chief likes to bully me, teasing her acolytes to kick me with a log and her heels slamming my belly and she slaps my face.

They tie me again at the wheel. I am their white American to punish.

I am patient now. I stand my ground. I kick back, I laugh, and I share this life, I understand, I am a part of this special garden.

Succulent fluorescent flowers emerge from the grass. A rose bush bloom profusely with pink perfumed roses. Eight glorious tricolour dahlias pompoms, some rows of spicy earth scented orange and yellow tagete.

A rooster runs around after the hens and the proudest brown hen is busy with seven yellow downy chicks following her pecking around.

Ducks, a white rabbit, a milking goat. Every animal belongs to someone here, the flowers, the corn, everyone is busy living fully in this prison nest.

I am put in a cell, locked with two women. One pesters me for the whole night. I bite hard in the fat of her invading unwanted belly.

The next night I am put alone in my own cell.

It's hardly sanity; I clearly hear the voices of ancestors and my parents, my friends and Rick, all my heroes. They all speak to me, sometimes all at once. I am mixed up between dreams and reality...

I wisely avoid speaking about this confusion approaching me to the doctor who comes to talk everyday with me. I only tell the doctor I don't sleep.

I count the days, since I am promised freedom, two weeks have passed.

Susy visits me again, she will take responsibility for me, in two days I shall be out.

I am ready, two policemen and two woman cops lead me through the medieval door, for the second time, I been in Jail Khanna for more than a month.

I get out by the grace of the brave Susy, my freedom grantor. She is here waiting for me at the police station signing a few papers for my release.

We walk out to the road, and we take a cycle rickshaw to the Quo Vadis. My hippie peers have saved some of my clothes from pillage, including my beautiful Puchinka. It's all there for me.

I am exalted and happy to dress up in my own clean clothes, to eat the food I can order. I've got no energy but laugh happily at my freedom.

I can't resist telling my own infectious tale.

I am exuberant again. Susy and I go dancing at the Cabin. Eddie eight fingers dance with me, he tells me about the latest party I've missed.

The hippies were invited to the King's palace!

King Mahendra, family and entourage, curious of this unusual hippie voyagers lingering in his kingdom, threw a party at the royal garden.

It started well, but S.T.P. and L.S.D. freak outs erupted in unacceptable disorder.

Therefore, a restricting police control is kicking out anyone without a valid stamp, that is most of the penniless hippies still scavenging happily in Shangri-La.

Mostly deported to India's border as we speak, any stamp valid only for the last two weeks is unrenewable.

Anyhow, it is the end of the monsoon season. Eddie himself will be leaving in two weeks to finish the rainy season in Pakistan, before going back to Goa.

Eddie repeats to me, I should go there!

With Susy, next morning, we go to the post office. There is a letter from Rick, back in Canada, he sends some money for me and my friends Peter and Miyeko.

Peter and Miyeko are gone and nowhere to be seen. Nobody knows where they are.

I dive into euphoria with the news from Rick; he still loves me. I can write to him now. I got his address now. it will all happen eventually.

I left Susy immersed in the paperwork, she must fill up before our planned departure.

Our passports must be recuperated at the Indian consulate with a valid visa.

Uncle saved my passport for me.

While Susy is working on that, I am invited for dinner by Therese and Danny. We are eating on a rooftop, it is raining hard, and we are under a partial roof. Therese and Danny propose me to tour and perform with them for the living theatre.

That makes me laugh, I have no more urge to get naked and flaunt myself, in a spectacle.

After dinner, back at the Quo Vadis, I pace from one room to the other eating, peanuts, mangoes, Nepalese triangular bananas and lychees. Ravenous, I consume all edible I see, I want to eat non-stop.

I am reconnecting to normality.

I keep losing my breath and encounter my departed ancestors, especially my brother Serge, and hiding behind him my grandpapa the baron Winspeare. They are there, waiting and signalling for me in streets corners and mysterious recess of Kathmandu old city.

In two more days, we should get our passport and money, then we can go.

I dance for two more days, with Eddie at the Cabin, before everyone split the scene. Before going I must walk to Swayambunat, to take a bath in the spring.

All has changed. To reach Swayambunat I discover, a new way, a spiral construction through the cosmic funnel from sky to underground. A huge theatrical setup, syphoning the whole universe like a giant rat trap.

The bait is eternal love and beauty.

The sky is a giant tarp over my head. It's full of holes, I perceive the many layers of many other skies.

My imminent departure with Susy is losing substance. I postpone conventional reality for now. I don't know where I am anymore.

I have lost all notions of time and distances. I walk incessantly. I roam a world I have yet to discover and assimilate as I go through. I believe I enter Calcutta, but I've never been there before. Each time I hesitate to advance on my way, I enter a city I have visited before.

I recognise the trees and the grass and the river. All is so familiar on my relentless way. I walk the map of my world, but I lost my way. I pass Paris, Brussels, Rome, Florence, Naples, Casablanca, Rabat, New York, Pittsburgh, Saint Louis, Laredo, Acapulco, Athens on my pilgrimage. I am returning home by jumping in the French Cancan split through the lost abyss. It's my shortcut onto the stage of the Crazy Horse Saloon, the best burlesque club in Paris.

I am wandering, absorbing shadows of my memories. I keep walking my map of a world I must identify.

I am a poor gypsy princess, very charming and cute, naïve and clumsily human, chosen by entities to sort chaos and change order.

I am the only living daughter of ascended mandarins. I use the invisible vehicle of the feather snake and all mythic beasts that my woken Kundalini strikes wildly.

The power fueling me is untamed and naïve, half is my power, and the other half is Rick's, who is blind. We will have to fight our way through more darkness before we meet and raise our love. I don't know how, but I am learning as I go.

To appease my sleepless furious immortal spirit, I must die and be still and will myself reborn.

I enter exactly through the heart of the spoon maker Katsiki's diamond, and inside it I find my pure self alone.

I offer my dance to Kali, my mother sister self. I dance, I follow the light beams refracted at the diamond's edges.

I open the heart of the diamond; I step in all the angles. I follow prismatic reflection; I reach the core dancing and die.

I sing Lucy in the Sky with Diamonds.

I crumble and my flesh turns to my skeleton, and I pick my bones up and dance. I cross the angular line with my death.

I rise up in the dance, regaining the prismatic flesh of my life again.

Death calls for me, thumping like a green and red sledgehammer. I continue my dance and it goes away.

I am free again to go on. I wander in the street again; I am in the city. A fruit seller hands me a gift of fruit and some red glass beads.

The children are escorting me inside the playful city. I enter this house stepping in from the street. I am offered perfect hospitality; I sip a drink of lassi and eat a samosa.

The people in the house seem to know me, they receive me, they feed me, and I do not need to say a word, and then I leave.

I thread the right line in the middle. Assaulting my way through a steep hill, then I tumble down the steep slope.

I follow my way guided by the parade of flowers free from stems lightly trotting on with the pack of dogs.

I recognise the flowers. They are grabbing me, hooking me with the help of sentient creatures alive or dead. From the living I hear the voices, their worried thoughts about me.

My dead brother Serge is here with me, barely hiding his longing ghost. We are helping each other way with the long story and the love to go on.

Nothing should be regretted, no one has renounced to exist, I greet occult power and convince it to my rescue.

I must remember who wants what. I must serve the occult purpose. The monks and the lamas come to greet me in the underground chamber.

I sit in Swayambunat in my own temple, awake and in peace, they come in solemn procession.

Monks, priests, and lamas come to me and bow in front of me. I keep silent, both aware and unaware of discarding despair and transforming into light guiding on.

After they all pass, I stand to go search for the spring. Before I find it, I lay to rest on a pile of red chillies drying on a cloth in the sun. The people working in the field run to me. They grab the corners of the cloth and toss me in the air with the chillies, not spilling any, it is a joyous game.

Moumoune

I notice the tree covered with small yellow apples. I go further down. The spring has transformed into a swollen deep tumultuous river flowing fast. I wonder if I should take my bath.

I see my Belgian grandmother Moumoune in her onion dress waiting for me on the other side of the spring. Closer to me, my Russian Bon-Papa is twisting his alpine cap on his head. He stands in front, barring me access to the river. I decide not to take my bath and not to cross.

I am searching for peace and love. The green and red sledgehammer pounds my head. I step into the mysterious focus of the diamond with my Kali dance.

Some dark man bent over me, pushes at my body with a long stick, while I am on the ground. I lay on twigs and small rock, clad in my lama dress, just emerging from my skeleton death.

I re-enter my laying inert body. With my hands just reborn I grip and push away the intruding stick. The dark man disappears running like a goat down the hill.

I dance my joyous way to renewed life inside the Kasikci diamond. I got rid of my fear.

I will remember not to judge and condemn what malaise guides me. I am at the compassionate mercy of what let me be.

I understand Earth's life is made of the shit of nourished creatures; nothing is lost.

Synchronicity makes the difference.

I cannot repair the net I have broken. I want through never to be compared, measured or consumed.

My bare feet pass lightly, hovering over the ground. I try with great effort not to crush all the creatures.

I am lucky and tolerant like I want my lover to be.

I can let my parents live and let go of me, I forgive them for the dangerous gift of life, they never owned me. They bred many unwanted children.

Bon-Papa

I accept to love them as they are, my wise brother and sister, still growing, observing the fitting discipline.

I am searching, so far away, for space. I am still walking down on my own. Clad in my lama dress, until two Gurkhas in a tiger jeep pick me up and bring me back to the Quo Vadis.

I see Susy who obviously lost herself when she lost me.

She forgot all about the passports and the bus tickets. I just remembered about them myself.

She hands me a bag full of my clothes, she walks with me, and I follow her on the road until she disappears.

The two Gurkhas cops take me inside the hospital to the waiting room. They stop to shackle my wrists, then we march on again. I'm still trying to hold my bag of clothes with my free hand, until I hand it to a tourist who then disappears.

We walk on, until I enter in Jail Khanna. The marshy pond is now a paddy full of tall rice grasses with plump grains ready for harvesting...

This is the third time I come here, and I don't understand why. I recognize the flower woman in the khaki sari. Once more, she chains me at the wheel by my shackled hand. What is this evolving recurrent nightmare...?

I cry again. I scream again. I speak loudly. I summon my protectors to love me enough and again come to my rescue.

I did ask them before, they tried, it is not so easy, the whole world is involved. I won't get out of here alive alone.

I need Rick. I need my parents. I need someone help to finish my work. I want out of here. It is not too late!

Now, I remember clearly how it is to cease and sink. I am watching with my patient self. My own disturbing presence.

One woman in a khaki sari thrashes me with bamboo sticks. Each time I feel a blow I feel alive. I laugh at her when she hits me. I scream, "very good, go on!"

She gets nasty and lashes at me again until she gets tired. I calm down, and I shut up.

In the morning the khaki sari one unshackles me with her key. I can dance again, and I roam developing a song of my story. I can hear my own voice chanting clearly.

The sun is set, and the night listen to my enchanted loving tale. I have the captivating voice of the small, charming girl I used to be. I have to win some time and space to grow up, and I must promise to be better and right.

I am not bored; my lively ancestors keep me company. They whisper irrefutable advice, "this is a crumbling world you are our mortal humans in constant peril, you must keep everything in the middle."

I must choose, I cannot roam the clashing realms, there is no order linking them. I must reach that raft of possible life in the middle and forget all this extra-terrestrial reality.

I have to get out. I am disturbed looking at the door of Jail Khanna. I still have a choice; I can go through the sky and join my spirit friends, the gods, the ancestors, the ascended masters.

I'll meet Jesus here, and Mohamed and Assurbanipal, and Ahura Mazda, Buddha Saskia muni, Mahavir, Mulana Rumi, Ezekiel, Doistoievsky, Montaigne and Ferdinant Celine, Hukleberry Finn and Tom Sawyer, and many other fascinating departed spirits. Through the earth I could go laughing through the old shit into the darkness with Gurdjeff and Poe.

Maybe I should forget the famous departed spirits, immemorial, and their embellished ulterior glory, I do not trust that either.

Eddie Eight Fingers come to visit and say bye before he goes to Peshawar, Pakistan.

He gives me some biscuits, some great books to read in English, some Charminar cigarettes and Ganesh beedis.

He is not too worried about me, he has been in jail in Denmark before, it's all part of learning.

He says, "see you later, and get out of jail, its better in Goa"

I am not a blind tool; I must willfully take care to renter into my skin to occupy my body temple.

I am now obsessing about how to get through that only access. The door is again closed to me.

I am resigned to choose the reasonable escape and presently cooperate to go back to my parents' home, my only opportunity.

I need to be cured, I feel weak and sick and tired, and I need help and deliverance.

I only can answer Rick or my parent's voices. I listen to Rick voice whispering, "sadly you are dead!"

I shout, "I am not, help me out of here!"

I hear my parent's exasperated voices whispering, "you are dead!"

I wail, "it is not true, help me out!"

I start to read the English books. It is easy for me to understand them now and in no time, I am transported into the author's mind.

I concentrate on my ply; I need to soften this severe omnipotent self that's watching me.

I answer with my clear innocent voice "my life is wanted by the precious love that shall judge me and help me grow."

I'm no longer seeking the challenging voices. I make that choice to go neither abused nor destroyed. I pray for the police and the doctor to save me. They put me in here, and they will let me out!

I request immediate assistance. I am fading and skinny and exhausted by all that turmoil.

My saviour shows up at the door.

He is that clingy shadow follower always on my trail since I roamed on my own or with Rick in Swayambu and Kathmandu. We met, before, I did not pay any attention to him, but I recognise him.

He is Pierre-Paul, a Mauritius student in medicine, he speaks French. He is devoted to me, happy to put himself at my disposal and rescue me.

He brings me news and offerings, fresh fruits, cookies, peanuts, cigarettes, soap, shampoo, tooth paste and candles and matches, and books.

He has contacted all the embassies in Kathmandu. Only the Swiss embassy agreed to help, they're already proceeding papers on my behalf.

My case is getting solved; I just have to be patient and cooperative while waiting for my relief. I am grateful. I have no choice. It will take time.

Pierre-Paul will be going to Mauritius before my release, but he will come again and visit me before he goes and keep in touch.

Now that I reintegrate into my tolerant mind, I chase the voices still so close.

I am no longer flying above the planet. I exploded like the atomic bomb, I fell back and marched on the dark desolate earth. My demoniac laughing body was teasing the world's war. I was laying trampled by the marching army and rolled over by tanks, bouncing back on me laughing, again and again.

I am now finding my breath again. Reintegrating into humanity.

I read my books. I share my cigarettes and my biscuits. I am starting from scratch. I feel predictably flat and empty. I aim to enter the world I left for this ending journey.

Self-emptiness discovery.

I restrict the part of me who still desires the intense frenzy. That restricted part still controls the voices.

The Swiss lady has taken official responsibility on my behalf. She contacted my parents and the Belgian embassy in Delhi, she is taking care of the first leg of my journey back to Delhi. I am yet to meet her.

My Mauritian saviour tells me of the progress on his second visit. He brings me more of the same gifts, a manna of treasures to share with my favourite inmates.

My parents have sent a blank ticket for my return; Kathmandu-Delhi, Delhi-Frankfort, Frankfort-Brussels. I am concerned, I feel inadequate irresponsible and selfish.

I have forced everyone's generosity to explore my limited freedom. It will cost a lot of money to get me back. I proved nothing but my parent's generous concern.

I would not have asked them for all that, I would have come back on the road, like I came! I want to say that, but obviously I lost that opportunity by freaking out.

Nobody listens to my protest. I just have to be thankful and wait.

I've been a resident inmate at Jail Khanna amongst criminals and mad women for over three months. The chief warden first cut my hair and now she combs my hairs gently.

I notice all things in perspective. My universal compassion dims, now I remember clearly who did what to me and still hold my grudges.

In Jail Khanna, we are old friends now. I share all my abundant gifts. I wonder why the inmates don't all cook together.

Each can cook and buy fruits, vegetables, tea, and tobacco from the Torcali every afternoon.

Each prisoner gets a daily ration of rice before noon, twice a week a bundle of wood to cook with, and some black blood pudding.

They sell their surplus rice to the guardian at the door, and that is their money for fruits, vegetable, tea, and tobacco.

Long timers prepare food for the transient prisoners like me and the Sherpa woman. Long timers feed the crazy ones with no money, prone to be beaten and chained up at the wheel.

Everyone is jumping for a cigarette butt, one cigarette shared by three inmates and the butt tossed for the poorest to fight for.

What I learned of decency is not expected in Jail Khanna, everyone washes naked at the fountain, including the wardens in the khaki saris.

Half the inmates naked and the other half in tattered robes.

Sundown is prayer time. For this daily ritual some dress like a man, and some groom nicely with their poor rags. During the celebrating festival they sing and dance and beat on pots with sticks to make music.

All night two woman are on watch, they call order before dark to count the prisoners. I can hear across the wall a man's voice doing the same routine check.

When the night envelops everyone, so do the screams and cries. Darkness begins a discordant concert.

Now I lay in the antechamber of the courtyard. Listening, and watching, between the Sherpa woman, and poxed face old Indra slightly mad.

She listens for airplane and runs and jumps in the middle of the garden chanting "America! America! Japan, Nepal, China, Dollars! Dollars!"

She jumps and dances, every time a plane flies over our head. Indra has a beautiful voice I love to listen to, full of sincere longing.

Indra shares her food and hay bed with me. When I had nothing, she was handing me her cigarette butts. She washes and de-lices me in the afternoon sun, and she call me souret, which means sun in Nepali.

Indra share fresh hay to lie comfortably resting on her half of the perfumed grass she gathers every day.

Indra and the Sherpa woman guard my things. I don't have to worry about the others stealing my stash of cigarettes and cookies.

Indra watches me dancing and pays attention to my songs. It pleases her to protect a white Apsara.

I get visits from Americans. I share my dollars gifts, we are sisters.

The Sherpa woman was living with her overdosed German hippie boyfriend. She grieved rejected from her tribe. She got lost wandering with no one caring for her, and she is waiting for help from the German brother of her dead boyfriend.

She shares some of her sprouted roasted wheat kernel with me.

When I am not reading my English books, I dream about the next chapter of my story. I am carefully learning how to survive, sitting on my heels watching how my two friends clean their grains, crush their spices and cook again and again the same thing which tastes different every day.

After I protested to the doctor, nobody beats me or ties me up at the wheel.

I got no more reason to fight for my freedom. I must swallow my thoughts, still rebellious and mad.

I am under the reforming scrutiny of charitable people. I cannot digest food, knowing I will get out of here, turned my stomach.

I build a strong desire to go away and call it freedom, even if I know humbling beauty and pleasure in my existence here.

I adapted nicely to this experience. I enjoy the harmony and the distress, the little flowers and the garden, the symphony of life in Jail Khanna and I love my friends I am about to leave.

The very white Swiss lady plain and pale, is here, she takes me through the medieval door. She hands me a pair of white leather sandals to put on my bare feet.

I thank her and I put the shoes on. The white sandals in new leather with small decorative holes, hurt my feet. I find them hideous; they remind me of the one of my first communions of church piety and a conformist world I never could live in.

I put on my clean Nepali cotton pyjamas and Nepali kurta with black and yellow block print. Overtop, my black and white felt vest that I got in Heraklion and the old felt corsair black hat, a bit out of shape. That's all that's left of my extravagant wardrobe, the hat feels good on my head, and I don't want to take it off.

My papers my tickets are ready. I somehow manage to paint a snake on my third eye. I need this sign for my identity, proof I changed.

The Swiss lady accompanies me to Delhi. She puts me in the hands of the Belgian ambassador at the airport.

I am thanking her formally when she goes away, with no feelings or emotion.

The Belgian ambassador chat nicely with me, he takes me himself to a hospital bed where I sleep, sedated by the nurses who looks after me for a week.

I eat the bland tasteless hospital food, wash up, walk ten steps to the bathroom and sleep until it's time to leave India.

The Belgian ambassador takes me to the airport. I am escorted by an Indian doctor who we meet at the gate. The doctor will only let me out his sight when I am received in my parents' hands.

Just before I leave the airport in Delhi, I discard the white sandals I got from the Swiss lady, I much prefer to be bare foot.

Delhi to Karachi takes less than one hour.

Forty minutes waiting on the ground in the same airplane, then a lingering ten-hour flight, Karachi to Frankfort.

I don't speak with the doctor, and I refuse to take any of his pills.

We land and walk outside to the transit lounge.

I am bare foot, I got a wilted flower mala necklace around my neck, my flowered Nepalese pyjama courta, my Cretan black and white shepherd felt vest, my black felt old pirate hat, my black snake tattoo painted on my forehead.

The tarmac of Frankfort is freezing and wet under my bare feet, I run.

I sit with the doctor in Frankfort transit lounge for three hours. I look at the grey sad foggy sky crying cold dirty water streaming on the big bay windows.

I remember the similar sky waiting in my forgotten home.

In the boring comfort of the waiting area, I got my dirty feet, warming, crossed under my thighs. I am sort of meditating, all of me, oriental style, resting on the grey cushy seat.

The German guards are scolding me to sit the German way. I tell them, with some insolence, "I don't speak German, speak to my doctor."

In time the voice on the speaker calls all the passengers aboard the plane and we fly to Brussels diving through dark clouds.

Fifty minutes later, we land.

Right away I see, my glowing parents, sticking out of the generic crowd, they are holding hands looking for me.

I am emotional, and I cry. We embrace.

My Papa is joking, "you come back from Buchenwald!"

We all laugh!

First, I say, "be careful, don't give any money to the doctor, he did nothing for me, he will ask!"

They thought I was crazy, but now they don't think it is so bad. They say, "tell us the story, then! What?"

Looking through that hermetic window plane, gliding silently in the approaching Boeing, over Europe, almost there, the darker hues, the darker greens, the red and gold foliage's at the end of October.

Something bleak wrapping it all efficiently.

I am in shock at the extravagant variety of that abundant food. It's the common market.

Soon, I am revolting again, about the excess of consumer greed, the blasting suffocating pollution and the conformist citizens banishing all bright colours from their routine.

Everyone hides and cheat behind that uniform façade...

I am personally suffering from the lack of clean air and sunshine. I doubt very much, I can ascend to a glorious destiny here.

I feel out of place like I always did in Brussels, I am not adapting in every way.

I arrived in Brussels, a perceptive precocious child, nine years old, aware to be a displaced country girl in that city.

My mother loves this comfortable city life, she was born here, and here she build a good family home.

She is satisfied with her chosen stability.

I am the only child preferring the country where I used to pursue the art of catching birds with putting salt on their tails.

In my parents' home I still have my own private entrance in the park like garden my Papa planted full of growing forest trees. With a tall edge of grown poplars to help us forget we live in a city.

I keep my door open for fresh air, my incense smoldering, and my small bee wax candle lit.

I got my copper wall, my empire sculpted bed in front, my life size plaster statue with a cat on the foot, my Agnes Sorel portrait, la dame de beaute.

My sculptures on the shelf above the heater, my oil paintings of mystic self, my stone carving in the garden guard my door.

This décor, with beads and necklaces and dress and shoes, I left in the sculpted worm-eaten antique wardrobe.

All of this waited for me, and now I am back. For the first month at home, I am alone with Maman and Jean-Hugues still growing.

Papa stays the week In Lille with his enamel business associate. He comes home only on the weekends.

My first mission is to get rid of my Nepalese lice and get examined by the family doctor. I have had no periods for months.

Maman handles me a metal tin of viscous grey paste, called grey salve, a radical treatment to get rid of crabs, body lice, and head lice.

Papa and Maman listen to my outpouring story, and watch me, exalted, crying, laughing and still fragile.

I share their suspicion about the price of my enlightenment.

Eager to get rid of my infesting parasites I don't bother to read the instructions in fine print on the box. I disappear with the box into the bathroom. And smear it all on every hair, combing it through my skull. My hairs form a grey glistening even skull cap up to my neck.

I wrap my head in a thick tattered towel, go down to the living room and show myself to Papa and Maman who are worried I put too much and risk losing my hair.

I keep that on for 24 hours, then wash and comb with a lice comb, for days. After a week of daily shampoo, no more lice.

It takes me a month, to write the first draft of my story.

My Brussels friends come to visit. I feel safe and emotional about it all.

I write letters to Rick. He writes me back and forth. The postman transports our delicate words. We commit and promise to a never-ending story. My next chapter will be with him.

My parents pass through multiple shocks listening to what I have to say. I am too much in it, too far out with radical experience.

I cry. I laugh. I protest. I dance. And I get better.

I wait, with hope to renew my self-worth and my wardrobe, to become again a desirable opportunity.

I design new dresses and I get them made by Madame Tassel. Papa is footing the bill, for me.

I heard he was considering coming to get me by motorcycle with my friend Philippe, they both were worried and curious at the same time. Curious and attracted by this complete escape.

My captive audience is shocked and flabbergasted, by such a passionate story without them. Maman suggests I start writing all I have to say, while I am still burning with it.

EPILOGUE - ALL MY DREAMS CAME TRUE

Over two months ago I got repatriated from Kathmandu.

I am still in Brussels at work to finish the book about my trip to other space in all detail. I want my readers to meet my funky friends and start choosing your own.

I type it all directly on my Remington portable, on the suggestion of my mother, an author of seven autobiographic novels, under the pseudonym of Sidonie Basil.

My story from the West to the East. Still happening right now.

Maman knew writing that book would be the solution for my therapy. We meet every afternoon on the weekend with Maman's mother Mamouche, a novelist under the pseudonym Ekaterina Darskaia, and Papa, not an author but a good critic.

With the three of them we read aloud and correct my work, word by word, phrase by phrase, we perfect it.

It takes only two months before it is ready to send to my publisher Ernest Flammarion,

I am one promising young author, now part of their team.

The subject of my book, my fresh hippie adventure, fit the hype of every media, in the press and the television.

I receive a contract proposal, with a substantial advance for my next voyage. I can't wait to say yes and go back on the road with Rick and all that money.

Philippe Dasnoy and Jean Antoine his cameraman assistant, produce an R.T.B. documentary film about me, the only hippie they know.

It is called Hippie Tribulation, aired on R.T.B French television.

I laugh and sigh and tell my story, smoke cigarettes, wave my cigarette holder, and blow smoke.

I dress up, go to the beauty parlour, and get my hair done with fresh flowers.

Professional discreet make up, with my cobra painted on the third eye.

I answer questions, dance and philosophize for thirty-five minutes, the rest of the film present my voyage with one animated map.

I decide on "Iron butterfly" and "I am a man" by Herbie Hancock, my choices for the background music.

The film ends up with a debate between three psychologists on the controversial hippie hype subject.

It barely aired once, late after the nightly news.

I appear on the little screen, in black and white, the timeless colour of immortality.

I am happy and triumphant against the traps of adversity.

A dangerous role model luring French speaking youth to get immediately a backpack on to dodge the unappealing system so hard to integrate.

And go tripping for ever if you can. You are free to try! Happy hippie trails!

I write my story while Maman is creating new wallpaper and textile design.

The French doors are open between us, and we can both work and listen to the music playing on the radio.

I type my story with gusto, on the table Papa carved in Croissy Sur Seine and Oise, near Paris. It's where I grew up, and the table where I hid under when I was two years old.

My teeny bopper brother Jean-Hugues goes to high school at the royal Athene of Uccle where I used to go, a three-minute walk from our family house.

He comes home for lunch; he is interested by my story.

Friends, family, schoolmates, neighbours and neighbourhood merchants, everyone is impressed by my story on the television. I become a star in the neighbourhood.

My three younger sisters are sneaking back, checking on the rejected family cocoon, provided for my prodigal repatriation.

I understand it is unfair. They need a part of that attentive concern and interest I get.

They look at me, their elder sister who's lucky to be alive. At ease in that home, we all had to leave with a virtual kick in the ass.

Right now, I am lovingly connecting and lingering with our parents.

Lucky I, we all heard I am the number one, the artist, the only one who was wanted. Like fame and success, with my second book, the proof of my talent.

That is all I could work on to gain freedom.

Rick can come to get me and share all I may win. I am so hopeful now; he only needs to buy his ticket from Montreal to Brussels. I am waiting for him. My parents, are like me, hoping him to be who I believe he is.

My sister Martine shows up for the weekend in Bruno's new Renault car, with her twin sister Claude acting as a foster mother during the week to care for Martine's two kids, Gilles, five and Emmanuelle, three.

The name of Bruno, temporarily, belongs to her.

My twin sisters waste no time ganging up on me with our youngest sister Papoum on their side. I soon start to cry. Overly sensitive to a resenting sibling cruelty. My two sisters are a pair, visibly overwhelming me, taller, bigger with whiter skin and a redder flame of thick long hair.

Jean-Hugues is here, Papoum is also here, still a minor siding with the twins. She attends art school, under police watch, prevented to elope with Carly, her thirty-ish older guy with a police record.

Maman has a lot on her plate still having to coach her four wild daughters. In this family, drama is always brewing.

I am called back and forth to Paris; my contract is pending. I do not listen to Papa who advises me to wait, they will propose more if I do. I know he is right, but I am impatient to leave.

I gain five kilos in two months. I get fit and well, my hormones are flowing again.

I attend eagerly my press campaign and the publication of my book.

I stay at Christiane's, my friend from Kathmandu. She rents a modern studio in Paris and offers me to stay on her sofa. She got in touch with my press agent after hearing my name and my voice on the French radio.

I appear on French, Swiss, Belgian, and Luxembourg Television. In Elle magazine, Marie-Claire, Femme d'aujourd'hui, Vingt ans …

I sign my books; pose for photographers, answer interviews. I am shown with my snake on and talked about in the daily paper.

Rick is in my heart. I am ready for him and wish him to come and fetch me soon.

I am certain no one else will do. I took care of business, I am sane for real, a part of daily news. Killing time by promoting my book.

I witness the rapid levelling of the differences. Everyone wants to be hip, it's now the main cultural fad. Everybody I meet is smoking hashish and trying acid, are we all the same?

That is so boring.

Maman is elegant and sober, satisfied with her inflexible set of acceptable good habits. She is a beautiful example to follow.

She fears loosening self-control and never will experience hashish and psychedelics.

Judging by my story everything she did not try, is bad. So, I proved special, not a conclusion.

I laugh like I cry, about my journey. I am insolent and proud of it. I smile knowingly to the camera, for the whole world to see, how cute, how wise, how psychedelic one can be.

My time to perform, just unplugged from recharging in the cocoon at my creative parents'.

I am one of many marginal space seekers.

This is not all about me, I had, my big moment under the microscope, but now I must run, and life goes on.

So, this is the last lines of this book, and it is complete.

I lean lightly on the vetust railing to gaze at a dilapidated part of my mansion. The railing snaps and falls in ruin.

Okay time for a change, to step further down and expand access to nature.

I enter a basement smelling of dust and rust and mold, with spider webs.

A corner table loaded with random things, indistinct and coated with the thick felt mold of forgotten dust.

I pick two clear glass bottles partially hidden by a rubbery web.

I examine through the clear glass, a luminous meadow, a minuscule diplodocus grazes on juicy leaves. There is water and others extinct creatures in his preserved world, we look with smiley eyes distracting each other, briefly.

I look in the other bottle, a tiny deer grazes grass in a forest clearing; light filters on him like a beam.

Like him, I am surprised and curious, the munching buck nods at me. I am enchanted.

All the transparent phases adding sensational, layers to this moment. Simply always fit. I close my eyes. I summon anyone dead or gone; nobody is lost.

In my new English version, I dive in this present past, and resurrect every moment echoing in my memory.

This is the good ending of To the Roof of the World. In the next book the story goes on, Via La Vie! Same heroes, same road, the next exciting phase.

CPSIA information can be obtained
at www.ICGtesting.com
Printed in the USA
BVHW040509261121
622568BV00006B/18